LAURENCE STERNE

A Biographical Essay

LAURENCE STERNE

A Biographical Essay

by

LODWICK HARTLEY

Original title: This Is Lorence

THE UNIVERSITY OF NORTH CAROLINA PRESS
CHAPEL HILL

Manufactured in the United States of America
Library of Congress Catalog Card Number 68-63753

PREFACE

If Thackeray's attack on Sterne in a famous (or infamous) lecture in 1851 was designed to bury the novelist, the effect was ultimately quite different. Up to the middle of the century Sterne's biography had not been taken seriously; and Thackeray himself was not in possession of the most reliable information about the man whom he glibly called "a worn-out old scamp," a "mountebank," and a writer who managed to show "a latent corruption—a hint of an impure presence on every page." In reaction to Thackeray's unfairness, the Reverend Whitwell Elwin set out almost immediately to correct the record in a long essay published in the *Quarterly Review* for April, 1854; and only a little later the young Percy Fitzgerald embarked on a pioneering biography that became—to the surprise of the economist-littérateur Walter Bagehot—two volumes long.

The most important biographical contributions, however, had to wait until our own century for the monumental work of Professor Wilbur L. Cross—published in three editions dated 1909, 1925, and 1929—and for the supplementary volumes of his student, Professor Lewis Perry Curtis—a monograph called *The Politicks of Laurence Sterne* in 1929 and an excellent edition of the *Letters* in 1935. It is safe to say that these three works provide most of what we know about the novelist in the way of factual material. A few facts, it is true, have been added and a few more letters have been discovered, but not many. And though some of the judgments of Cross are subject to argument, his biography as a whole is indispensable. Unfortunately for the lay reader, it is so rich in details, not only of the life but also of the works and times, that it may be discouraging. Furthermore, it is now available only in a rather expensive reprint.

Aside from Cross, there have been a fairly generous number of other biographies in one or two volumes. But the most significant twentieth-century effort has been in criticism—in short, in the attempt to understand the man and artist by achieving a closer reading of his works. Almost every aspect of Sterne's literary product has been studied: its rhetoric, style, technique, structure; its relation to the intellectual traditions, current ethics, and popular philosophy of the age; its literary influence in England, America, and on the Continent. Literally hundreds of monographs, articles in learned journals, and doctoral dissertations have appeared.

Of many of these enthusiastic and often illuminating efforts, the author himself might have conceivably remarked, as he once did of the French people, "If they have a fault, they are too *serious.*" Yet in spite of the earnestness of the effort, almost everyone would agree that the enigma of Laurence Sterne has not yet been solved. Nor do I make any claims of doing so. Somewhat like the Hamlet with whose jester Sterne claimed affinity, the Reverend Mr. Sterne has a fine chance of meaning many different things to many different people. Though few now will accuse him of such prurience as Goldsmith and Thackeray did, few will venture to call him a saint. His sincerity, his morality, and his sensuality are likely for a long time to maintain their baffling ambivalences. No one, on the other hand, can fail to call him a genius.

The original title of this book—*This Is Lorence*—was derived from a story about an early incident in the author's life and was intended to indicate how Sterne as an artist persisted in caricaturing himself as a man. Thus it was designed to suggest an informal sort of thesis and at the same time (and naturally) to indicate the limitations of the portrait that it presented. But the main purpose of the volume was simply to provide an introduction to the man who wrote two of the most fascinating books in the language through an essay light enough to do justice to the Shandaic mood and to please the palate of the lay reader, yet accurate enough to be useful to the student who falls somewhat short of being a specialist.

The job of writing any sort of biography of Sterne, scholarly or popular, is exceedingly perilous because in the available evidence the subject appears to be not one but several people, some of whom are (to complicate matters) provided with interchangeable masks. First, one may isolate some sort of "objective" Sterne—"the man Sterne" (in a phrase to which Dr. Johnson gave his own slanting) revealed in relatively easily documented opinion and comment of people who knew him in the flesh. Then there is, for want of a better term, the "subjective" Sterne who permeates *Tristram Shandy*, the *Sermons*, and *A Sentimental Journey*. Admittedly, the two are not the same; yet they are so closely and subtly related as often to seem so. Then there is the Sterne of the letters—which often differ so little in style and method from the fiction as to seem not to warrant a separate category. Here the criminal prudence of a brother-in-law who burned some of them and the unscrupulousness of a daughter who mutilated others in the attempt to edit them decidedly reduced their total reliability as biographical evidence. Finally, there is the Sterne of local and other legend, as eccentric and heterodox a clergyman as one could desire in fact or fiction. The material is, therefore, most complex; and the code book of much of it was lost forever when Yorick drew his last phthisic breath. The task of extracting the portrait is, finally, not unlike one of the labors of Hercules; and, in the language of a television show, if the "real" Sterne ever stands up, half of the audience will likely reject the identity, having better notions of their own as to what the reality should be.

In preparation for the original edition of this book, I read all the biographies and a large part of the accessible scholarship. Thus my debt to predecessors is large, indeed. In the present reprinting I have corrected a few errors; but in the absence of a sizeable amount of fresh biographical evidence, I have seen no reason to make important changes.

As often as possible, I have, of course, allowed the subject to speak for himself, at times to the point of employing incidents from the novel to fill in the narrative when other more nearly factual material has not been present. Of the dangers of this method, I have been fully cognizant. Accordingly, I have made a conscientious effort to keep my readers from being led too far astray. No one need believe, for example, that the incident of the dead ass occurred exactly as Sterne reported it or that the author actually adapted for his own billet-doux a missive from a drummer to a corporal's wife. Sterne was an artist, not an historian. He not only dramatized reality—he created it. Rarely did he feel a binding obligation to strict truth when he picked up his pen to write anything—letters, journals, or fiction. And if sometimes we cannot tell the exact difference between fact and fiction in his life, it is safe to assume that he could not always do so either.

If in this respect I might have unintentionally misled the reader, I might also have done so in another. In every way I have tried to keep the narrative moving, with as little documentary and other impediment as possible, in the firm belief that Sterne's story is worth telling in and of itself. In doing so, some distortion was inevitable. More leisurely pages, to be sure, might have set a more realistic tempo for those periods of Sterne's life that were not so alive and hectic as the most characteristic periods of his biography seem to have been. Obviously, his relatively short and exciting periods of residence in London and in Paris at the height of his fame were in sharp contrast to the twenty years when he was attempting to attend the parish duties and farm his glebe at Sutton in Yorkshire. It should be clear where the longer treatment is necessary, and no serious imbalance should be involved.

At this point, I should mention another kind of license that I would not have taken if I had intended the book for the specialist: namely, in some modernization of spelling, capitalization, and punctuation. For the full flavor of the style—especially as indicated by an elaborately complex system of dashes in varying lengths to achieve various purposes—I can recommend any one of the recent editions listed in an appended bibliography.

The irony of twentieth-century Sternean scholarship has been that in its very richness, its zeal, and its enthusiasm for the exploration of every cranny of the novelist's mind, thought, and art the victim may be what Virginia Woolf called the "common reader," for he may become easily convinced that so complex a masterpiece as *Tristram Shandy*, in particular, must be a novelist's novel or a scholar's novel—and not for one who refuses to be overwhelmed by what he does not know about classical rhetoric, Hermetic philosophy, the tradition of "learned wit," and theories of comedy and the comic. Actually, the novel will never be popular for too "common" a reader. It is far too subtle for that. But it can be read by ordinarily sensitive and intelligent readers who may adopt the attitudes of such quite uncommon people as Elizabeth Bowen who is willing to "consign [herself] dizzily to it," Thomas Wolfe who reveled in the way it "*boils* and *pours*," or Katherine Anne Porter who takes keen delight in its "living breathing people."

My own comments on the fiction are largely incidental

to the narrative and are limited to suggestions of the ways in which Sterne's contemporaries read it and in which it may be read today by any one who regards a book as an object of delight. More elaborate guides to its secrets will be found elsewhere. For those who wish to pursue such ends I have provided an updated list of books both biographical and critical at the end of this volume containing a selection both from the material I used in the writing of it and from the best of the more recent scholarship.

Back to the man and his biography, Sterne like many another humorist created a role for himself that he deliberately set about establishing and perpetuating. If he did much to create the word *sentimental* (as we shall see), he is even more directly responsible for the verb phrase *to Shandy it.* "Joy," he argued in one of his sermons, "is another name for Religion." And "Laugh, my lord, I will," he replied to a bishop who sought to inhibit him. In his life as in his fiction it is true that there is often an intermingling of the comic and the pathetic–if not the tragic–and it is not inappropriate to speak of his "sad hilarity." But it is the laughter rather than the sadness that is most readily and charmingly apparent.

It was Coleridge who first spoke of Sterne's "dallying with the devil." It is still possible to see the Yorkshire parson selling his soul for the literary fame that came so suddenly and with such abundance. But one remains free to decide whether this drama should have a Marlovian or a Goethean ending. In the light of the verve and the joy that Sterne gamely put up as a defense against his constant pursuer, Death, most people will doubtless choose the latter.

All biographical treatments aside, the novelist has surely given the only reliable directions to anyone who really wants to know him. Of *Tristram Shandy* he said simply, " 'Tis a picture of myself." He should be taken at his word.

CONTENTS

PART FOUR: ALAS, YORICK

PART ONE: LORENCE

CHAPTER I

POOR RELATION

ORKSHIRE IS A LONG way from Tipperary—not merely in miles or kilometers but in the racial traits that distinguish the sturdy and stolid dweller of the northern English moors from the easy and resilient inhabitant of Southern Ireland. The meeting of the twain in the person of Laurence Sterne might well have been expected to produce a creature wonderful and strange.

The walled cathedral-city of York first appears in history as Eboracum, capital of the Roman province of Britain. Having acquired its pride, its dignity, and its severity at an early date, it has since been reluctant to relinquish them. Although in the eighteenth century it was by no means a large city in the modern sense, it was queen of the north: the seat of an archbishop and the possessor of one of England's most magnificent cathedrals. Its narrow streets stumbled through rows of half-timbered houses mellowed by smoke, moisture, and the years, finally debouching in a northern corner upon a rich and vast pile of Gothic architecture, miraculously hidden from view of most of the city. From the minster's astonishing windows gleamed a priceless treasure of glass, and from one of its splendid towers boomed "Great Peter," the biggest bell in the kingdom. Of the Chapter House the loyal Yorkshireman could exclaim with pride: "As a rose among flowers is this building of ours." The pageantry of the Assizes and of the Church furnished frequent drama for York's streets; and the summer racing seasons brought gay sporting crowds to the metropolis of the Ridings. Yet, situated as it was in a featureless plain, the city could not escape a certain ugliness and drabness that travelers have long taken for granted. ("York is an old town," wrote a French tourist in 1811, "and of course very ugly.") Furthermore, there was a coldness and narrowness in its social and ecclesiastical life that belied the warm glitter of the Assembly Rooms and the candle-glow of the minster's altar. Around the stronghold of God whirled a vortex of pettiness and frustration that often threatened the very foundations; and political and ecclesiastical rivalries took their toll in souls and bodies.

To the staid capital of Yorkshire the bustling Irish town of Clonmel was in marked contrast. It was not without historical importance, for it had been the scene of Cromwell's severest defeat in Ireland. Indeed, its beginning may have antedated that of York, although its pride was of a vastly different origin. According to a story redolent of Celtic imagination, the primitive settlers let off a swarm of bees and erected their circular fort where it settled, calling the spot Cluian-mealla–the plain of honey. It was a simple town, situated most pleasantly on the Suir River, a broad stream dotted with picturesque islands. In the last half of the eighteenth century Arthur Young found it to be a busy and prosperous place, a center of flour milling and woolen manufactory. Its inhabitants were largely plain people living simple, industrious lives. It had no minster to command the traveler's awe. Its chief attractions lay neither in its traditions, its architecture, nor in the exciting life of its streets. Its greatest charm was its natural beauty. Instead of the flatness and shadow that marred the beauty of York, it had as a setting the green loveliness of Tipperary, with rolling hills and fertile valleys, Irish sunshine and Irish laughter. And to the south rose the blue Comeragh mountains.

The archepiscopal Svernes and the fashionable Jaqueses fraternized in the veins of Roger Sterne, and the fact that they did not produce an illustrious scion of two of Yorkshire's first families was a quirk of fate rather than a consequence of blood. In the body of Roger's son these august and snobbish strains found themselves in uncomfortably close quarters with what Laurence himself has led us to believe were unspeakables—the strains contributed by the Nuttles or Nuttalls of Clonmel. What resulted, it is safe to assume, is explainable both as a quirk of fate and as a consequence of blood—an unpredictable creature and an enigma, ever elusive and ever fascinating, in whom the secular and the sacred, the serious and the humorous, the comic and the tragic, the moral and the immoral, the admirable and the contemptible are hopelessly jumbled. Sometimes one feels that Laurence Sterne may best be understood in Alice's through-the-looking-glass world. Certainly, he so often eludes conventional standards of judgment that one is almost tempted to suspend their application.

By all normal laws of expectation great-grandfather Richard Sterne (God rest his soul!) should have been the most famous of the Sterne clan. He was an irascible and determined body who published a work summarizing the 3600 faults "in our printed Bibles" and who advanced himself to the second highest ecclesiastical post in England. That Providence had predestined him to be Archbishop of York even the least Calvinistic reader will be inclined to believe. In his youth he fell into a sluice and miraculously escaped being mashed to pulp in the mill wheel; moreover, he again tempted Providence by falling from a church steeple. Nothing could kill the man until he had run his appointed course—not even his loyalty to King Charles, which brought him no nearer the scaffold than his attendance, as spiritual comforter, upon Archbishop Laud on the occasion of his execution. Every evidence points to the fact that he was a sober and bigoted gentleman who took himself with complete seriousness, and who did the right things with an important air. So, as he deserved, he was a complete success. His great-grandson was destined to be a greater success for almost exactly opposite reasons, through no fault either of logic or of what Grandfather Sterne bequeathed to his progeny.

What of his solid qualities the Archbishop passed or did not pass on to his sons are yet matters of conjecture. At least, none of the sons attained real eminence. The most important fact known about the third son, Simon—Laurence's grandfather—is that he had the acumen to marry a rich heiress from the socially prominent Jaques family of Elvington and York. Even before the Archbishop was elevated to his see, the bride's mother had been a great lady of York, with a house on the fashionable Pavement, a resplendent coach, and a blackamoor. Indeed, Mary Jaques was as good a catch as the third son of an archbishop could wish. The lady fulfilled her conjugal duties not only by bringing an ample dowry but also by presenting her husband, in the course of time, with three sons: Richard, Jaques, and Roger. Richard turned out to be a Yorkshire country gentleman more or less after the usual pattern. Jaques went into the Church, where he became something of a chip off his grandfather's block. Roger, alas, was the black sheep—who turned out to be more important than the rest perhaps because he least deserved to be.

As the third son of a third son, Roger was, in the scheme of primogeniture, bound to be handicapped. But there is no reason to believe that Roger made good use even of the opportunities that he had. Neither the university nor the Church seemed to appeal to him. At the tender age of sixteen he made the third possible choice and entered the army, probably as the line of least resistance. The Cumberland Regiment of Foot, to which he attached himself, was not without distinction; but its traditions did not inspire the amiable ne'er-do-well to eminence in army life. Four years after his marriage he was listed as an ensign. His only advance in rank came just before he died. About the best that his son could say of him was that he was "a little smart man—active to the last degree," adding that he combined a quick temper with a kindly and sweet disposition. Ambition had little place in his character.

In the early eighteenth century the British Army was in a deplorable state of discipline and morale. Even one of the best regiments offered to a soldier little promise of regeneration through military training. Exactly the opposite was more nearly true; the transformation of gentleman into boor seemed considerably more frequent than the transformation of boor into gentleman. Later in the century Cowper was to express himself indignantly on the brutalizing effects of army life, especially on the simple country lad:

> To swear, to game, to drink; to show at home
> By lewdness, idleness, and sabbath-breach,
> The great proficiency he made abroad;
> T'astonish and to grieve his gazing friends,
> To break some maiden's and his mother's heart;
> To be a pest where he was useful once;
> Are his sole aim, and all his glory, now!

Roger Sterne was no simple country lad, but he was a mere boy when he went into the army and was thus highly susceptible to deleterious influences. One should hardly be astonished at Roger's forgetting the Sterne mitre and the Jaques crest to the extent of allowing himself to be captivated by a woman beneath him in class. Laurence insinuated not only that his mother was of lowly origin (the daughter of "a noted sutler in Flanders in Queen Ann's wars") but also that Roger married her to square a debt with her father (or step-father, as he seems to have been),

Incredibly enough, it has been strongly suggested that Sterne's account of his mother's origin is a fabrication motivated and colored by his later revulsion to her selfishness and coarseness. Mrs. Sterne has been identified as Agnes Nuttall, youngest daughter of Captain Christopher Nuttall, a poor but respectable member of an old Lancashire family. If this identification is correct, the facts that she was poor and that she was a victim of army life may explain the absence of ladylike qualities in Agnes. At any rate, whatever may have been her background, she was able to get two husbands: first, a Captain Hebert or Herbert ("of a good family," said Laurence) and, finally, Roger Sterne.

What Mrs. Sterne did not bring in the way of dowry or polish she made up in iron constitution. She married Roger on September 25, 1711, and, as the quaint custom was, lost little time in finding herself with child. Marrying a soldier, as Agnes knew well in advance, was a matter of being off to the wars and offering oneself up in line of duty. The first child, named Mary, was born in Lisle in July, 1712. Many years after, her famous brother wrote her history with classic bluntness:

> This child was most unfortunate–she married one Weemans in Dublin–who used her most unmercifully–spent his substance, . . . and left my poor sister to shift for herself–which she was able to do but for a few months, for she went to a friend's house in the country, and died of a broken heart. She was a most beautiful woman–of a fine figure, and deserved a better fate.

Laurence came along in schedule during the next year. "My birthday was ominous," he himself wrote. Since his father's regiment had been disbanded, Agnes and Roger, "broke and set adrift into the world," had come from Dunkirk to Clonmel in order to have the family roof over their heads. It was thus that Sterne came to be born in Ireland in November, 1713.

Soon afterward, Roger and his family returned to Yorkshire, remaining for some ten months at his mother's place in Elvington. Here they waited until Roger's regiment had been reorganized. There comes now a sorry story of camp-following by Agnes and her babies to Dublin, to Exeter, and back to Dublin. This included a rigorous journey by land from Liverpool, a lying-in to give birth to another son, Joram, and a narrow escape from a leaky vessel in the Irish Sea. However vulgar Mrs. Sterne may have been, her vicissitudes in following her husband command sympathy. Traveling conditions in the eighteenth-century England were fraught with enough rigors and perils to daunt even the stoutest of heart and body. In 1736 Lord Hervey wrote that the road between Piccadilly and the court suburb of Kensington was so bad that residents of Kensington were isolated by "an impassable gulf of mud." If such was the condition in the purlieus of London, what could be expected of provincial roads? Here, the dust of summer and the mud of winter were equally obstructive. Arthur Young wrote of a Lancashire road with "ruts, which actually measured, four feet deep, and floating with mud... The only mending it receives in places is the tumbling in some loose stones, which serve no other purpose but jolting a carriage in the most intolerable manner." An upset was no rarity. Add to insufferable road conditions the menace of highwaymen and the discomforts of a crowded coach, and a land journey from Liverpool to Plymouth becomes a major and perilous undertaking for a man, much less for a pregnant woman with two babies in tow. We do not wonder that Mrs. Sterne buried children with almost the same regularity with which she bore them. The miracle is that she herself survived to a reasonably advanced age.

Sterne's early childhood was governed by the instability

of army life. When he was six, his father was ordered to Spain on the Vigo Expedition, and the Sternes had to go, bag and baggage, to the Isle of Wight. En route Joram was carried away by smallpox; but his place was soon to be taken by Anne, who in September, 1719, entered the world for a brief sojourn. "This pretty blossom," Laurence wrote in his autobiography, "fell at the age of three years, in the barracks of Dublin—she was, as I well remember, of fine delicate frame, not made to last long, as were most of my father's babes." The return to barracks in Wicklow, Ireland, necessitated another trying journey. Then came a brief half-year of calm at the home of a generous clergyman-relative near Wicklow. Here Laurence seems to have done nothing more exciting than to fall through a mill-race while the mill was running (in emulation, we suppose, of the Archbishop). There was another stretch of life in barracks in Dublin, followed by brief residences at Mullingar and Carrickfergus. At Mullingar another relative had taken the family on his bounty. In these somewhat kaleidoscopic years, other fragile blossoms than Anne had faded after brief periods of blooming: for example, there was Devijeher [*sic*], who was named for his father's colonel and who might well have sunk under such a burden; then there was Susan, most ephemeral of all. In her son's autobiography Mrs. Sterne's fecundity is endowed with the casualness of that of Defoe's great heroine, Moll Flanders. So frequent were arrivals and departures in the family that the undertaker seems almost to jostle the midwife. It is difficult to figure out the roll-call of the Sternes for any given year.

The psychological and physical effects of barrack life on Sterne are not easy to determine accurately. Little Laurie may be pictured, as Thackeray suggests, with tricorne hat on head and drum-sticks in hand playing at soldier with his friends. His heart may have thrilled to the sound of martial music and to the spectacle of scarlet-clad troops. He may have made friends of soldiers, old and young, and listened to their stories with boyish awe and admiration. Obviously, much of the uncertainty and hardship that dogged his elders went unnoticed by him. Later in his life he was able to utilize his experience for his greatest creative effort without any reflection of bitterness or disapproval. But undoubtedly something of the unhealthiness of an unstable life became a permanent part of his nature, and no small amount of what is mercurial in the mature Sterne is traceable to these early years.

At the age of ten an important break came in Laurie's life. At this time he was sent away to school near Halifax, in the West Riding of Yorkshire, ostensibly because his Uncle Richard could there keep him under his surveillance. This separation from family was fortunate. Now for the first time Sterne was able to taste of stability. For the rest of the Sterne family, however, another move was imminent—this time to Londonderry, where Mrs. Sterne gave birth to another daughter and from where Ensign Sterne's regiment was dispatched in 1727 to defend Gibraltar.

Roger Sterne's army record at Gibraltar is undistinguished, but at least one private "war" makes his stay at the post fatefully significant. There is no reason to believe that Gibraltar was better than the average English garrison town like Portsmouth, for example, in which General James Wolfe saw only a collection of "dirty, drunken, insolent scoundrels improved by the hellish nature of the place, where every kind of corruption, immorality, and looseness is carried to excess." Convivial and cocky little Roger Sterne could well be expected to ameliorate the tedium of garrison life by occasional carousing with his fellow officers. Over the wine glasses one day there was an argument—"about a goose," his son recorded laconically. When an officer named Phillips undertook to oppose, Roger flared up, a duel ensued, and Roger emerged with a severe sword wound. So powerful was Phillips' thrust that Roger was completely run through and pinned to the wall; whereupon the luckless ensign with miraculous presence of mind begged his opponent to brush off any plaster adherent to the point before withdrawing the blade. Thus began the last phase in the life of "the smart little man" who fell so far short of proving a worthy scion of the Yorkshire Sternes. He never fully recovered from the wound. His subsequent history is briefly and pathetically chronicled by Laurence:

> ...he was sent to Jamaica, where he soon fell by the country fever, which took away his senses first, and made a child of him, and then in a month or two, walking about continually without complaining, till the moment he sat down in an arm chair, and breathed his last—which was at Port Antonio, on the north of the island.

The year of his death was 1731.

In the meantime Laurence had continued under the care of Uncle Richard, who apparently had received the child as a poor relation—with a stolid sense of duty rather than with any scintilla of warmth or affection. After all, he probably argued, the child was the fruit of a brother's mismatch and was nothing to be proud of. Whatever dislike the uncle may have borne toward his charge was reciprocated by the nephew, who in later years never referred to his uncle as a benefactor. The boy's conduct in the Halifax school may have strengthened Uncle Richard in the view that his nephew was an Irish brat. Life in barracks imposed little discipline on soldiers and less on their children. We should not be surprised if the master of the school had plenty of difficulties with a young rapscallion who held studies in contempt and constantly engaged in pranks.

However, Laurie's rebellion against his prescribed studies should not be taken to mean that he had no interest whatsoever in books. Horace and Ovid, the *Iliad* and the *Aeneid* he read with relish and enthusiasm—sometimes too overt:

> Was I not as much concerned for the destruction of the *Greeks* and *Trojans* [he wrote in his great novel], as any boy of the whole school? Had I not three strokes of a ferula given me, two on my right hand, and one on my left, for calling *Helena* a b**** for it? Did any one of you shed more tears for *Hector?* And when king *Priam* came to the camp to beg his body, and returned weeping to *Troy* without it,—you know, brother, I could not eat my dinner

And perhaps the master was not always unsympathetic. In his later years Sterne told with some complacence a story on which serious doubts have been cast. Whether or not it is true, it is too famous to be omitted. One day, the story ran, young Laurie clambered up a tempting ladder and painted his name in large letters on the freshly white-washed ceiling of the schoolroom. The usher, failing to take the matter as a joke, administered a stiff lacing. The master, on the other hand ("able," indeed, and gifted with rare prescience), "was very much hurt at this, and said, before me that never should that name be effaced, for I was a boy of genius, and he was sure I should come to preferment—this expression made me forget the stripes I had received." One wonders how long the master's patience continued when he found that Laurie, while he should have been filling his copy books with exercises, had drawn hens, soldiers, and heads of women. Perhaps if he was really prescient, he saw something far different from future ecclesiastical preferment in a caricature that Sterne one day made of himself: a long-chinned, long-nosed face labeled, "This is Lorence."

CHAPTER II

A LADY IN LITTLE ALICE LANE

WHEN ROGER STERNE died, Laurie was a lad of eighteen, ready for the finishing touches of a gentleman's education but without visible means of getting them. The death of Uncle Richard in 1732 did not simplify the situation. And a visit by Sterne's mother and sister to England was not likely to increase the interest of the Yorkshire connections in Roger's brood. The attitude of the Sternes at the time is reflected in an accusation that Laurence made against Uncle Jaques when his own treatment of his mother was in question:

> My Father, as you remember died in the King's Service in the West Indies. My Mother was then with her own relations in Ireland and upon the first news of his death came over to England; she was then in some difficulties about her pension and her business was with you to solicit your interest to procure it for her upon the English Establishment.
>
> But I well remember she was forced to return back, without having so much interest as to obtain the favor of being admitted to your presence (not being suffered even to reach York)—

Poor, disagreeable Agnes Sterne was destined never to storm successfully the bastions of her husband's proud relatives, although she may have died trying. At this time she had to content herself with going back to Ireland to her pension of twenty pounds a year and to the income from an embroidery school which she conducted.

But for Laurie himself fate was not unfavorable. Sons

cannot always be depended upon to assume their father's obligations in regard to poor relations; hence it is a wonder that the heirs of Uncle Richard did not encourage Sterne to shift for himself. In the year after Richard Sterne's death, however, the eldest son was kind enough to stake the lad for at least a part of his college expenses. The act earned for the benefactor an affectionate mention in the memoirs: "... by God's care my cousin Sterne, of Elvington, became a father to me, and sent me to the university..." Yet in another mood Sterne asserted that his cousin was not too lavish with his bounty. He referred to "the expenses of my education at the University, too scantily defrayed by my Cousin Sterne with only thirty pounds a year, and the last year not paid, but with money I borrowed."

Neither Laurie nor his relatives could have had any hesitation in choosing the proper college. Jesus College, Cambridge, had for generations been honored by the Yorkshire Sternes. Not only had Uncle Jaques and Cousin Richard been students there, but great-grandfather Sterne had been a Master. Laurence was entered as a sizer—a designation which, although no longer indicating a "self-help" student assigned to menial duties, still bore the stigma of poverty. The contemporary attitude is expressed by Thomas Gray—a milliner's son who had been able to nourish his fastidiousness at one of England's most fashionable schools—in a letter to his aristocratic friend and fellow Etonian, Horace Walpole. Gray wrote that sizers were "graziers' eldest sons, who come to get good learning, that they may all be Archbishops of Canterbury" and further suggested that for their sustenance they were forced to "feast upon the leavings of the rest." Although the social position of the ordinary sizer may not have been enviable, Sterne had the advantage of having distinguished connections. In time he was awarded one of the county scholarships founded by his great-grandfather, the Archbishop.

Laurence entered Cambridge in 1733; thus he was twenty years old when he began his college career. At such a mature age for college entrance a student dependent in a measure upon charity might be expected to devote himself with some seriousness to his studies. However, two things made such a circumstance unlikely for Sterne: first, the state of university life at the time; and, second, his own temperament.

Throughout the eighteenth century both the great universities were notorious for their lax educational standards and for their general rowdiness. In his "Essay on Modern Education" Swift wrote that he had heard "more than one or two persons of high rank declare that they could learn nothing more at Oxford or Cambridge than to drink ale and smoke tobacco." Dr. Johnson revealed the laxities of discipline at Oxford, and Gibbon attested to the worthlessness of his own education. As late as 1776 the pious and great William Wilberforce was shocked at the licentiousness in talk and habit that he found when he entered Cambridge. It was notorious that gownsmen made bonfires in the courts, drank uproariously, and acted like Mohocks in insulting townsmen in the dimly lighted streets.

Gray wrote of the universal addiction to tobacco and to drinking parties. "There's nothing but whiffing from fellow to sizer," he exclaimed; "nay, even the very chimneys, that they mayn't be thought particular, must needs smoke." The "guzzling affairs," in which the young undergraduates participated, he described with vividness: "... imagine me pent up in a room hired for the purpose, and none of the largest, from 7 o'clock at night, till 4 in the morning! 'midst hogsheads of liquor and quantities of tobacco, surrounded by 30 of these creatures, infinitely below the meanest people you could even form an idea of; toasting bawdy healths and deafened with their unmeaning roar." The effeminate bookworm of Peterhouse (sometimes called

"Miss Gray" by his fellow-students) further delivered himself on the subject of Cambridge:

> Surely it was of this place, now Cambridge, but formerly known by the name of Babylon, that the prophet spoke when he said, "the wild beasts of the desert shall dwell there, and their houses shall be full of doleful creatures, and owls shall build there, and satyrs shall dance there; their forts and towers shall be a den for ever, a joy of wild asses; there shall the great owl make her nest, and lay and hatch and gather under her shadow; it shall be a court of dragons; the screech owl also shall rest there, and find for herself a place of rest."

In the absence of actual records, it is easy to surmise that Sterne acted at Cambridge at least to some extent like the son of his father and like his schoolmates. His earliest associates are uncertain; but on June 16, 1735—at the end of his second year—entered the man who was to be for the rest of his life his most constant friend. This lad called John Hall was later to be known as John Hall-Stevenson —a poetaster, eccentric, and country gentleman whose bibulous and bawdy propensities marked him for mild infamy. It is not difficult to imagine Hall, Sterne, and perhaps Tom Gilbert (a fellow of Gray's own college and eventually a member of Hall-Stevenson's "Demoniacs") taking part in just such drinking bouts as Gray describes, bandying salty jokes and obscene verses with all comers. If Laurence found any real deterrent to a life of conviviality at Cambridge, it was most probably a lack of money. But such an obstacle was not insuperable to one who could be the life of the party and who chose wealthy friends.

In his Cambridge days Laurie was already hollow chested and marked for the disease that was to hound him to his grave. One night he awoke to discover his bed wet with blood and to experience for the first time the horror of a hemorrhage from the lungs. But in spite of such an ominous portent, he seems in outward appearance to have reflected his precarious health remarkably little. Hall-Stevenson describes him as being very handsome. And, indeed, he must have been if he looked at all like the full-faced young man painted by Allan Ramsay, a painting without any of the consumptive suggestion of the usual portraits. In roundness of face, at least, the portrait suggests the comfortable smugness of a young Samuel Richardson rather than the thin resilience of Yorick; but the mischievous smile about the corners of the mouth and the twinkle in the eye suggest Shandean devilishness. The later Sterne gave a notably different appearance: a bloodless face with large lips, deep-set and luminous eyes, and a prominent nose.

We can depend upon Laurie's not having taken too much interest in his studies; that is, in so far as the formalities were concerned. He could not have been a joy to his tutors. He disliked anything that required mental exertion and shared with Gray a thorough distaste for Cantabrigian metaphysics and mathematics. Naturally, logic and rhetoric under the guidance of a dry-as-dust don were dull and repulsive if they kept him from sprawling with Hall-Stevenson under the favorite walnut tree in the court of Jesus College, a volume of Rabelais in hand. And nothing that a tutor could offer or the college library supply could be so exciting as the poems of the scandalous Lord Rochester or a novel by the equally scandalous Aphra Behn. Hall-Stevenson described the scene of arboreal education in his typically clumsy verse:

> At CAMBRIDGE, many years ago,
>   In JESUS, was a walnut-tree;
> The only thing it had to shew,
>   The only thing folks went to see.
> Being of such a size and mass,
>   And growing in so wise a College,

I wonder how it came to pass,
  It was not call'd the Tree of Knowledge.
Indeed, if you attempt to run
  (The air so heavy is, and muddy)
Any great length beyond a pun,
  You'll be obliged to sweat and study.
This is the reason 'tis so good for tisics,
  And will account why no one soph,
  No Fellow, ever could hit off,
To call this Tree the Tree of Metaphysics;
Though in the midst of the quadrangle,
  They every one were taught their trade;
They every one were taught to wrangle,
  Beneath its scientific shade.

Logic, Sterne was later to ridicule in *Tristram Shandy*, which is on the surface as colossal a violation of the science as one can find. Pedantry in general he was also to ridicule, though—lacking chiefly the *saeva indignatio*—he was never of the temperament to ridicule it exactly in the vein of Swift, Arbuthnot, and Pope. He kept his love for the classics, and in philosophy he found a real and enduring love. That love was John Locke, whose *Essay on the Human Understanding* was to be one of the most important influences on his thinking and was to give plan and purpose to his novel.

Although to people of pious or serious turn of mind university education in the eighteenth century was often a total loss, it was certainly not so to Sterne. The Shandean mind found guzzling affairs and tobacco smoke no real hindrance to its amorphous growth, for its development was not dependent upon books on tutorial lists or upon the sober and painstaking pursuit of knowledge. At all events, Cambridge in the end gave Laurie two degrees—and it gave him at least one life-long friend.

Sterne received his bachelor's degree from Cambridge

in January, 1737. Since he had no fortune of his own, he was forced to choose a profession.

In Sterne's day the matter of going into the Church involved no necessity of a devout life either before or after the choice was made. Laurence's citation for "exemplary life, good morals, and virtuous qualities" upon his being admitted to the diaconate was a mere convention. To many the Church was a career, somewhat in the same way that the army was; and jockeying for preferment often took precedence over the cure of souls. Indeed, the typical attitude of churchmen seemed to be that one could do most for God by doing as much as one could for oneself. Even a man of such superior intelligence and character as Jonathan Swift might allow himself to become deeply embittered by the failure to get the advancement for which he considered himself eminently fitted. Materialism, of course, did not grip the whole of the Church, which on occasions still had the power to change a man of the world into a man of God. But for Sterne, putting on the cloth worked no such profound religious change as that which came in the lives of two literary clergymen of the preceding century, Donne and Herbert.

The Church was an obvious choice for Laurie. Archbishop Sterne had established the tradition, which Uncle Jaques was carrying on in becoming style. The young aspirant's chances seemed good from the start. Another reason for the choice was that Laurie was hardly fitted to do anything else. A paraphrase of the frequently quoted slander against the teaching profession would have been explanation enough in a century in which the professions open to a gentleman were severely limited: "He who can does; he who cannot *preaches*." So, as Dr. John Hill observed, Sterne "seated himself quietly in the lap of the church; and if this was not yet covered with a fringed cushion, 'twas not naked."

Laurie was ordained deacon by the Bishop of Lincoln at Buckden Hall, near Huntingdon, about two months after he had received his degree in neighboring Cambridge. Equipped with a license for a curacy, he went to St. Ives, a sleepy little town on the sluggish Ouse River. Here he spent a year in obscurity so deep that the research of two centuries has not penetrated it. But Uncle Jaques's eye was on him, and after a year he was moved to an assistant curateship at Catton, another post that was dismal but that had the virtue of being only seven miles from York.

As Sterne neared priesthood, there was a considerable quickening in the interest of Uncle Jaques, now Archdeacon of Cleveland and Canon and Precentor of the York Cathedral. On August 20, 1738, Laurence was ordained priest in the bulky red sandstone cathedral at Chester with the laying on of hands by the resident bishop. Immediately, the Archbishop of York presented Sterne with the living of Sutton on the Forest, a village a few miles north of York. Again, the parish was unattractive, but it paid forty pounds a year and the incumbent, if he so desired, could live in York. Soon there came additional preferment. The award of the prebend of Givendale made Laurence a member of the cathedral chapter and gave him the opportunity of preaching in his turn in the great church.

Especially during the racing season, York lost its quaint torpor and took on an atmosphere of smartness and fashion; and much of the briskness was carried over into the winter gaieties for which it drew widely from the "county" families. The center of social life was in the Assembly Rooms designed by the Earl of Burlington and surpassed in elegance and importance not even by those of Bath and Tunbridge Wells. The main room was an antique Egyptian hall from Palladio, richly carved and ornamented, and equipped with thirteen dazzling lustres with an even more dazzling center lustre, the magnificent gift of the Earl. Here were held balls and musicales; and here the loveliest belles of the county were displayed to eligible young bachelors.

The newly ordained clergyman cut an unusual figure in the assemblies of his first winter as Vicar of Sutton. He was not one to allow the black of his garb to cloud the brightness of his spirit. Neither in dress nor in manners was he a Beau Brummel; but, assuredly, many a young lady fell under the spell of his sentimental conversation.

Among the young ladies who moved in the fashionable throng of the ornate Oriental hall was one Elizabeth Lumley, the daughter of a well-to-do country clergyman who after her father's death had taken up residence in a rambling old house in what was then called Little Alice Lane (the present College Street). Since she was in the middle twenties, Miss Lumley was not in the first flush of girlhood, but she managed to conceal her age with superior skill. No one ever claimed beauty for her. A pastel portrait by Francis Cotes shows her as having an almost expressionless face with a small, sullen mouth, a receding chin, a fairly large nose, and eyes somewhat heavily lidded. Gossipy John Croft spoke of her with bluntness:

> Tho' she was but a homely woman, still she had many admirers, as she was reported to have a fortune, and she possessed a first rate understanding.

It should be added that she was a capable musician and had a passable voice. It is entirely possible that her prospects of a fortune should have made her attractive to an impecunious young clergyman like Sterne, and her intellectual and musical accomplishments may have deluded him into the thought of a marriage of true minds. Otherwise, it is difficult to explain why he did not devote his attention to the younger and more beautiful belles who came to York from the surrounding countryside to grace the assemblies and to snare husbands.

Sterne's wooing of Miss Lumley took on several aspects of the medieval courtly love affair. It was by no means a whirlwind match: it covered a period of two years in which sentimental extravagances played an important part and in which the climax was reached in a scene that would have graced that remarkable anomaly for which the eighteenth-century stage is famous or infamous, the sentimental comedy. The procedure of the courtship in Little Alice Lane, the tender attentions that Laurie paid his Bess at the assemblies, and the languishings while he was briefly away at Sutton are not matters of record. But a visit paid by Miss Lumley to her sister in Staffordshire in 1739-40 provided the occasion for Sterne's writing a series of letters giving a remarkable insight into his exaggerated emotional life.

When Sterne gets down to the serious business of delineating his passion, it is difficult to decide whether rhetoric has run away with feeling or whether feeling has run away with rhetoric. Not Troilus in all his pangs for the yet unyielding Criseyde could strike a pose of more exquisite pain. When Miss Lumley left town, Laurie moved into her lodgings, which he fancifully regarded as a rustic cottage surrounded by roses and jessamines and romantically named, for no easily apparent reason, "D'Estella." "The hour you left D'Estella," he wrote in what seems to be his first letter, "I took to my bed." He continued:

> The good Miss S—, from the forebodings of the best of hearts, thinking I was ill, insisted upon my going to her.—What can be the cause, my dear L., that I never have been able to see the face of this mutual friend, but I feel myself rent to pieces. She made me stay an hour with her, and in that short space I burst into tears a dozen different times—and in such affectionate gusts of passion that she was constrained to leave the room....

He was seized by a sudden paroxysm when he was confronted at the dinner table by "one solitary plate, one knife, one fork, one glass!" And his heavy sighing, his loss of appetite, and his general debility moved the maid, Fanny, to pity—and to the application of hartshorn as a remedy. The letter ends in a superstroke of elaborate melodrama: "Ah me!—but adieu!—the vesper-bell calls me from thee to my God." (Neither of whom did he ever serve with consummate devotion.)

In another letter Laurence pictured himself in retirement in a "little sun-gilt cottage, on the side of a romantic hill" with Love and Friendship for his sole companions. And then the extravagance of his imagination took a Rousseauistic turn: "We will build, and we will plant, in our own way—simplicity shall not be tortured by art—we will learn of nature how to live—she shall be our alchymist, to mingle all the good of life into one salubrious draught."

This was an exhausting pace that could hardly have lasted. Twice later Sterne was to wish this same Elizabeth Lumley dead so that he could marry two other ladies—not, however, simultaneously. It may also be argued that he borrowed some of the very language of his most profusely sentimental letter to apply it to the object of his last and almost incredible love affair. These incidents run far ahead of our story, it is true; but Sterne's passion seems not even to have outlasted Miss Lumley's Staffordshire visit, for the lady was eventually accusing him of failure to write. Although his apologies are couched in language that is sufficiently sentimental, the protestations of an acute love malady are lacking. Laurie pictures his beloved walking in a Staffordshire garden in the spring and casts her, conventionally enough, in the rôle of handmaid to Flora and Pomona, who "will load thee with their sweet blessing." "Sweet as this may be," he continues, "return—return—the birds of Yorkshire will tune their pipes, and sing as melodiously as those of Staffordshire." But when she speaks of coming back to York, his ecstasy tapers off into a sentimental consideration of how the shrubs and flowers of Staffordshire will droop and fade with her departure:

> Who will be thy successor to nurse them in thy absence? –Thou wilt leave thy name upon the myrtle tree.–If trees, and shrubs, and flowers could compose an elegy, I should expect a very plaintive one upon this subject.

A man more genuinely in love would have preferred the contemplation of a hymeneal hymn to such a pastoral elegy.

In the midst of the affair Sterne's friend and "cousin" John Hall-Stevenson had acquired his hyphenated name and had assured himself financial security in a way that the *York Courant* for February 12, 1740, reported like a transaction on the exchange: "Last week John Hall of Skelton Castle, Esq; was married to Miss Stephenson, a young lady of 25,000l Fortune. The Ceremony was perform'd by the Rev. Mr. Sterne of Sutton-Forest." Such an event might have inspired Sterne to see himself safely settled, although he could not have hoped for so dazzling a fortune.

At any rate, Miss Lumley's interest did not flag; nor perhaps did her ability for stratagem. "I believe she was partly determined to have me," Sterne asserted in his little autobiography, although she held back because she "thought herself not rich enough, or me too poor." The climax is dramatically presented in the brief but astonishingly compact memoirs. The setting is one evening in the Assembly Rooms. Miss Lumley had had what seemed a touch of consumption. While Sterne was sitting by her "with an almost broken heart to see her so ill," she remarked: "My dear Laurey, I can never be yours for I verily believe I have not long to live–" Then came the master-stroke. "But," she added, "I have left you every shilling of my fortune." (She had just fallen heir to a portion of the estate of a distant relative at Leeds.) By the time Sterne wrote this account he was too thoroughly the artist to be capable of telling the unadorned truth. But even if it is partially true, few men were ever taken at a less fair advantage. When the lady produced the will, Laurence was lost.

"It pleased God that she recovered," he recorded with eloquent pithiness, "and I married her in the year 1741." Needless to say, Mrs. Sterne outlived her husband. In scarcely more than a decade after their marriage whatever physical attraction Elizabeth Lumley had had for Laurie had vanished and their relations had ceased to be conjugal. Before the end of the second decade Sterne was disposed to write in dog-Latin to Hall-Stevenson that he was tired and sick of his wife. In one of his sermons, "The History of Jacob Considered," he rationalized with his usual facility:

> Listen, I pray you, to the stories of the disappointed in marriage!—collect all their complaints:—hear their mutual reproaches; upon what fatal hinge do the greatest part of them turn?—They were mistaken in the person.—Some disguise, either of body or mind, is seen through in the first domestic scuffle;—some fair ornament,—perhaps the very one that won the heart,—"the ornament of a meek and quiet spirit," falls off.

Undoubtedly his own marriage was not made in heaven.

The couple were married by the Dean of York on Easter Monday, March 30. A scandalous story is told to the effect that when Sterne appeared before his congregation (including, of course, his bride) at Sutton on the following Sunday, he based his sermon on the text: "We have toiled all night and taken nothing." This is typical of the kind of story—unauthenticated, to be sure—for which Sterne was to prove a convenient peg. We do know on good authority, however, that before his marriage he had got a reputation not entirely becoming a clergyman. A few weeks after the wedding a half-cousin of Mrs. Sterne, Matthew Robinson, wrote from Bath to his sister Elizabeth, later the famous Mrs. Montagu:

> Our cousin Betty Lumley is married to a Parson who once delighted in debauchery, who is possessed of about £100 a year in preferment, and has good prospect of more. What hopes our relation may have of settling the affections of a light and fickle man I know not, but I imagine she will set about it not by means of beauty but of the arm of flesh.

Neither the nature nor the extent of the alleged debauchery has ever been made clear. Mrs. Montagu herself seems to have given some credence to this report, for she later wrote of Sterne: "He was a great rake, but being japanned [i. e., ordained] and married has varnished his character." The debauchery and the subsequent varnish may have been of equal depth. Perhaps the gaieties of his college days, his delight in ribaldry, and his friendship for Hall-Stevenson were his blackest sins. But in the face of persistent rumors to the contrary, it would be unsafe to argue for anything like pre-marital chastity in Sterne. As a matter of fact, there is even an ominous possibility (as we shall see) that his youthful indiscretions may have tainted him with a disease which, though unperceived as such by him or his wife, may have determined some of his marital difficulties to a greater extent than anyone has yet dared to suggest. Whatever his vices were, "the arm of flesh" could scarcely hope to be highly efficacious against them. Betty Lumley might better have employed "the ornament of a meek and quiet spirit."

CHAPTER III

"A WHIG IN A PARSON'S GOWN"

i

MARRIAGE OFFERED to Sterne the first real home that he had ever known, and he could not have failed to find satisfaction in the thought. But, unfortunately, the bridal pair were not able to move directly into a "sun-gilt cottage" on a "romantic hill," nor was Laurie to be allowed to live his own life as country parson and paterfamilias. Sutton was a small community in a flat and marshy area north of York. It consisted of the grange of Squire Harland, a little row of cottages, a square-towered stone church, and a parsonage well concealed by shrubbery. Laurence described the parsonage as a "large ruinous house" that demanded many repairs before it could be occupied: there had to be stuccoing and bricking and, to conform to the latest fashion in construction, sashing. Moreover, a house had to be built for the carriage of the parson's lady. All these matters were obliged to produce some exasperation, for building and repair costs always have a way of getting out of hand. Well might Sterne end a statement of renovation costs with an item charged to "God knows what–"

Real pleasure was later to come in laying out walks, in planting shrubs and trees, and in doing other things toward making the rectory a comfortable and attractive place to live in for twenty years. But whatever may have been Laurence's inclination to anticipate Voltaire's advice and dig in his own garden, plans had been made for him to dig in the political gardens of other people. Like many another frocked Yorkshireman, Uncle Jaques had for years dabbled in politics. In York the Tories and the Whigs were sharply divided; and almost as much of the maneuvering for the Whig cause went on in the Minster Yard as in the less sacred precincts of the George Inn in Coney Street. As far back as the election of 1734 seeds of a deep animosity had been sown between the Precentor (Dr. Sterne) and Dr. John Burton, who was a Tory, a scholar of sorts, and an obstetrician considerably in advance of his time. In the 1734 election Dr. Sterne was on the Whig bandwagon—as he was to be many times afterward—with an eye on any and all preferment that might be grasped as a plum for ardent electioneering. In this election, which was a clear success for the Whigs, there were plums; and a very fine one, the Archdeaconry of Cleveland, fell into the lap of Dr. Sterne. On the losing side in the contest was Dr. Burton. When this gentleman a few years later attempted to build a hospital for the poor in York, he found no support in the Whiggish purlieus of the Cathedral. Chagrin may have made him vindictive. At any rate, he decided to air the dirty linen of the political clique in the Minster Yard, bringing against Dr. Sterne and his associates the grave charge that they had planned to use the Sacrament Money, traditionally assigned to the poor, as a campaign fund for the next election.

One can readily see why the Precentor, guilty or innocent, should have been consumed with ire for the Tories even before the next campaign got under way. But there was an additional reason why feeling should run high. The Whig government in London had fallen on lean years, and Sir Robert Walpole's power was teetering. Since every man counted as the straw that might save or break the Whig party's long ascendency, the Yorkshire Whigs were on their toes, and a fight to the death could be expected whenever their representation was seriously threatened. In April, 1741, the retirement of Cholmley Turner, long a Whig M.P., had necessitated an effort to return another Whig member in his place; but the election of the following month had occasioned no particular trouble. Sir Miles Stapylton and the young Viscount Morpeth were elected to hold Whig seats. However, the real struggle began in the summer of the same year with the untimely death of Lord Morpeth and the consequent candidacy of the Tory George Fox, a wealthy Londoner who owned a Yorkshire estate. The Whigs regarded the situation as particularly dangerous; for, since Turner was in retirement, they had no strong candidate to offer. The only solution that presented itself to them was to insist upon Turner's standing once again for the Shire and to campaign furiously against Fox.

Before the May election Dr. Sterne seems to have planned to go into politics on an extended scale with a bishopric as his goal and had conceived the idea of establishing a paper to offset the influence of Caesar Ward's Tory *Courant*. Thus it was that Laurie was drafted from whatever pleasures he might have got from a honeymoon or from gardening at Sutton to take a job as political journalist—a writer of "paragraphs," as he called it—on the *York Gazeteer*, which was issued from the press of John Jackson in Grape-Lane. After the demise of Lord Morpeth the contest between the *Gazeteer* and the *Courant* waxed warm, turning into a mud battle in which Laurie, although he later denounced the whole affair as "dirty work," was far from being clean-handed. In spite of the fact that Turner was returned, Laurie's political efforts were not conspicuously successful. His attacks on Fox naturally met with answers from the Tories who gave as good as Laurie sent, and sometimes better, until at least in one instance the matter turned out to be a personal combat between Sterne and an anonymous Foxite. Laurie's spindle legs and frail physique were not immune to attack, and at times he found himself the victim of such a Popean paraphrase as the following:

> Let L———y *Scribble—what? that Thing of Silk,*
> L———y *that mere white Curd of Ass's Milk?*
> *Satire or Sense, alas! can* L———y *feel?*
> *Who breaks a Butterfly upon a Wheel?*

Other attacks were just as severe and were decidedly more Rabelaisian, the upshot being that the youthful journalist was before long to find the whole business distasteful and annoying.

In the midst of the campaign there arose another circumstance that tended to make Laurie's life uncomfortably complex. We have seen how, after the death of Roger Sterne, Agnes Sterne and her daughter Catherine attempted to throw themselves on the Yorkshire relatives and how, having been given no encouragement, they were forced to return to Ireland, where they lived on a government pension of £20 a year and the income from an embroidery school. So far as the facts can be determined, mother and sister had been contented to stay in Ireland until they heard a rumor that Laurie had married an heiress. Immediately their interest in Sterne increased, and they set out for Yorkshire, ostensibly with the idea of attaching themselves to their kinsman and playing ladies for the rest of their lives. For Laurence the situation was a most delicate one. There can be little doubt that Mrs. Sterne and her daughter were loud-mouthed and uncouth. Even Dr. Jaques Sterne and Mrs. Custobadie, the wife of the Registrar of the Chapter, had spoken of Agnes's "clamorous and rapacious temper." Sterne had had almost no contact with his mother and sister since he was ten years old, and his associations and training of the intervening years had widened the social gulf between them. All emotional ties between mother and son had been severed long before, and poor Agnes could have been nothing but a stranger to her child.

To a young clergyman who was struggling to establish himself, who was trying to remodel a parsonage, and who was embroiled in a distasteful political campaign, the news of Mrs. Sterne's landing at Liverpool came as a severe and terrifying blow. Laurie dropped everything and rushed to Liverpool in the hope of heading off his mother and convincing her that the situation would be better for everybody concerned if she and Catherine remained quietly in Ireland. Sterne's main line of argument was an attempt to disillusion his mother as to his wealth. In his representations on this point, he did not scruple at exaggerating in his own favor. He later wrote to his Uncle Jaques:

> I convinced her, that besides the interest of my wife's fortune, I had then but a base hundred pounds a year, out of which my ill health obliged me to keep a curate, that we had moreover ourselves to keep, and in that sort of decency which left it not in our powers to give her much: that what we could spare, she should as certainly receive in Ireland as here; that the place she had left was a cheap country—her native one, and where she was sensible 20 pounds a year was more than equal to 30 here, besides the discount of having her pension paid in England where it was not due; and the utter impossibility I was under of making up so many deficiencies.

For "convinced" in the first sentence, we should read "attempted to convince." The "base hundred pounds" was an understatement of at least fifty pounds. Aside from these discrepancies of fact, Sterne's logic appears irrefutable. Mrs. Sterne had foolishly and needlessly thrown away the income from her embroidery school and had jeopardized her pension, and furthermore, she had attempted to thrust herself on her son at a most unpropitious moment. If she had come when Sterne was better established, she might have had a warmer reception. With such facts in mind, Sterne's statement about the conclusion of his argument does not appear quite so ridiculous and reprehensible as it does out of its context:

I concluded with representing to her, the inhumanity of a mother *able* to maintain herself, thus forcing herself as a burden upon a son who was scarce able to support himself without breaking in upon the future support of another person whom she might imagine was much dearer to me.

But Mrs. Sterne was not to be moved by what she evidently considered to be specious reasoning. Her son was too zealous in his argument to be convincing. Besides, she had come to England to live at her ease either in York or Chester, and stay she would. Sterne's hasty trip to Liverpool, therefore, turned out to be unsuccessful in its main object; but Laurence did convince his mother and sister that they should remain in Chester. And it must be said to his credit that he contributed to their support. Laurie describes his parting from Mrs. Sterne with the melodramatic touch that we may expect when he is arguing his own case: "I took my leave with assuring her—that though my income was strait, I should not forget I was a son, though she had forgot she was a mother."

To return to the Whig campaign, after some ten months of pamphlet and newspaper controversy Sterne was heartily sick of his part in it. And when the election was all over, what did he get as a reward? The Reverend Robert Hitch, man of God that he was, overheated himself in December while canvassing for votes and, a martyr to the Whig cause, passed on to seek heavenly preferment. As a result, Laurie was presented with Hitch's prebend of North Newbald, somewhat richer than that of Givendale which he already held. (The living of Stillington, which he acquired about the same time, did not come in payment of political service.) For ten months' service of body and soul Sterne felt that he had been paid in a way that was niggardly enough. Then on top of the hard contest came the worst possible blow: Walpole's government fell. Thus everything that Sterne had worked for must have seemed to collapse like a house of cards. If the Tories were to be in power, little good it now did to be a rampant Whig. Partially as a result of the dêbacle, George Fox was elected in July, 1742, to represent the city of York in Parliament. A disillusioned Sterne recanted in a letter to Caesar Ward, the editor of the *Courant:*

Sir,

I find by some late preferments, that it may not be improper to change sides; therefore I beg the favour of you to inform the public, that I sincerely beg pardon for the abusive Gazetteers I wrote during the late contested election for the County of York, and that I heartily wish Mr. Fox joy of his election for the City.

Tempora Mutantur, & nos mutemur in illis.
I am, Sir, your Penitent Friend and Servant,

L. S.

Times might change and so might Laurie, but not Uncle Jaques, who had a memory like an elephant and who could have looked only with cold fury upon the apostasy of his protegé. "He quarrelled with me afterwards," Sterne later wrote, "because I would not write paragraphs in the newspapers—though he was a party-man, I was not and detested such dirty work, thinking it beneath me." This is another classic example of understatement. Dr. Jaques could have regarded the matter as no trivial one. He was betrayed and the Whig cause was betrayed; thus his wrath was to be implacable and he was to take his revenge in due time.

ii

The culmination of Sterne's unfortunate political activity left him more time to consider his duties as parish priest and head of a household. In May of 1743 he was writing in answer to a questionnaire sent out by the Archbishop that he resided personally upon his cure and in his parsonage house, that there were about three hundred and twenty families in his parish, that he had made an effort to prevail upon the Quakers in his parish to attend church, and that he was particularly zealous in conducting his confirmation classes.

> I catechise every Sunday in my church during Lent, but explain our religion to the children and servants of my parishioners in my own house every Sunday night during Lent from six o'clock till nine. I mention the length of time as my reason for not doing it in church.

Only Laurie could have kept heads from nodding during such lengthy sessions—if, indeed, he did so.

The parson also developed notions of indulging in the gentlemanly sport of farming. The impulse was perfectly natural for one who liked pottering about among flowers and fruit trees. Moreover, he had rights in the glebe of his benefice, and he was never averse to augmenting his income. Nothing is so enchanting as farming in the air or on paper. A handful of seed multiplies as if by a magician's touch into a groaning harvest; a hen and a cock produce a lucrative commerce in eggs and poultry. By the time Sterne wrote *Tristram Shandy* he knew the folly of calculations that leave nothing out of account but Nature. Through Mr. Shandy, Sterne reflected what must have gone on in his own naïve mind:

> ... it was plain he should reap a hundred lasts of rape, at twenty pounds a last, the very first year—besides an excellent crop of wheat the year following—and the year after that, to speak within bounds, a hundred—but in all likelihood, a hundred and fifty—if not two hundred quarters of pease and beans —besides potatoes without end.

The vision was an alluring one; but one could be disillusioned in time. In the last year of his life Laurence summed up his disillusionment in a letter to Sir William Stanhope:

> I was once such a puppy myself, as to pare, and burn, and had my labour for my pains, and two hundred pounds out of pocket.—Curse on farming (said I) I will try if the pen will not succeed better than the spade.—The following up of that affair (I mean farming) made me lose my temper, and a cart load of turneps was (I thought) very dear at two hundred pounds....

While the prospects looked rosy, Laurence borrowed enough money from his wife to buy a farm. They stocked it with cows and geese, and embarked on their experiment. Inexperience was not long in taking its toll, and the novelty began wearing thin. Although Sterne was eventually convinced that he had assumed more responsibility than he could handle with pleasure, in one way or another over more than a decade he increased his holdings of land; and his letters give evidence of the attention—sometimes grudging—that he gave to his crops.

Sterne is responsible for a remarkable self-portrait or caricature (as it actually is) that delightfully reflects the early years at Sutton. He introduces this aspect of himself in the first book of *Tristram Shandy* in the person of Yorick, a parson mounted on "a lean, sorry, jackass of a horse, value about one pound fifteen shillings." The exaggeration is a waggish attempt both to cast himself in a Cervantic mould and also to see himself as others were inclined to see him. Jest-loving, irresponsible, naïve, good-naturedly wayward and eccentric—he presented a curious and amusing phenomenon to his parishioners:

> In the several sallies about his parish, and in the neighbouring visits to the gentry who lived around him—you will easily comprehend, that the parson, so appointed, would both hear

and see enough to keep his philosophy from rusting. To speak the truth, he never could enter a village, but he caught the attention of both old and young.–Labour stood still as he passed –the bucket hung suspended in the middle of the well–the spinning wheel forgot its round,–even chuck-farthing and shuffle-cap themselves stood gaping till he had got out of sight; and as his movement was not of the quickest, he had generally time enough upon his hands to make his observations,–to hear the groans of the serious,–and the laughter of the light-hearted; all which he bore with excellent tranquillity.–His character was,–he loved a jest in his heart–and as he saw himself in the true point of ridicule, he would say he could not be angry with others for seeing him in a light, in which he so strongly saw himself.

In his parish of Stillington Laurie made such a close friend of the genial squire, Stephen Croft, that a warm reception always awaited him at Stillington Hall. With Philip Harland, the more hard-bitten and practical Tory squire of Sutton, the matter was somewhat different. At least at the outset this redoubtable gentleman refused to see anything charming or amusing in a Don Quixote in clerical dress. As time went on, however, his attitude softened.

Unbiased information about the years at Sutton is scanty, especially if we discount (as, indeed, we should) much of the gossip passed down to us in *The Whitefoord-Papers* and in *Scrapeana* by a brother of Squire Croft. "It grieves me to speak harshly of any member of the family of Crofts of Oporto," wrote the late Dr. Saintsbury some years ago, "... Stephen's brother John tittle-tattled in his later years to Caleb Whitefoord and otherwise a good deal of stuff about 'Yorick,' which is obviously spiteful, which almost confesses itself to be second- (or further) hand, and which I venture to regard as almost to the last degree untrustworthy. John was a mere child (he was born in 1732) when Sterne came to Stillington; he left to join the business in Portugal; when he came back he admits that he found Sterne 'much taken up in the gay world' which made 'a wide gap in [their] intimacy.'" A lurid example of John Croft's tid-bits is his version of Laurie's quarrel with Uncle Jaques, manifestly gossipy in the extreme:

> In his younger years he [Sterne] was a good deal employed by his Uncle, in writing political papers and pamphlets in favour of Sir Robert Walpole's Administration, when they afterwards fell out about a favourite mistress of the Precentor's, who proved with child by Laury and the cause of their breach is now living. The Lady is said to resemble Sterne very much, though at the time of their rupture, he gave out as a reason in the public coffee house, that it arose from that he would not continue to write periodical papers for his Uncle.

This is the kind of story that the Yorkshire Tories might have told to discredit their Whig opponents in the Church, but it could hardly have commanded wide credence.

The most famous story (although it was admitted by the narrator to be an "idle tale") concerns the parson's custom of preaching at Sutton in the morning and walking over to Stillington to repeat his sermon in the afternoon. Once, relates Croft, while Laurie "was going over the fields on a Sunday to preach at Stillington, it happened that his pointer dog sprung a covey of partridge, when he went directly home for his gun and left his flock that was waiting for him in the church in the lurch." Sterne himself would have enjoyed both the story and the grotesque sentence structure; but there is no reason to believe that the incident ever happened. Croft would also have us believe that the Sternes' lack of success in farming was due to their improvidently selling produce more cheaply than their neighbors did. Then he passed on two stories apparently designed to contradict Laurence's own suggestion in the portrait of Yorick that he was beloved of his parishioners.

Once while Sterne was skating on the pond in Stillington Common, the first story ran, the ice broke and none of his parishioners would attempt to save him. "Another time a flock of geese assembled in the churchyard at Sutton, when his wife bawl'd out 'Laurie, powl 'em,' i.e. pluck the quills, on which they [the parishioners] were ready to riot and mob Laurie."

Obviously, these gossipy bits do not shed much real light on Sterne's early activity as a parish priest. Except for Laurence's protestations of his love for his wife during his attempts to convince his mother not to become an additional responsibility, we know little of the domestic situation at the parsonage. Croft asserts categorically that from the outset Sterne was unfaithful and that serious disagreement between him and Elizabeth was early in getting a start. For the first part of the charge there is no clear evidence. For the second, there is the support of Laurence's own intimation to the effect that the discovery of incompatibility came soon after the marriage. The preoccupation with obstetrics in *Tristram Shandy* suggests the unfortunate and even tragic cause of some of the turmoil in the Sutton parsonage during the early years of Sterne's married life. After at least one miscarriage, Mrs. Sterne gave birth to a girl baby in 1745. Like many of Agnes Sterne's babies, this bit of humanity proved ephemeral, dying the day after birth. The baby lived just long enough to be named Lydia in compliment to Mrs. Sterne's sister. Two years later another baby was born and was also named Lydia. Four or five years after the second Lydia's birth a still-born child arrived. There were no more children. To a modern gynecologist the syndrome just described might possibly produce suspicion of venereal disease, especially since Lydia turned out to be a frail and (as it was rumored) epileptic child and since Mrs. Sterne herself developed a significant neurosis. That Laurence ever sensed any real tragedy in the situation he never once intimated; and Mrs. Sterne was by nature so unattractive to almost everybody that she has eternally cut herself off from some of the sympathy that she deserves.

Although Croft tells us that Laurence's parishioners considered him "crazy or crackbrained," he makes no specific comment on the way in which Sterne's preaching was received at Sutton and Stillington. He does have something to say about the attitude in York. "When it was Sterne's turn to preach at the Minster," he reports, "half of the congregation usually went out of church as soon as he mounted the pulpit, as his delivery and voice were so very disagreeable." Charming though his printed discourses are, Sterne was certainly no great pulpit orator. But again Croft's testimony is subject to question. At least on two special and important occasions during his first decade at Sutton, the gaunt and eccentric parish priest mounted pulpits in York without causing a general exodus. The first occasion came on Good Friday, in 1747, when he preached the annual charity sermon in St. Michael le Belfrey and succeeded through his persuasive powers in bringing in something over sixty-four pounds for two local schools.

In 1750 as chaplain to Sir William Pennyman he preached to a large congregation at the close of the summer Assizes. The Assizes usually brought a carnival spirit to York, in spite of the fact that the prisons might be full and that many sordid cases might be on the calendar. The streets were filled with townspeople in dark blue coats, glossy black hats scrupulously brushed, and mirror-like boots; officers and soldiers added a dash of red; and young ladies in white muslins floated down the narrow streets like little perfumed clouds. On the opening and closing Sundays of the Assizes, the Minster was the scene of colorful pageantry. First came the judges with their jet-black robes and enormous powdered wigs. Then came the mayor and the corporation followed by footmen in white livery, large nosegays in their buttonholes. Add to this the usual pageantry of a great cathedral and one has the setting for the sermon that the Vicar of Sutton and Stillington preached before "the Hon. Mr. Baron Clive and the Hon. Mr. Baron Smythe, the high sheriff, the grand jury, and about a thousand less important people." Laurence assuredly felt his own importance and treated the occasion with all the eloquence that he commanded. The sermon that he chose for the day was one of his best. It was well organized and, as Mr. Shandy was later allowed to comment, "dramatic." Taking as his text Hebrews XIII 18—"For we trust we have a good conscience"—Sterne artfully began with a half denial of it. Before he had finished, he had inserted a little of everything that would have made a sermon successful for the particular audience for which it had been carefully planned. There were character sketches with serious and humorous suggestion; there were touches of sentiment; there was a warm coloring of anti-Catholic feeling in the vivid description of the horrors of the Inquisition. But, best of all, there were frequent references to legal procedure, and the whole sermon could be taken as a subtle compliment to the judges. That it was one of Sterne's own favorite sermons is suggested by the fact that he included it in *Tristram Shandy*, waggishly allowing Dr. Slop to go to sleep while he was listening to Corporal Trim's rendition of it.

iii

Dr. Jaques Sterne could wait for his revenge on his nephew. For a few years after the beginning of their quarrel the Precentor contented himself with making life unpleasant for the Jacobites and for Dr. Burton. Never had the reverend gentleman had such a brilliant opportunity to display his noisy patriotism as he had during the excitement of 1745. When Bonnie Prince Charlie and his Highlanders invaded England, Dr. Sterne was galvanized into action. With godly zeal and eloquence he defended King George, "The Defender of the Faith"; he attacked popery on every hand; he helped ferret out Jacobites and to see that they found their way to the gallows. During all the excitement, Laurence was considerably less active than his relentless uncle, although he showed his loyalty by a very generous contribution to the Archbishop's defense fund and by eloquent sermons preached against the Mass and other Popish practices. In a day when few people chose to make a clear distinction between Tory and Papist, Dr. Burton was not so discreet. While he was out of the city on a visit to his estates, he allowed himself to be captured by the Highlanders. His subsequent release cast grave suspicions on him as a Jacobite. Dr. Sterne pursued him with a passion and would no doubt have relished seeing the doctor marched to the gallows to have his heart cut out if evidence could have been found to prove Jacobite connections.

Dr. Burton was fortunate enough to escape such a violent fate only to achieve an undesirable immortality at the hands of Dr. Sterne's recalcitrant nephew. Laurie's dislike for the pompous little doctor could hardly have arisen out of sympathy for Uncle Jaques' attitude toward him. He must have had a reason of his own. John Croft suggested in an anecdote such a simple (or complex) reason as a natural antipathy:

> Sterne meeting Dr. Burton, in the Minster Yard, York, and entering into discourse some difference arose, on which the Doctor, vehemently said, 'Sir, I never give way to a fool!' Sterne, stopping him short, replied, 'but I always do, Sir;' and directly gave him the way.

But had it not been for Dr. Burton's turning author with scholarly pretentions, and had it not been for his ridiculous fiasco in supporting the son of George Fox in the election of 1758, the "man-midwife" might not have proved such ready material for satire just when Laurie was embarking upon *Tristram Shandy*. The mere fact that he had issued an ostentatious folio, called *Monasticon Eboracense* and purporting to be an ecclesiastical history of Yorkshire, might alone have tempted Sterne to deflate the turgid and excessively ambitious author.

When the alarm of the '45 was over, the Minster Yard could return to its own disagreements. In such a place it was only natural that jealousies and rivalries should be burning away briskly under godly chasubles and stoles. In a somewhat complicated and extended controversy between Archbishop Hutton and Dean Fountayne, we find Dr. Jaques arrayed on the side of the Archbishop, whereas Laurie was on the side of his college friend, the Dean. Of course, the situation could not be calculated to lessen the breach between uncle and nephew. More strongly than ever did the Precentor feel the need for putting the ungrateful prebendary in his place. One of the most direct means of doing so was through an attempt to cut off some of Laurie's income.

Preaching in the Cathedral was done by members of the Chapter according to a pre-arranged calendar; but a member was not forced to preach his turn if he could provide a substitute. For one reason or another, members of the Chapter quite frequently found it convenient not to serve; consequently, the business of substitute preaching became a fairly lucrative one. Often the preaching itself was little more than a formality. One might dust off an old sermon of one's own, or lift a message from one of the divines whose printed sermons were easily accessible. On special occasions, as we have seen, the great church might be filled with an impressive throng, and there might even be enough lovely ladies to charm the roving eyes of certain prebendaries. But the kind of congregation that might just as likely turn up is suggested by an autograph note that Sterne made on one of his printed sermons: "Made on All Saints and preached on that day 1750 for the Dean.—Present 1 bellows blower, 3 singing men, one vicar and 1 residentiary." No matter how perfunctory one's performance might be, a pound was paid for the job. Sterne seems to have been rather zealous in picking up an additional income by taking over the turns of other members of the Chapter. For several years after the beginning of his quarrel with the Precentor, he even took over on occasion the turn of Dr. Jaques himself, although never at the Precentor's request. As the breach between uncle and nephew widened Dr. Sterne determined to put a stop to Laurence's profitable business.

A sort of clearing house for the substitute preaching was the bookshop at the sign of the Golden Bible in Stonegate. Apparently, in most cases Hildyard, the proprietor, was allowed to arrange substitutions according to his own judgment in the matter. Late in October, 1750, however, when Archdeacon Blackburne requested the bookseller to fill his turn he hinted that Laurence would not be acceptable, since the choice of him might offend the Precentor. Sterne has delightfully described the amusing scene that ensued between himself and Hildyard:

I stepped into his shop just after the sermon on *All Saints*, when with an air of much gravity and importance, he beckoned me to follow him into an inner room. No sooner had he shut the door but with the awful solemnity of a premier who held a *lettre de cachet* upon whose contents my life or liberty depended—after a minute's pause—he thus opens his commission:

"Sir, my friend the Archdeacon of Cleveland not caring to preach his turn, as I conjectured, has left me to provide a preacher—but before I can take any steps in it with regard to you—I want first to know, Sir, upon what footing you and Dr. Sterne are."

"Upon what footing!"

"Yes, Sir, how your quarrel stands."

"What's that to you?—How our quarrel stands! What's that to you, you Puppy!"

"But, Sir, Mr. Blackburne would know."

"What's that to him?"

"But, Sir, don't be angry. I only want to know of you whether Dr. Sterne will not be displeased in case you should preach."

"Go, look. I've just now been preaching and you could not have fitter opportunity to be satisfied."

"I hope, Mr. Sterne, you are not angry."

"Yes, I am; but much more astonished at your *impudence.*"

I know not whether the Chancellor's stepping in at this instant and flapping to the door did not save his tender soul the pain of the last word. However that be, he retreats upon this unexpected rebuff, takes the Chancellor aside, asks his advice, comes back submissive, begs quarter, tells me Dr. Herring had quite satisfied him as to the grounds of his scruple (though not of his folly), and therefore beseeches me to let the matter pass and to preach the turn.

At first, Sterne was very angry, but when Hildyard actually produced the letter from the Archdeacon and demonstrated that it contained only a "cautious hint," Laurence swallowed his pride and consented to preach the turn. Later he apologized to the Archdeacon for his heat and asked for any other turns that Blackburne might wish to pass along to him. "You would even do me a *favor* to let me have them," he wrote; "I say a *favor*, for by the by my daughter will be twenty pounds a better fortune by the favors I've received of this kind from the Dean and Residentiaries this year... You who are a *Father* will easily guess and as easily excuse my motive." (Lydia was now a young lady of five and the apple of her father's eye.)

Dr. Jaques, of course, could not be won by such paternal sentimentalism. He was quick to make protest:

Good Mr. Archdeacon,

I will beg leave to rely upon your pardon for taking the liberty I do with you in relation to your turns of preaching in the Minster. What occasions it is Mr. Hildyard's employing the last time the only person unacceptable to me in the whole Church, an ungrateful, an unworthy nephew of my own, the Vicar of Sutton; I should be much obliged to you if you would please either to appoint any person yourself, or leave it to your Register to appoint one when you are not here. If any of my turns would suit you better than your own, I would change with you.

This affair should have been sufficient notice to Laurie that his uncle was definitely on the warpath and that attrition would follow. Through his friendship with the Archbishop, Dr. Sterne was capable of proving a serious barrier to any advancement that might come his nephew's way. But, fortunately, Laurie had strong friends in the Chapter and he had won the friendship of the middle-aged Thomas, Viscount Fauconberg, lord of the manor in which Sutton lay. These friends succeeded in annoying Dr. Sterne by looking out for the interests of Laurence. For example, Lord Fauconberg secured for him the appointment as Commissary of the Peculiar and Spiritual Jurisdiction of Alne and Tollerton, and later that of Commissary of the Peculiar Court of Pickering and Pocklington. It was impossible for Dr. Jaques to block either of these appointments; for they were the rights of Dean Fountayne, and the Archbishop had no jurisdiction over them. For the latter appointment, however, Dr. Sterne supported the grasping ecclesiastical lawyer, Dr. Topham–shortly to become one of Laurie's prime antagonists.

But if Dr. Sterne was in a measure foiled in blocking preferment for Laurie, he had another ace up his sleeve; and he used it in a way that should blacken his character forever. Unfortunately, the affair did not leave the victim himself unsmirched.

Dr. Jaques was not unaware that his sister-in-law, Mrs. Roger Sterne, was still in England and that she and Catherine persisted in the idea that one day Laurence would or should treat them handsomely. On an earlier occasion of a trip to England by Mrs. Sterne, the Precentor had refused to receive the "clamorous" lady. However, circumstances can alter cases. A strong bond of sympathy now developed between the two. As early as 1744 Catherine used a visit to her brother as an occasion for making a complaint to Dr. Jaques. On the same trip it seems that Laurence and his wife had tried to get Catherine interested in some sort of trade, suggesting that of a mantua maker and offering to make the necessary financial arrangements. Perhaps Elizabeth Sterne was guilty of a tactical blunder when, as an alternative, she suggested service in the "family of one of the first of our nobility." According to Laurence's version of the story, Catherine rejected such ideas in scorn, "telling me I might send my own children to service when I had any —but for her part, as she was the daughter of a gentleman, *she would not disgrace* herself, but would live as such."

The precentor's sympathetic attention to complaints did not mean that the worldly and materialistic prelate (Warburton called him a *bon vivant;* Croft, "a rich and opulent man") had developed humanitarian feelings. Just the reverse was true. We can expect only a rigid auditing of past accounts from a clergyman who once stated in giving his most important qualification for additional ecclesiastical preferment: "I have now spent upwards of thirty-five years in a faithful service of the Crown, at an expense that I believe no clergyman else has done." Dr. Jaques now saw the chance of using the aging Mrs. Sterne as a convenient rod with which to chasten his apostate nephew. Therefore, when

Agnes herself came to York in 1747, the Precentor received her kindly and listened to her complaints with patience and sympathy. Laurence himself was not blind to the direction in which events were moving, but he could not have foreseen the outcome. Several times he tried to bring about a truce between himself and his uncle, once attempting to use his wife as a mediator. He was not successful. Dr. Sterne finally had his revenge in 1751 when by a stroke of malevolent genius he was successful in placing Mrs. Sterne and Catherine in the local workhouse, managing to circulate the report that they were there on account of Laurence's neglect.

On April 5, 1751, Laurence wrote to his uncle a defense from which a part has already been quoted. The whole must be somewhat discounted as a masterpiece of rationalization. Again, Laurie makes out too good a case and indulges in his typical trick of dramatizing himself as the sentimental hero of the piece. But much of the defense is convincing. The letter is climaxed by a statement that has brought horror to many readers. Sterne had the temerity to say that his mother "brought not one sixpence into the family—and though it would give me pain enough to report it upon any other occasion that she was the daughter of no other than a poor suttler who followed the camp in Flanders—was neither born nor bred to the expectation of a fourth part of what the Government allows her, and therefore has reason to be contented with such a provision." Indeed, this is no appropriate Mother's Day sentiment. And it is a little difficult to defend it, especially since we now have some reason to believe that Sterne was exaggerating the baseness of his mother's origin. But one should remember that the statement was addressed to a member of the family, that it was not designed for publication, and that it arose out of consummate chagrin over the impossible position in which his mother and Dr. Sterne had placed Laurence. The thought that his mother had allowed herself to be used to the diabolical ends of his uncle would explain, if not excuse, his angry rejoinder. Being good to one's mother has for a long time been a too easy criterion of essential virtue, and the reverse has been equally easy to apply as a criterion of baseness. Only the wilfully blind can refuse to see that Sterne has a case.

The Precentor was at least partially successful in his maneuver. There was fairly widespread gossip to the effect that Sterne had neglected his mother and that he finally let her die in jail. In 1776 the Reverend Daniel Watson, who had the neighboring parish of Leake when Sterne was at Coxwold, wrote to a friend: "Shall I tell you what York scandal says? *viz:* that Sterne, when possessed of preferment of £300 a year, would not pay £10 to release his mother out of Ousebridge prison, when poverty was her only fault, and her character was so good that two of her neighbours clubbed to set her at liberty, to gain a livelihood, as she had been accustomed to do, by taking in washing." In 1795 Croft, ever eager to show Sterne at a disadvantage, repeated the story:

> Sterne's mother died in the common gaol at York in a wretched condition, or soon after she was released. It was held unpardonable in him not to relieve her, when he had the means of doing it, as a subscription was set on foot for the purpose... Never anyone dwelt more upon humanity in theory but it does not appear that he put so much of it in practice.

And the great Horace Walpole sneered that he knew on "indubitable authority" that Sterne's mother would have "rotted in jail" if a subscription had not been raised for her. "A dead ass was more important to him," he continued, "than a living mother." Lord Byron adapted the sneer to purposes of personal melodrama when he wrote: "I am as bad as that dog Sterne, who preferred whining over 'a dead ass to relieving a living mother'–villain–hypocrite–slave–sycophant! but *I* am no better." Thus the black hand of Dr. Jaques laid its smirch on Laurence for years to come.

The actual facts in the case are by no means clear; but it seems that they have been grossly exaggerated. Several times in 1758, seven years after the "incarceration" Sterne mentions visiting his mother in York. Once he mentions "my poor mother" whose "affair . . . is by this time ended, to *our* comfort, and I trust, hers." Such a statement suggests that some sort of reconciliation has been brought about and some settlement made. Agnes Sterne was buried from the parish church of St. Michael le Belfrey in York on May 5, 1759. Uncle Jaques survived only a month longer, going to his grave without making his peace with his nephew. Croft wrote that Catherine married a publican in London. When Sterne wrote his memoirs in the last years of his life he stated that his sister was "still living, but most unhappily estranged from me by my uncle's wickedness, and her own folly."

It will be noticed that there is no immediately contemporary account of Sterne's "disgrace." And there is no reason to believe that Sterne's real friends in York placed such an interpretation on the incident as gossip was later destined to do.

CHAPTER IV

"CRAZY CASTLE"

When a tilt in the Cathedral precincts became disagreeable, the knight-errant could always withdraw. He had friends enough in York to support him in his verbal joustings or to amuse him in whimsy; and he had others in the country who furnished him effective sanctuary.

Now that he had freed himself from the tentacles of his uncle, he could dig in his own garden—not only metaphorically but actually. Not yet completely disillusioned about farming, he was still increasing his holdings of land. This practice he continued throughout a large part of his life, especially when he could do so without outlay of funds. Having improved his relations with Philip Harland, he found it possible as time went on to share with the Squire and Lord Fauconberg in the land that they were acquiring by that elegant form of robbing the public, enclosures. Through the extension of his farming activities by one means or another, Laurence was eventually growing such quantities of oats, potatoes, wheat, and barley that he was something of a squire in his own right.

One may be assured that he did not develop the zeal or the efficiency of a real farmer and that his farming, in spite of his protestations concerning the amount of time it entailed, was never a great deal more than a hobby. He, of course, delighted in playing the part of a country gentleman. Not yet had he become the more Chesterfieldian figure that he was later to be. He was still, in his own words, "a lousy prebendary," and the carelessness of his dress would have identified him as he shuffled like a dirt farmer through the streets of York. Boswell's verse description of the way the parson looked in his Sutton days is probably accurate:

> A threadbare Coat with sleeves full wide
> A formal nightgown's place supply'd.
> He wore, his new ones not t'abuse,
> A pair of ancient, downheel'd shoes;
> He roll'd his stockings 'bove his knees,
> And was as *dégagé's* you please.

But in the sports and social activities of the North Riding he had plenty of opportunities to develop into a man of the world.

In the North Riding, as well as in other parts of England, hunting was an important pastime for peers, squires, and clergymen alike. The *Connoisseur* for January 29, 1756, presents a satirical portrait of the fox-hunting Yorkshire parson:

> Hunting and shooting are the only business of his life; fox-hounds and pointers lay about in every parlour; and he is himself, like Pistol, always in boots. The estimation in which he holds his friends is rated according to their excellence as sportsmen; and to be able to make a good shot, or hunt a pack of hounds well, are the most recommending qualities. His parishioners often earn a shilling and a cup of ale at his house, by coming to acquaint him that they have found a hare sitting, or a fox in cover. One day, while I was alone with my friend, the servant came in to tell him, that the clerk wanted to speak with him. He was ordered in; but I could not help smiling, when (instead of giving notice of a burying, christening, or some other church business, as I expected) I found the honest clerk came only to acquaint his reverend superior, that there was a covey of partridges, of a dozen brace at least, not above three fields from the house.

Although the "Reverend Jack Quickset," the subject of the sketch, had a living in the North Riding, he hardly represents Sterne, who was less of a professional in the sport. It is interesting to note, however, that the account in the same *Connoisseur* paper of Quickset's delay on his way to church is strikingly similar to Croft's much later story about Sterne and the covey of partridges. There is no record that Sterne's clerk—his "Sinful Amen"—was employed in spotting game, although he performed other duties equally Shandean.

Sterne's hobbies had a way of coming and going. He took up shooting until he became a good shot; then he found other diversions. "At certain intervals and changes of the moon" he was (on his own testimony) "both fiddler and painter, according as the fly stings." Since most of his painting was a matter of copying portraits, he developed little originality; but he did become a rather respectable draughtsman, and his interest in art was later to have its literary value. His dabbling resulted in two interesting acquaintances. One was "Count" Christopher Steele, a Frenchified English painter who had been a pupil of Vanloo in Paris and who had set up a studio in York. The second and more important was George Romney, Steele's most distinguished student.

Social life for the Sternes had its interests. There were dinners at the Harlands'; warmer and more intimate gatherings at Stillington Hall, the seat of the Crofts; and now and then elegant parties at quadrille on the invitation of Lady Katherine Fauconberg, who presided graciously over Newburgh Priory, an ancient Augustine religious house converted into a magnificent estate. For Sterne there were, in addition, the boisterous and orgiastic gatherings in the decaying Gothic pile of his college mate, Hall-Stevenson—scandalous gatherings that made the North Riding buzz with gossip.

It is significant that one of Sterne's few original artistic attempts was a Hogarthian caricature of his wife. This highly uncomplimentary performance, which in the last century M. Stapfer found in the possession of the Bailiff of Guernsey, is a pen and ink drawing of a lady with a masculine face of which the dominant features are a hooked nose and a sharp chin. Lack of femininity in her visage is emphasized by a lace cap, a ribbon around her neck, and a bow behind. Below the drawing is written in Sterne's hand, "Mrs. Sterne, wife of Sterne"; and in the corner, "Pigrich fecit." It was easy enough to caricature the lady. Francis Cotes almost did it in his crayon drawing of her. The unattractiveness of her features caused Nathaniel Hawthorne to wonder how "Sterne ever contrived to live a week with such a woman."

As the caricature suggests, the domestic relationships of the Sutton vicarage were not sweetened by the vicar's pursuit either of his hobbies or of his social life. Mrs. Sterne had become a neurotic woman who apparently resented that it was her husband and not she who was the welcome guest at Stillington Hall and Newburgh Priory. She was naturally cut off from Laurence's gay jaunts to Hall-Stevenson's Skelton Castle. The fact that she had a still-born child in the early 1750's could not have improved either her psychic or her physical condition. In this sad experience Sterne, who could usually be counted on to perform creditably in a period of actual distress, acted the part of a sympathetic husband. We find him writing with something suggestive of pathetic simplicity to Theophilus Garencieres, Vicar of Scarborough and medical practitioner of York:

> Mrs. Sterne was last night delivered of a dead child. She is very weak and I think wants some comforting liquid or other to take of every two or three hours.

Mrs. Sterne's own state of mind in March, 1753, is reflected in a letter that she wrote to her famous half-cousin, Mrs. Elizabeth Montagu. The purpose of the letter is to thank Mrs. Montagu for a message informing Elizabeth of the illness of her sister, Mrs. John Botham. Indirectly, Mrs. Sterne reprimands her fashionable relative for neglect:

> For being thus cruelly separated from all my friends [she writes], the least mark of their kindness towards me, or remembrance of me, gives me unspeakable delight... I spare no pains to improve every little accident that recalls you to my remembrance, as the only amends which can be made for me those unhappinesses [*sic*] my situation deprives me of. As a proof of this, I must inform you, that about three weeks ago, I took a long ride through very bad weather and worse roads, merely for the satisfaction of enjoying a conversation with a gentleman who though unknown to you, had conceived the highest opinion of you from the perusal of several of your letters...

Mrs. Botham, for whom Lydia Sterne was named, had also been neglectful, having given her sister practically no information about her children:

> ... I know no more whether they are black, brown, or fair, wise, or otherwise gentle, or froward, than the man in the moon. Pray is this strange silence on so interesting a subject owing to her profound wisdom, or her abundant politeness?

These paranoid traces in Mrs. Sterne were to increase and were to be augmented by the feeling that she was a burden to her husband. Ultimately, a strange kind of megalomania developed.

Whatever escape Sterne might have needed from the unhealthful atmosphere of the vicarage, he found in abundance at Skelton Castle—better known as "Crazy Castle" on account of the desire of its master and the vagaries of his guests.

Although the *York Courant* had indicated that Hall-Stevenson had made a profitable match, the dowry of his lady seems to have turned out to be disappointing. But the handsome and convivial young gentleman had been lucky enough to inherit an ancestral estate. In the affair of '45 he had romantically organized a cavalry unit on the Hanoverian side. However, when fears of invasion were past and all was tranquil again, the dashing cavalry officer had doffed further activity or adventure in favor of settling down to an indolent, dilettantish, and hypochondriac existence as lord of his castle and as host extraordinary. His musty library was filled with curious books, many erotic. Here in Gothic half light he could toss off—as the spirit moved him—a bawdy verse tale, a fable in imitation of the most obscene strain in La Fontaine, or a coarse political satire. These he from time to time had the temerity to publish; and in 1795 (after his death) they were collected in three volumes of the *Works* for all of posterity who can stand tedious pornographic verse. Acquaintance with John Wilkes was responsible for most of Hall-Stevenson's excursions into political satire. Like Churchill and other Wilkesites, he attacked Bute and all professional politicians. He even dared to beard Ursa Major in his den by addressing "An Essay Upon the King's Friends" to Dr. Johnson. The redoubtable doctor, however, seems to have taken little notice. Perhaps Hall-Stevenson's most reprehensible actions were his attempts to capitalize on Sterne's popularity when his friend held the literary spotlight in London and his indiscretion in writing an obscene continuation of *A Sentimental Journey*. Among the limited number who professed to find Hall-Stevenson's verse witty was Horace Walpole. Gray branded it "absolute nonsense," and the *Critical Review* attacked it vigorously. Against the *Critical Review* the author fought back in a futile and tedious attempt to castigate the editor, Smollett, and his henchmen.

To judge Hall-Stevenson entirely on the basis of his verse would be to misjudge him. To many friends he was attractive, and often in his friendships, as particularly in his relationship to Sterne, he was both constant and generous. Even on chance acquaintances he made a good impression. His hospitality was fabulous. His board was ever groaning, and the steps to his wine cellar were in a chronic state of wear.

If we can accept the owner's whimsical description, the nearest literary counterpart of "Crazy Castle" was the House of Usher. Its tower—"threatening destruction every hour"—and its turrets rose above two terraces, which in turn rose above a dark moat. Of bats and owls and jackdaws (all of which would have been appropriate to Roderick Usher's plight) there were many. A more cheerful note was to be found in the pigeons that nested in the turrets and strutted on the terraces. Hall-Stevenson can speak for himself:

> There is a Castle in the North,
>   Seated upon a swampy clay,
> At present but of little worth;
> In former times it had its day.
> This ancient Castle is call'd Crazy,
>   Whose mould'ring walls a moat environs,
> Which moat goes heavily and lazy,
>   Like a poor prisoner in irons.
> Many a time I've stood and thought,
>   Seeing the boat upon this ditch,
> It look'd as if it had been brought
>   For the amusement of a witch,
> To sail amongst applauding frogs,
> With water-rats, dead cats and dogs.

And so on with mock Swiftian realism.

The dampness of the place might have been hopelessly depressing had not the interior of the house been so constantly brightened by conviviality. The master, it is true, did not entirely escape the evil effects of the atmosphere; for rheumatism dogged him from the dampness, as did poor digestion from rich foods and a sedentary life. In time he became a typical *malade imaginaire,* sleeping in a room in sight of a weathercock and refusing to be budged from his bed if the damp and marrow-piercing northeast wind were blowing. Sterne's attempt to work a cure by tying the cock in a westerly direction is a classic story, regardless of whether it is true. The deception is said to have worked until, the string breaking, the vane swung smartly around to northeast, and Hall-Stevenson popped back into bed.

About this splenetic, eccentric, and withal amiable individual revolved a mildly decadent fellowship known as the "Demoniacs." Practically everybody in the eighteenth century who was, in Dr. Johnson's language, "clubbable" belonged to some kind of fellowship. There is a long list of eighteenth-century clubs of various sorts and purposes ranging from the Scriblerus Club of Swift and Pope and "The Club" of Dr. Johnson himself through the Nonsense Club of Cowper and Churchill to the infamous Medmenham brotherhood. Hall-Stevenson's group was not a fixed one but was a somewhat shifting circle of indiscreet country parsons, comfortable squires, army officers, and schoolmasters. These came to Skelton Castle for what amounted to houseparties. Tom Gilbert wrote in March 1741 (before Laurence had definitely identified himself with the Skelton group):

> On *Monday* morning, every vassal
> Cries whip and spur for *Skelton-Castle,*
> Where bounty, wit, and mirth appear,
> And pleasure crowns each smiling year.

The host himself also had a verse description:

> Many a grievous, heavy heart,
> To Crazy Castle would repair,
> That grew, from dragging like a cart,
> Elastic and as light as air,

Some fell to fiddling, some to fluting,
Some to shooting, some to fishing,
Others to pishing and disputing,
Or to computing by vain wishing.

The spirit was that of Rabelais' Abbey of Thélème (a favorite affectation of the time): *Fais ce que vouldras*. During the day the guests were left to their own devices. In the evenings they lapped up their host's Burgundy, reeled off salacious stories by the yard, and sang when the spirit moved them or when Laurie tuned up his fiddle. Most often included in the rollcall were the Reverend Robert Lascelles, vicar of Gilling and commonly known as "Panty" among the fraternity; Andrew Irvine, master of the Kirkleatham school; Squire Nathaniel Garland; Colonel George Lawson Hall, a brother of the owner of Skelton Castle; Colonel Charles Lee, who is remembered without too much credit in American history; and in at least one respect the most fabulous of all, Zachary Moore, who was so prodigal on one trip to the Continent as to have his horses shod with silver. There also drifted into the group the excessively lean and sufficiently eccentric Colonel William Hewett ("Old Hewet") of the Leicestershire Volunteers. No one better deserved a place among the "Demoniacs." Smollett called him "one of the most original characters upon earth" and described his death in Italy in 1767 in a remarkable note appended to *Humphrey Clinker:*

Being taken with a suppression of urine, he resolved, in imitation of Pomponius Atticus, to take himself off by abstinence; and this resolution he executed like an ancient Roman. He saw company to the last, cracked his jokes, conversed freely, and entertained his guests with music. On the third day of his fast, he found himself entirely freed of his complaint; but refused taking sustenance. He said the most disagreeable part of the journey was past, and he said he should be a cursed fool indeed, to put about ship, when he was just entering the harbour. In these sentiments he persisted, without any mark of affectation, and thus finished his course with such ease and serenity, as would have done honour to the firmest stoic of antiquity.

The "Demoniacs" offered a weak version of the much more scandalous "Medmenham monks," whose erotic and sacrilegious orgies are among the most astounding instances of eighteenth-century decadence. The Medmenham group, sometimes called the "Hellfire Club," consisted of a number of libertines whose only strength apparently lay in their sexual virtuosity. Except John Wilkes, who was associated with the group, none was of superior intelligence. The doyen, Sir Francis Dashwood, rebuilt West Wycombe Church in Buckinghamshire, excavating beneath it a cave for the highly blasphemous and profligate rites of the brotherhood. Their ritual was a parody on that of the Catholic Church. The monks garbed themselves in Franciscan habit, addressed their worship to "Bona Dea," the goddess of love, and made prayers to Satan. Wilkes is credited with breaking up the group. According to the accepted story, he concealed in the cave a baboon dressed as the devil and arranged to release it just as the weak-minded Lord Orford was reciting a prayer to Satan. When the baboon pounced on the peer, the meeting ended in disorder.

Dashwood was an occasional visitor at Skelton. John Wilkes knew both Hall-Stevenson and Sterne in London. Hence a connection between the Medmenham and Skelton group is inevitable. However, one would have little inclination to ascribe to the Skelton circle even a fraction of the sickening debauchery engaged in by the Medmenham libertines. The "Demoniacs" were probably not a great deal more vicious than ordinary middle-class gentlemen when they are freed from the restraints of their normal lives. A juvenile holiday spirit prevailed at Skelton, and the parsons and the squires got somewhat the same pleasure from their ribald stories and repartee that small boys get from scribbling obscene words on fences. Coleridge spoke expressively of Sterne's "dallyings with the devil." There are many evidences that Laurie liked the adventure of being naughty, especially if it did not involve the violation of a fundamental moral principle. Skating delicately and skilfully on the thin ice of depravity provided a thrill like skimming along over the pond in Stillington Common in early winter. At Skelton, we may be sure, he did not lag behind the other "Demoniacs." If he told tales approximating "My Cousin's Tale of a Cock and a Bull," assigned to him in *Crazy Tales*, he exhibited prurience enough. But all his contributions to the group were not necessarily ribald. In one period he fancied himself a poet and produced surprisingly serious and unShandean verses on the soul and the universe. These he very likely read to his Skelton friends. The poetry, to be sure, was not very successful. If Hall-Stevenson had been capable of telling Sterne the truth about it, he might have paraphrased Dryden's remark to Swift: "Cousin Shandy, you will never be a poet." But he seems not to have realized that he himself was no poet; thus he was probably unable to discern that there was more cleverness than inspiration in Sterne's strange "The Unknown"–in which symbols are substituted for the words *world*, *heaven*, *soul*, and *God* somewhat remotely in the manner of Old English runic verse.

If the host set the tempo of the group, the chief wildness of Hall-Stevenson (known as Anthony or St. Anthony on account of his monastic aversion to the outdoors) seemed to be telling bawdy stories, drinking a little too much, going with Sterne on visits to Mrs. C[haloner], Miss C[haloner], etc. in Guisborough, and racing his chariot along the plage at Saltburn with one wheel in the sea. Sterne credits himself with attempting to make his friend more temperate:

"If I was you, quoth *Yorick*, I would drink more water, Eugenius.—And if I was you, Yorick, replied *Eugenius*, so would I." (It is Sterne's little irony that the master of Skelton is allowed to appear in *Tristram Shandy* as Eugenius, the discreet counselor.) However mild Hall-Stevenson's vices may have been, his parties were not the most becoming ones for men of God. Nor was he exactly the kind of person that wives consider to be the best influence on errant husbands. One scarcely wonders that Mrs. Sterne may have been uncertain about the salutary influence that the "Demoniacs" had on Laurence.

The literary influence of these associations is not easy to determine. *Tristram Shandy* did not grow quite so directly out of the "Demoniacs" as *Gulliver's Travels* and the *Dunciad* grew out of the earlier and more decorous Scriblerus Club; but there is an important connection. On many occasions Sterne deserted the hunters and fishers (among whom the host himself was not often found) to turn over the mouldy and curious volumes of Hall-Stevenson's library. From such foraging he undoubtedly acquired some of the military and medical lore that he incorporates with much glibness in his novel; and thus he may have acquired other recondite material. One may accept such an assumption without discounting the importance of the browsing that he did among books in York, or the importance of his own book-collecting instinct in determining his literary sources. But the most important consideration is the fact that among the "Demoniacs" he nurtured the ebullient and whimsical spirit that comes to such wonderful flowering in *Tristram Shandy*. And the "Demoniacs" themselves probably provided enough eccentric material to fill several novels of the length of his masterpiece.

CHAPTER V

"A POLITICAL ROMANCE"

BEING ABLE to retire conveniently to the country was one matter; being kept a prisoner in the country either by wheat or barley or by impassable roads was another. Sutton could quickly become desolate when Sterne was cut off from his friends in the Chapter and his cronies who gathered at Sunton's Coffee House. "If you have three or four of the last York's Courants, pray send 'em us," Sterne wrote to a friend in the winter of 1758, "for we are as much strangers to all that has passed amongst you, as if we were in a mine in Siberia." The trouble had been caused by heavy crops with consequent involvement in matters of gathering and selling, as well as by torrential rains that had all but washed away the road to York. To add to Sterne's miseries, the dampness of the valley in which he lived racked his weak chest, and he was afflicted with coughing and asthma. Moreover, another illness of Lydia, now eleven years old, distressed her doting father.

Laurence's letters to the Reverend John Blake, Master of the Royal Grammar School in York, show his growing dissatisfaction and indicate that another hobby-horse—the farming that was just now promising good returns—was in a fair way to be discarded. Sterne's retirement from York after the quarrel with Dr. Jaques had by no means been complete. He had preached his turns in the Cathedral, he had found time for visits with Blake, and he had slipped away for an occasional concert with his friend of Dickensian name—Marmaduke Fothergill, bibliophile and surgeon to the County Hospital. He had visited his mother, for whom he seems to have made some kind of satisfactory arrangement. Doubtless, he had discreetly kept out of the way of Dr. Sterne. As time went on, Sterne joined a convivial group of ecclesiasts and laymen who met at Sunton's Coffee House. So convenient was Sunton's to the George Inn and to the Minster that it was the proper milieu for political gossip concerning the Cathedral, the shire, or the nation. Evenings were filled with gay rapier thrusts of wit, which the "President" of each occasion hardly attempted to hold in order.

Nothing was more ravishing to Laurence than the play of wit, and Sunton's Coffee House provided splendid opportunities for the exercise of his talent either in the select evening gatherings or among the daily clientele. Dr. John Hill told an amusing story that, however unreliable it may be in detail, reveals the kind of by-play for which Sterne developed some reputation. One day in Sunton's a gay young officer who affected a dislike of parsons, was interrupted in the midst of a bawdy joke by the entrance of a gaunt vicar. Taking his cue, the officer changed his tack and began abusing the clergy. Sterne, who was the vicar in question, stood the abuse as long as he could. When he could take no more, he accosted the speaker: "Sir, I'll tell you a story. My father is an officer; and he's so brave himself, that he is fond of everything else that's brave, even to his dog: you must know we have at this time one of the finest creatures in the world, of this kind, . . . the best natured that can be imagined; so lively that he charms everybody; but he has a cursed trick that spoils all; he never sees a clergyman, but he instantly flies at him." "Pray how long has he had that trick?" asked the captain, falling neatly into the trap. "Sir, ever since he was a Puppy," replied Laurence. The officer, if we may believe the story, was won by the reply.—But Sterne did not always win friends with his jests. How venomously barbed his tongue might be and on whom his wit would turn, few could predict. He himself suggests that his cleverness won him more enemies than friends:

> Trust me, dear Yorick [he makes Eugenius say in the first book of *Tristram Shandy*], this unwary pleasantry of thine will sooner or later bring thee into scrapes and difficulties, which no after-wit can extricate thee out of...'tis no extravagant arithmetic to say, that for every ten jokes,—thou hast got an hundred enemies; and till thou hast gone on, and raised a swarm of wasps about thine ear, and art half stung to death by them, thou wilt never be convinced it is so.

Indeed, he continues, a "grand confederacy" was finally formed against him, just as Eugenius had predicted.

Since coffee house companionship provided stimulation and amusement, it is a matter of no wonder that such deterrents as bad roads and heavy crops could be the subject of serious complaint. When the overseers of the highway for Clifton neglected their duties in the summer of 1757, Sterne joined squires Croft, Harland, and Chomley in a sharply worded protest: "...if you don't directly set about effectually repairing the Horse Fair or lane to your town from the Forest and also make sufficient bridges for carriages over the several letches [streams] on the Forest (now that the weather is good) you may depend upon being indicted the next Assize." Whether this unequivocal demand brought action is not recorded. We do know that for some time afterward the roads continued to furnish a frequent subject of complaint.

As for the nuisances of farming, Sterne wrote Blake in July, 1758:

> I should have beat up your quarters before now, and but for the vile roads and weather, together with the *crisis* of my affairs, namely the getting down my crop—which, by the way, is in danger of sprouting. However, I will come over at your

desire, but it cannot be tomorrow because all hands are to be employed cutting my barley, which is now shaking with this vile wind.

In the following December he was still complaining:

> I have four threshers every day at work, and they mortify me with declarations that there is so much barley that they cannot get through that species before Christmas Day—and God knows I have (I hope) near 80 qrs. of oats besides. How I shall manage matters to get to you, as we wish for three months, half distracts my brain.

He had already taken a tenant, and he hoped soon to clear "hands and head of all country entanglements."

The anxiety to see Blake arose from the fact that Laurie was doing some *sub rosa* maneuvering and counseling in a curious entanglement of his friend. The Master of the Royal Grammar School was engaged in an effort to make a marriage settlement involving himself and Margaret Ash, the daughter of a well-to-do widow of York. Blake's chief objectives seem to have been to secure a sufficient dowry, whereas Mrs. Ash's aim was to get her daughter off as inexpensively as possible. The widow was a redoubtable lady: a "Loup Garou," Laurie called her, "or Raw Head and Bloody Bones to frighten Master Jacky into silence and make him go to bed with Miss, *supperless* and in peace." While Blake was dickering with his fiancée's lawyer, Sterne sent him a "stubble goose" for consolation. Another he dispatched to the stubborn widow, apparently in an effort to pour oil (or goose grease) on troubled waters. However, Laurie's attempts to aid Blake in circumventing the Widow Ash involved more than dispatching "gooses," to use his own word. In fact, he became so involved behind the scenes that he quaked lest his part against the influential widow should come to light. The real involvement he was particularly eager to keep from Mrs. Sterne, although she knew something of the situation: "I tore off the bottom of yours [i.e., your last letter]," Sterne wrote Blake at one point in the affair, "before I let my wife see it, to save a lie.—However, she has since observed the curtailment and seemed very desirous of knowing what it contained, which I conceal and only say 'twas something that no way concerned *her* or *me*.—So, say the same, if she interrogates." Some of Mrs. Sterne's womanly curiosity was later immortalized in Mrs. Shandy, who got erroneous impressions from listening at key holes. Sterne is only human in not wanting his wife to catch him in a lie, whatever else the matter might have involved.—After all the commotion, the whole affair proved futile, for negotiations reached an impasse and Miss Ash married somebody else. Blake, too, found other consolation and, we trust, an adequate dowry.

An irrepressible love for intrigue was at least a partial cause for Sterne's embroilment in another squabble in the Chapter—always a fertile field for petty jealousies and rivalries.

The roots of the new quarrel lay in Dean Fountayne's appointment of Sterne to the Commissaryship of Pickering and Pocklington in 1751. It has previously been mentioned that the post was also sought by Dr. Francis Topham, who had the support of Dr. Jaques Sterne. Dr. Topham, a leading ecclesiastical lawyer who was as obsequious as he was treacherous, attempted to get revenge for the slight by attempting to effect a breach between Dean Fountayne and the Archbishop, then Dr. Hutton. A clever game of bootlicking got for Topham the lucrative patent of Commissary and Keeper General of the Exchequer and Prerogative Courts. However, he found that he could not circulate with impunity his story of the Dean's perfidy in giving to Sterne an appointment promised to him. At a public Sessions Dinner, the Dean confronted Topham with his libel and in a scene of dramatic tenseness proved him a liar.

Sterne was a delighted participant in the fray, the memory of which he embalms in *Tristram Shandy* in the story of one Phutatorius who at a Sessions Dinner suffered having a hot chestnut dropped on an unmentionable part of his anatomy.

In the interest of truth, one must admit that back of Sterne's interest in the affair was not merely his love for a fight. He, too, had political motives and hopes for preferment. When his friend and college mate, Fountayne, had become Dean in 1747, Sterne seems to have looked to him to balance the loss of his uncle's favor. He had served the Dean as private secretary, writing his Latin oration when he received an honorary doctorate from Cambridge and in general supporting him in his feud with Dr. Hutton. It is not until some years later that we realize Sterne's disappointment in the dividends that his friendship for Fountayne paid. In a memorandum written in 1761 and labeled "In case I should die abroad," he expressed his bitterness for not receiving adequate preferment by characterizing the Dean as a "very corrupt man" and expressing doubt that Dr. Topham deserved the severe handling that he got as "Trim" in Sterne's first important satire, *A Political Romance*, and as Didius and Phutatorius in *Tristram Shandy*.–But we run ahead of our story.

To return to the matter of the Sessions Dinner, the Dean's silencer seems to have worked. At least, we hear no more of Topham until 1757, when Dr. Hutton became Archbishop of Canterbury and was succeeded in York by the physically weak and morally ineffectual Dr. Gilbert. Of the new archbishop Horace Walpole wrote trenchantly: "On the news of Gilbert's promotion they rung the bells at York backwards, in detestation of him. He opened a great table there, and in six months they thought him the most Christian prelate that had ever sat in that see." Dr. Topham lost little time in using his blandishments to make himself welcome at the episcopal palace at Bishopthorpe. When he got the ear of the Archbishop, he took pains to impress His Grace with what a queer lot the Dean and the Chapter members were, at the same time offering his services for the best interests of the see. Moreover, he translated his offer into action, and convinced the prelate of his handiness.

About a year after Dr. Gilbert's installation, Topham, pursuing legal research to his own advantage, discovered precedent for conferring a patent for two lives instead of one and conceived the brilliant idea of making his best patent safe for his son Edward–subsequently an inferior dramatist and a superior rake. Topham's blandness at first won the infirm Archbishop to the idea; but as Gilbert pondered the matter, he had misgivings. Since such a matter had to be approved ultimately by the Dean and Chapter, Topham unblushingly sought the favor of his old enemy, the Dean. But the Dean turned a cold shoulder. When an adverse decision was rendered, a small pamphlet war began: Dr. Topham published a letter attacking the Dean. The Dean answered–putting the matter aside, he thought, once and for all; but Topham came back with a reply to the answer, in which he described "a late notable performance" of the Dean as being "the child and offspring of many parents." The suggestion was that Sterne and others had had a hand in the affair.

If Sterne had not given assistance before, he was now ripe for the fray, and he entered the fight with a brilliance the appreciation of which is limited only by the local significance of the contest. Whatever may have been the value of his apprenticeship in writing political "paragraphs" for Uncle Jaques, he now emerged as a satirist of dangerous potentialities. In January, 1759, appeared *A Political Romance*, better known as *A History of a Good Warm Watch-Coat*, which excoriates Topham as thoroughly as

Macflecknoe excoriates Shadwell, although it gained for its subject a less spacious immortality.

Sterne looks at the squabbles of the Chapter House and the Minster Yard through the large end of a telescope. Instead of placing the setting of the satire in a cathedral town, he places it in a country parish where the "sexton and dogwhipper," Trim, has caused dissension by starting a dispute about the height of the parish clerk's reading desk as compared with that of the parson's. He had unsuccessfully sought from the clerk a pair of old velvet breeches and he now begs of the parson an old watch coat, "in order to have it converted into a *warm under-petticoat* for his wife, and a *jerkin* for himself against winter." Trim is easily identified as Topham, the parson as the Archbishop, John the parish clerk as Fountayne, the breeches as the double Commissaryship of Pickering and Pocklington, and the watch coat as the patent that Topham wanted to retain for his son. Sterne includes himself as Lorry Slim, who takes malicious delight in getting the pair of breeches that Trim wanted. Trim is handled with nothing like Christian charity. Sterne boldly paints him as "a little dirty, pimping, petty-fogging, ambidextrous fellow" who "had blacked the parson's shoes without count, and greased his boots above fifty times." And as if that were not enough, Sterne slings after Topham the epithet, "greedy hound." Those were fighting words; and the fact that Sterne did not get his nose mashed by Topham can be only an evidence of Laurie's luck and Topham's spinelessness. Roger Sterne had been run through with a sword for less; but he had had the misfortune to insult a soldier rather than an ecclesiastical lawyer.

The spirit of the satire is Swiftian in its severity, its coarseness, and in its clothes symbolism. In the latter respect the similarity to *A Tale of a Tub* is easily apparent. Another

Swiftian touch was the attachment of a key purporting to make the whole an allegory of European affairs. There is also a discussion of the key by a "political club" meeting near the Cathedral, an obvious reference to Sterne's friends at Sunton's. Finally, Sterne affixed a letter to Topham in which he clears up a detail or two of the case and begs God "as it is my duty" to forgive Topham for his "many coarse and unchristian insinuations"!

The boldness of *A Political Romance* was enhanced by the fact that Sterne did not hide behind anonymity. He requested his publisher Caesar Ward (against whose *Courant* he had once written) to filiate "the child" upon himself. The request that the pamphlet be priced at one shilling is amusing. Topham's *Reply*, Sterne remarks, has sold for sixpence:

> But mine, my dear friend, is quite a *different story*:—It is a web wrought out of my own brain, of twice the fineness of this which he has spun out of his; and besides, I maintain it, it is of a more curious pattern, and could not be afforded at the price that his sold at, by any *honest* workman in *Great Britain*.

Dr. Topham seems to have struck his flag as soon as the pamphlet issued from the press and to have promised silence if the satire were withdrawn. Such an offer seemed reasonable even to Sterne's friends, who did not relish having the affairs of the Minster Yard made so ridiculous to the public. Thus for Sterne's brilliant effort the Chapter organized a private burning, much to the disappointment of the author. Fortunately, Laurie was able to save a few copies from the flames.

A production so short-lived could naturally give its author little more than local fame. But it did not represent an entirely inauspicious start, for it was plainly successful in laying the enemy low and it gave Sterne confidence in his ability to wield a pen effectively. From now on the demon of writing was to be in his blood. Nor was there an end to chances for flaying Dr. Topham in print. The lawyer was merely filed for future appearances in *Tristram Shandy*.

PART TWO: TRISTRAM

CHAPTER VI

AT THE SIGN OF TULLY'S HEAD

i

LTHOUGH BY THE time he had reached forty-six Sterne had gained some local prominence, he seemed far from making his mark in the world. In his periods of melancholy and reflection this fact added materially to his discomfort. For almost twenty years he had been anchored in an unattractive little parish. His maneuvering for advancement in the Church had involved him in arguments and feuds without gaining for him any considerable returns. He had married a wife who for one reason or another had become progressively harder to live with. He had become the adoring parent of a child who seemed, like himself, doomed to ill health. He had achieved some success in farming only to have his avocation become irksome to him. In short, he had neither health, worldly goods, position, nor happiness to show for two decades in which he had carefully masked his struggles by engaging in eccentric and often unorthodox gaieties. Now the ashes of his first important literary work had been scattered to the same damp Yorkshire winds that wracked his weak chest. Certainly the burning of the pamphlet was not a complete defeat; but it was hardly the brilliant triumph for which he longed. Even his friends were glad to see the document out of the way. Nevertheless, out of whatever frustration he may have felt came neither a poem like "The Vanity of Human Wishes" nor a bitter diatribe on mankind like *Gulliver's Travels*. Rather, there came a curiously wonderful Yorkshire "epic" in which he settled old scores, indulged his delightful whims, and won for himself an immortality of fame.

Suddenly in the burning of the pamphlet he seems to have caught a vision of the possibility of using his talents for his own ends. Writing for Uncle Jaques had brought only quarrels; writing for Dean Fountayne, ashes. This time he would write for himself. So back to Sutton he rode, put on his slippers, his dressing gown and cap, sharpened his quill pens, pulled Burton's *Anatomy of Melancholy* from his bookshelf, and embarked on a real adventure in literature. It mattered little that conditions in the Sutton parsonage were hardly propitious for literary production. Mrs. Sterne's neurosis was now rapidly developing into dementia, little Lydia was ailing as usual, and the winds of January were provocative of asthma. Nevertheless, by the end of the month Laurence's quill pen had been jabbed countless times into the ink well and had flown rapidly over sheets of foolscap, strewing drops of ink in all directions; and the tallow had streamed into the candleholder unheeded.

When he had discovered some of the paces of his Rosinante, Yorick settled into a merry canter. By March 9 he had reached the eighteenth chapter, and two weeks later he was well into the twenty-fifth. On May 23 he was packing off the manuscript of Volume I to Robert Dodsley, the famous publisher in Pall Mall, promising "If you publish it now—a second volume will be ready by Christmas or November."

Though London publication had probably been in his mind from the start, he had already allowed some of the York booksellers to see his manuscript. There had been no takers for several possible reasons. In the first place, the eccentricity of the work was a deterrent; and the fate of his previous pamphlet was no recommendation. Who could guarantee that the new work, with Topham and Burton pilloried as Didius and Dr. Slop, would fare better? Croft reported that even Sterne's closest friends failed to see its attractions. The author, we are told, read his work one night after dinner at Stillington Hall and failed to keep some of his auditors awake. Forthwith he impetuously threw the manuscript into the fire, where it would have met the fate of his earlier work had not the Squire saved it. But unless revisions made by Sterne in the summer of 1759 were very sweeping indeed, it is hard to believe such a story. The dinner, the wine, and the warmth of the fire might more easily have been the real soporifics than the opening chapters of *Tristram Shandy;* and the story of Laurence's loss of temper fits ill with his delightful bit of pleasantry at his own expense in Book II of the novel when he allows Dr. Slop to go to sleep in the midst of Corporal Trim's rendition of one of the author's sermons. At all odds, whatever his misgivings might have been in regard to the possible success of the book, he discreetly concealed them in his letter to Dodsley in which he assured the publisher that the book would sell and asked £50 for the manuscript. He also took some pains to minimize the local color of the work, giving the impression that it was a sort of new *Memoirs of Martinus Scriblerus.* "The plan, as you will perceive," wrote Sterne, "is a most extensive one,—taking in, not only the weak part of the sciences, in which the true point of ridicule lies—but everything else, which I find laugh-at-able in my way."

Dodsley, too, was doubtful. But Sterne was not to be discouraged. If the London bookseller did not want to take the risk, the author suggested, he himself would bear the expense of bringing out a "lean" quarto in York and putting it on sale there to test the pulse of the public—"that I may know what price to set upon the remaining volumes from the reception of these." There would be a great convenience, he continued eagerly, in being able to read the proof so near the actual place of printing. In a postscript he undertook to reassure his urbane prospective publisher on the really doubtful point: "All locality is taken out of the book—the satire general." This statement is, of course, no more accurate than the one he later made to Garrick that *Tristram Shandy* had gone forth into the world "hot as it came from my brain, without one correction."

While negotiations were going on, some of Sterne's closest friends were voicing their misgivings. Marmaduke Fothergill was insistent: "Get your preferment first, Lory! —and then write and welcome." To Fothergill's argument, Laurence replied that preferment was slow in coming and that he refused to suffer the pangs of thwarted authorship. He was later to remark, paraphrasing Colley Cibber, that he wrote "not to be *fed*, but to be *famous*." For brothers of the cloth who observed that his humor was unbecoming to a clergyman, Laurence merely countered dryly that Dean Swift was guilty of worse, admitting, tongue in cheek, that what he had written was not so becoming as a "meditation on Death." In mock defense against charges of lack of restraint, he proclaimed with literal accuracy that he had burned more wit than he had published. He also argued with exquisite logic that to remake the book according to the criticism of others would be to spoil it. He now had sublime confidence in what he was doing, and no amount of fear for him on the part of his friends or condemnation of his unpublished work by his enemies could deter him. As a silencer to the disapproving clergymen, he did offer to submit his novel to the Archbishop. If the tradition is correct, the none too exciting Dr. Gilbert showed surprising perspicuity and approved enthusiastically. He is even reported to have said in later years that he read *Tristram* once every six weeks.

In the meantime domestic matters continued unsettled. While he was writing the first two volumes of his masterwork, he had enough cares and worries to break a man several times stronger than he. His mother died in May, 1759. Uncle Jaques followed in June of the same year. Neither death could have caused him great sorrow. But the fact that Dr. Sterne's will cut off Laurie's chance of inheriting his uncle's property produced a feeling of frustration. Sterne refused to wear the customary mourning. The situation at the parsonage had gone from bad to worse. Gossip of the neighborhood continued to insist that the Sternes did not "*gee* well together," and there were stories of bickerings. Mrs. Sterne's mind was seriously disordered, and rumor had it that she was driven crazy by her husband's philandering. Laurie was usually ready to admit that he had a will-o'-the-wisp fancy and that he was always "miserably in love" with some one. We shall soon see evidence that the rumor may have had some real foundation in fact. But the story of Mrs. Sterne's catching Laurie in bed with the maid can be regarded as little more than rank gossip; nor can we accept the story that on another occasion he was caught rifling a strong box in which savings for Lydia were kept. Even if the stories were true, Mrs. Sterne's condition, as it should now be apparent, was not explainable by causes so immediate.

Much that we know positively about Sterne's conduct at this time (and we know it on the authority of the man who was more likely to tell the worst than the best) is unmistakably to his credit. When his wife's mental malady took the form of her imagining that she was Queen of Bohemia, he set about manfully to cure her, humoring her whim and treating her as if she were actually the imagined character to the extent of inducing her to go driving by attempting to reproduce coursing as practiced in Bohemia.

> For that purpose [John Croft reported] he procured bladders and filled them with beans, and tied them to the wheels of a single horse-chair. When he drove madam into a stubble field, with the motion of the carriage and the bladders, rattle bladder, rattle; it alarmed the hares, and the grayhounds were ready to take them.

Throughout the summer and early autumn Sterne endured the strain of life in the Sutton rectory. By November 19, 1759, however, he had decided to move to the Minster Yard in York. The immediate reason he gave was that residence in the city would furnish Lydia a better opportunity to begin dancing and other schooling. On his own behalf, he could hardly have helped feeling that he could bear his burdens better in York, where his scope of activity was greater—whatever might have been the other inducements. A few weeks after his removal he wrote to a friend that his wife had lost her senses by a stroke of palsy, that the sight of the mother had thrown little Lydia into a fever, and, in general, that the early books of *Tristram Shandy* had been produced amid great trials and heaviness of heart.

If Mrs. Sterne had been seriously upset by her husband's philandering, she could hardly have consented cheerfully to moving the family near the object of Laurence's latest flirtation. Nor could she have derived any satisfaction from the fact that the flirtation thrived in the same Assembly Rooms where almost two decades ago her own sentimental affair with the gay but impecunious young clergyman had both beginning and climax.

Just when this new affair began is uncertain. Those who wish to believe that Sterne is shadowing forth his *amour* in the references to "Jenny" in *Tristram Shandy* are forced to place the beginning in the early months of 1759. However, there is no evidence that Miss Catherine Fourmantelle, a professional singer from London, had come to York to grace the concerts in the Assembly Rooms until the autumn. At any rate, in the fall and winter of 1759 Sterne had laid siege to the attractive young lady, who had been escorted up to York with due propriety by her mama. For Laurence, Kitty was a complete stunner; and the middle-aged clergyman, who almost single-handed invented the word *sentimental*, acted the part of a young stage-door gallant, keeping Miss Fourmantelle up late on Saturday nights, sending her sweetmeats, honey, and bottles of Lisbon wine, and even on one occasion dispatching a copy of one of his sermons in which, he averred, the "tender and compassionate mind in the picture of Elijah" reminded him of her!

> If this billet catches you in bed [he wrote one Sunday morning], you are a lazy, sleepy little slut—and I am a giddy foolish unthinking fellow for keeping you so late up—but this Sabbath is a day of rest—at the same time that it is a day of sorrow—for I shall not see my dear creature today—unless you meet me at Taylor's half an hour after twelve—but in this do as you like—I have ordered Matthew to turn thief and steal you a quart of honey—
>
> What is honey to the sweetness of thee, who art sweeter than all the flowers it comes from.—I love you to distraction, Kitty—and will love you on so to Eternity—so adieu and believe what, time only will prove me, that I am
>
> Yrs.

If the letter were a youthful outburst, it might pass unnoticed. Written as it was by a middle-aged married man, spindle-legged and otherwise unhandsome, it is another evidence of the amazing extent to which he allowed his emotional vagaries to carry him. His own rationalization of his philandering is exactly what one should expect. In his extraordinary sermon on the Levite and his concubine he defended irregular attachments with a sentimental argument:

> ...Let me be wise and religious,—but let me be man. Wherever thy providence places me, or whatever be the road I take to get to thee,—give me some companion in my journey, be it only to remark to, How our shadows lengthen as the sun goes down!—to whom I may say, How fresh is the face of Nature! How sweet the flowers of the field! How delicious are these fruits!

Lack of congeniality in his married life and his constitutional demand for emotional reciprocity are the keys to Laurence's affairs with women. There is evidence that when his wife was willing and capable of offering tenderness and understanding, Sterne gave tenderness and understanding in return. When she was not willing or not capable, he simply sought to satisfy his needs elsewhere.

There is little reason to believe that Kitty was actually Sterne's mistress. Whether or not Kitty and "Jenny" are the same, Laurence adequately explained not only this affair but many of his others in the first book of *Tristram Shandy:*

> Nor is there anything unnatural or extravagant in the supposition that my dear Jenny may be my friend.—Friend!—My friend.—Surely, Madam, a friendship between the two sexes may subsist, and be supported without—Fy! Mr. Shandy:—Without any thing, Madam, but that tender and delicious sentiment, which ever mixes in friendship, where there is a difference of sex. Let me entreat you to study the pure and sentimental parts of the best French Romances;—it will really, Madam, astonish you to see with what a variety of chaste expressions this delicious sentiment, which I have the honour to speak of, is dressed out.

But however guileless may have been the relations of the two, the flirtation was at best indiscreet. The extent of Sterne's indiscretion would, of course, depend upon how openly he flaunted his attentions. Meeting Kitty quietly at the homes of his friends was indiscreet enough. If he made a spectacle of his attachment for her in the Assembly Rooms and if he accompanied her on shopping expeditions (as he hints that he did with the elusive "Jenny"), it is a wonder how, even in an age of relaxed moral standards, he escaped serious censure. That he was so brazen we have no positive proof.

In considering the whole affair with Miss Fourmantelle, one must not forget that Sterne's real mistress was his new-found art, and that no sentimental considerations were allowed to offer an obstacle to what he intended to do. Even while he was declaring his love for Kitty, he was busying himself with more practical matters in the company of another lady, Mrs. Ann Ward, widow of the late editor of the Tory *Courant* and able successor to her husband's printing establishment. And the gay Saturday evenings with Miss Fourmantelle were not more exciting than the mornings spent over proof sheets. Late in December, 1759, the first two volumes of *Tristram Shandy* appeared on the shelves of John Hinxman (successor to Hildyard) in Stonegate. Not many days later the book came out in London.

In York, Sterne's faith in the popularity of the book was quickly justified. Everybody of importance in the city knew the stir that *A Good Warm Watch-Coat* had caused, and for several months it had been noised about even as far as London that the Vicar of Sutton was engaged on an "extraordinary" book. Both curiosity and fear took many a frocked gentleman to Mr. Hinxman's shop on a damp December day. Satire was an exciting game in eighteenth-century England. Swift and Pope had cracked the whip and had made the high and the low jump alike. Sterne had already given promise of being another Swift, and had even himself suggested a comparison with the earlier master of satire. Who could tell what the new work would bring forth?

Whatever the first readers may have expected, they were certainly surprised; for no novel like *Tristram Shandy* had ever before come from an English pen. The humorous "shock" of the first amazing chapter set the tempo; but it was by no means adequate preparation for the seemingly topsy-turvy narrative that was to follow. The book began as an obstetrical romance and eventually became unclassifiable. The title invited readers to the "life and opinions" of a "gentleman" whose conception was an important consideration in the first book but whose birth had to wait for the third (not yet published). Chapter VIII of the first book had a blank dedication, which was offered for sale (price: fifty guineas) in the following chapter. With a bow to Voltaire and his recently published *Candide*, there was finally a dedication to the moon. The typography was as mad as one could imagine: italics and black letter type were sprinkled through the text, passages were set up in large capitals and in small, and there was miscellaneous decoration of brackets, hands, asterisks, and dots. There were long passages in French and short ones in Greek and Latin. Chapter lengths varied from sixty pages to four lines. One page had an oblong smudge of black ink. Among the insertions were a long burlesque legal document and a sermon. If at the beginning the sentence structure seemed reasonably orthodox, sentences soon began to be riddled with dashes; and digressions sprang up on nearly every page.

The whole could not have helped having about the same effect on the good *douce* people of eighteenth-century York that the novels of James Joyce and Gertrude Stein had on the same kind of people everywhere in the postwar decades of the twentieth. The attitude expressed by Sir Horace Mann in a letter to Walpole may be taken as illustrative of a common type of reaction even among the very intelligent: "You will laugh at me, I suppose when I say I don't understand it. It was probably the intention that nobody *should*. It seems to me *humbugging*." But Sterne did not leave his readers entirely in the dark. Early in the game he asserted plainly that Tristram was a product of the widely discussed psychology of Locke—in short, that he was the result of "an unhappy association of ideas, which have no connection in nature." Thus readers were warned of the "calamities" that would come from what Locke considered a disease of the mind—"the foundation of the greatest, I had almost said of all the errors in the world." Not only the characterization, the author suggested, but the structure of the whole book would be organized on the tenet of Locke's philosophy that held association to be the parent of confusion and chaos. Like Fielding before him, Sterne later took the reader into his confidence regarding his method. "I fly off from what I am about," he wrote, "as far and as often too, as any writer in Great Britain; yet I constantly take care to order affairs so that my main business does not stand still in my absence." And he ended the first book with the warning: "If I thought you was able to form the least judgment or probable conjecture to yourself, of what was to come in the next page,—I would tear it out of my book." After such a *caveat* had a reader the right to complain if attention had become a monkey, swinging from limb to limb in the forest of the mind?

Another important idea of Locke, the author suggests, would be embodied in the structure of the novel: the idea of duration as the train and succession of ideas. Sterne had the notion of attempting a realistic time-scheme in which the reading time of the novel would be designed to parallel the duration of the action. For example, when we are informed some seventy pages after the announcement of Dr. Slop's entrance into the Shandy's back parlor that the "man-midwife" had been in the house two hours and ten minutes, the succession of ideas furnished to the reader's mind by the seventy-odd pages is supposed to approximate the passage of the stated time. In the same way, the first day of Tristram's life ends after several hundred pages. Both these illustrations, of course, run beyond what the first readers of *Tristram* actually read. Sterne's ideas about duration are only suggested in the first two books. But in the third book two whole chapters are devoted to the subject, and the author's plan is made clearer. Sterne had, of course, attempted the impossible. Thousands upon thousands of pages would have been necessary to cover the first year of the hero's life. But although the scheme failed in its original intent, it is a fascinating precursor of experiments with time in the writing of fiction practiced by James Joyce and Mrs. Virginia Woolf, working in our own day under the influence of Bergson's psychology very much in the same way that Sterne wrote in the eighteenth century under the influence of Locke's.

In spite of Sterne's avowed removal of all local references, there was plenty of recognizable satire to keep the first purchasers from being disappointed. Local attention was caught by satire on the legal profession including parody of its phraseology, and especially by the introduction of Dr. Topham as Didius. The second book abounded in satire on Catholicism reminiscent of the warm feelings that had developed in York during the '45; and Dr. Burton was scandalously pilloried as Dr. Slop:

> Imagine to yourself a little squat, uncourtly figure of a Dr. Slop, of about four feet and a half perpendicular height, with a breadth of back, and a sesquipedality of belly, which might have done honour to a serjeant in the horse-guards.

The anti-Catholic satire is as naïve and provincial and obscene as it could very well be. Not until he went to the

Continent did Sterne learn that not all Catholics were depraved.

The author himself figured everywhere in his novel. His asthma is introduced into the fifth chapter of the first book, and chapters ten and eleven present the famous picture of Yorick as knight errant and wit. No reader in York could have failed to recognize the portrait; and some, no doubt, saw in it the *apologia* of the whimsical vicar, who like most satirists imputed the best of motives to himself. Finally, there was the recognizable sermon on the Inquisition, preached nine years before during the Summer Assizes and published in pamphlet form.

Plenty of spice was to be found in the Rabelaisian humor. The real charm, however, was in the characterization. Never before had there been such a pair as Mr. Shandy and Uncle Toby. The first stood as an incarnation of the fallacy of rigid faith in logic:

> —he was systematical, and, like all systematic reasoners, he would move both heaven and earth, and twist and torture every thing in nature, to support his hypothesis.

Nothing in the literature of eighteenth-century anti-rationalism had excelled the portrait. Uncle Toby, on the other hand, was the warm and ridiculous embodiment of the sentimentalism for which his creator became deservedly famous and infamous. Not since Falstaff had there been such a superb comic creation.

ii

According to a letter that Sterne wrote for Kitty to relay to London friends, two hundred copies of *Tristram Shandy* were sold in the first two days of its appearance in York. If the letter is telling the strict truth, the bookshop at the Sign of the Golden Bible must have had two unusually busy days. A local success, however, was naturally a means rather than an end. Sterne had now to stimulate sales in the capital. For this purpose he cannily enlisted the aid of Miss Fourmantelle in bringing the book to the attention of her dramatic, musical, and literary friends, notably the great theatrical idol of the day and joint patentee of the Drury Lane Theatre, David Garrick. The letter that Sterne composed for Kitty to copy is a masterpiece of subtle advertising. Not only is the new novel pictured as a popular success in York, but it is described as "a witty smart book" by a local celebrity well worth knowing. And there is a final clever touch to emphasize its naughtiness:

> The graver people, however, say 'tis not fit for young ladies to read his book; so perhaps you'll think it not fit for a young lady to recommend it. However, the nobility and great folks stand up mightily for it, and say 'tis a good book tho' a little tawdry in some places.

A few weeks later Sterne heard indirectly that Garrick had spoken well of the book; so he set himself down to compose a flattering letter that would clinch the great man's approbation. "My first impulse was to send it to you," wrote Laurence (not scrupling to "lie abominably" if necessary), "to have your critique upon it before it went to press." He concludes with a plethora of expansiveness:

> I sometimes think of a Cervantic comedy upon these [the first two volumes] and the materials of the third and fourth volumes which will be still more dramatic...Half a word of encouragement would be enough to make me conceive and bring forth something for the stage.

The proper encouragement was never forthcoming. And Sterne's greatest success in the dramatic was destined to be either in *Tristram Shandy* or in his own life—in both of which drama exists in generous measure.

About March 1 came the great turning point for Laurence, a circumstance that metamorphosed the country parson into the first literary lion of the realm and gave him an astonishing career in London society scarcely less meteoric and brilliant than Lord Byron's later triumph after the publication of *Childe Harold*. Unfortunately, for the first part of this unusual story we have no more reliable authority than John Croft; but since the account has few inherent improbabilities, it may be accepted with reasonable assurance.

As chance would have it, Squire Croft of Stillington Hall had occasion to go to London on business, and he offered to take his parson along, with all expenses paid. For Sterne such a golden opportunity was almost irresistible. However, he at first declined, pleading that his wife's malady made it difficult for him to leave York. "But you can't do her any good by staying here," the Squire argued. The argument seemed valid enough. So, begging an hour's time in which to pack his "best breeches," Laurence accepted; and soon the two were on the highroad.

The momentous journey took parts of four days. While the coach jogged along Londonward, even the wildest flight of Laurence's imagination could not have suggested the events of the ensuing weeks—events that enabled him to return to York in his own coach and pair, so famous that a letter addressed "Laurence Sterne, Europe" would reach him.

Evening had fallen when the travelers from Yorkshire rolled into Chappell Street and drew up before the house of Nathaniel Cholmley of Whitby, Squire Croft's son-in-law. Here the two were to lodge. If Sterne slept a wink during the night, it would be a matter of surprise. At all odds, in the morning he was up well before breakfast and on his way to the shop of Robert and James Dodsley with all the anticipation of a young author whose brain-child has just come from the press.

The Sign of Tully's Head marked the most fashionable and famous bookshop in London of the mid-century. It stood on the sunny side of Pall Mall, then an unpaved roadway running from St. James's palace to Carlton House; and behind its bulged green panes and slanting sunblinds were enshrined in cool dimness the best of morocco bindings and the most exciting productions of contemporary letters. In the spring of the preceding year its shelves had offered an Oriental tale, *The History of Rasselas, Prince of Abyssinia*, written by a frequenter of the shop who walked with a rolling gait and who was not noted for impeccable linen. It had also offered an essay called *An Enquiry into the Present State of Polite Learning* by a pock-marked and otherwise unprepossessing physician and hackwriter known as Oliver Goldsmith. For years Robert Dodsley himself had received his customers with a sober and quiet manner faintly tinctured with an obsequiousness suggestive of his early years in domestic service. Dodsley had had a remarkable career beginning with a position as a footman and ending with that of an extremely important bookseller, with a reasonably distinguished career as a dramatist included. In the service of the Honorable Mrs. Lowther he had written two poems advising servants how to behave. (The eighteenth-century Muse admitted any diet.) A dramatic success with a one-act satire, "The Toy Shop," together with a loan from so eminent a personage as Mr. Alexander Pope, had given him an opportunity to set up as bookseller. The time had been propitious, for such established booksellers as Lintot and Tonson were passing off the scene. Literary treasures were ready to fall into his lap. Dodsley had paid the struggling Samuel Johnson ten pounds for "London" and had stimulated the publication of his great dictionary. At the urgent request of Horace Walpole he had brought out a singularly successful poem called "Elegy Written in a Country Churchyard." His personal literary successes did not end with the beginning of his career as publisher. Even as late as 1759 his tragedy *Cleone* was an important ornament of the London theatrical season. But by 1760 Robert Dodsley had retired from much of the active management of the firm in favor of his brother James.

On account of the early hour of the new author's arrival at the shop on a morning in March, 1760, Laurence hardly entered upon the heels of either of the brothers. Instead, he more probably encountered a sleepy clerk who was just opening the blinds. In the early morning darkness the Yorkshire vicar assuredly fingered an expensive leather binding or two before he acquired the casualness to ask whether the shop offered for sale the works of a certain Mr. Sterne.

"Sir," replied the clerk forthwith, "they cannot be had in London either for love or money."

No angel's song could have been sweeter music to Laurence's ear. His heart turned a handspring. That his novel was being read in London he knew. He also knew that the *Gentleman's Magazine* and the *London Chronicle* had published excerpts from the portrait of Yorick as a delightful delineation of the author himself and that thus he had acquired some reputation in the great city as an unusual personality. But such popularity as the clerk suggested he could not have anticipated. Now he could talk real business with the Dodsleys. No longer would there be wheedling for a mere fifty pounds. Much bigger game was in sight. There were sermons to be published; moreover, Sterne had visions of a long series of Shandean volumes, stretching away enchantingly into the future. He knew that he had "arrived." Apparently, James Dodsley, too, recognized the fact, although in his meeting with Sterne an hour or so later he was inclined—like a good business man —to make the best possible bargain for himself and thus to argue concerning terms with the now extremely confident author.

If we may continue to follow Croft's account, during the negotiations with Dodsley the Squire of Stillington and Mr. Nathaniel Cholmley drove down Pall Mall; and Sterne, happening to see them, ran out to say that he was mortgaging his brain to Dodsley. When the two friends learned the terms, they advised Sterne to haggle no longer but to close the deal at once. An agreement having been reached, Laurence went gaily back to Chappell Street, "skipping into the room" where he announced to the Squire and Cholmley that he was "the richest man in Europe." However, that this part of the account is not strictly accurate is suggested by the fact that the tentative written agreement was not signed until three days later. In the meantime, according to Sterne's intimation in a letter to Kitty, Garrick had had his word to say to the bookseller. Richard Berenger, the actor's close friend, was on hand to witness the paper when it was finally drawn up. Whenever the document was signed, it was a signal victory in the parson's campaign for fame.

The letters to Garrick had been miraculously efficacious. The arbiter of elegance had liked the book, and his approval was in effect the golden smile of success. Two days after Sterne's arrival in London, Garrick was sending seats for the theatre—most likely for a performance of *The Siege of Aquileia* by the highly praised Scotch dramatist, John Home. A warm intimacy sprang up immediately. In two more days the new author was taking up lodgings in Pall Mall. By this time there had been a wild-fire spread of his popularity. He had so little time to himself that he had to compose a letter to Kitty in breathless snatches:

> I have the greatest honours paid me [he wrote] and most civilities shown me that were ever known, from the great; and am engaged already to ten noble men and men of fashion to dine.

Another evidence of his astonishing rise to eminence is the fact that on the day he signed the contract with Dodsley he could dispatch his new friend Berenger to the great Hogarth on a successful mission for "ten strokes" of his "witty chisel to clap at the front of my next edition of Shandy." In spite of Sterne's having burlesqued Hogarth's *Analysis of Beauty*, the caricaturist thought enough of the novelist's genius to venture going "down together hand in hand to futurity," as Sterne had suggested. Not only did he furnish the requested drawing of Trim reading the sermon, but he also did the christening of Tristram as a frontispiece for the third volume.

The demands on the novelist's time grew apace, and great and near-great crowding into his apartments to sip his tea and to demand him for their salons. Laurence outlined his triumphs to Kitty back in York, calling the roll of celebrities with all the glibness of a true parvenu:

> From morning to night my lodgings, which by the by are the genteelest in town, are full of the greatest company. I dined these two days with two Ladies of the Bedchamber—then with Lord Rockingham, Lord Edgecumbe, Lord Winchelsea, Lord Lyttleton, a Bishop—etc., etc.

As time went on, the Duke of York invited him to supper; he dined with the aging symbol of an earlier era, Lord Chesterfield; he went to Windsor Castle in the suite of Lord Rockingham to see that gentleman and Prince Ferdinand of Brunswick installed (the latter by proxy) as

Knights of the Garter with all the usual medieval pomp and ceremony. Old Lord Bathurst, who had hobnobbed with the giants of the golden Augustan age, was consummately flattering:

> He came up to me one day, as I was at the Princess of Wales's court [Laurence recorded]. 'I want to know you, Mr. Sterne; but it is fit you should know, also, who it is that wishes this pleasure. You have heard, continued he, of an old Lord Bathurst, of whom your Popes, and Swifts, have sung and spoken so much: I have lived my life with geniuses of that cast; but have survived them; and, despairing ever to find their equals, it is some years since I have closed my accounts, and shut up my books, with thoughts of never opening them again: but you have kindled a desire in me of opening them once more before I die; which I now do; so go home and dine with me.'–

"I have not a moment to spare," Sterne wrote on April 1, giddy with success, "–dine today with a dozen Dukes and Earls." In corroboration, Thomas Gray remarked, ". . . one is invited to dinner, where he dines, a fortnight before." Further claims to immortality were fastened on him when his portrait was painted by Sir Joshua Reynolds and his bust was modeled by Roubiliac. The portrait shows definite traces of the sitter's dissipation during the kaleidoscopic weeks. According to one story, Laurence had to be propped up during the sittings. It is a miracle that the delicate frame of the parson could have held up under the hectic rush from Ranelagh to Windsor and back to Pall Mall again. Compared with this, the dissipation of the house-parties at "Crazy Castle" was inconsequential.

In this dazzling April Sterne had the good fortune to meet a young Scotsman of nineteen who was as yet obscure but who had already developed a true flair for celebrities and for biographical details. Manifestly impressed by the great lion of the season, this new friend was to record in verse the metamorphosis of the Yorkshire parson:

> By Fashion's hands compleatly drest,
> He's everywhere a wellcome Guest:
> He runs about from place to place,
> Now with my Lord, then with his Grace,
> And, mixing with the brilliant throng,
> He straight commences *Beau Garcon.*
> In Ranelagh's delightfull round
> Squire Tristram oft is flaunting found;
> A buzzing whisper flys about;
> Where'er he comes they point him out;
> Each Waiter with an eager eye
> Observes him as he passes by;
> 'That there is he, do, Thomas! Look,
> Who's wrote such a damn'd clever book.'

The same James Boswell reported a conversation that took place a few years later when the statement was made in the presence of Dr. Johnson that there was little hospitality in London. "Nay, Sir," said the Doctor, "any man who has a name, or who has the power of pleasing, will be generally invited in London. The man, Sterne, I have been told, has had engagements for three months." "And a very dull fellow," put in Noll Goldsmith, who was himself no brilliant star in the drawing room. "Why, no, Sir," maintained the Great Bear with a marked show of firmness.—As a matter of fact, the secret of Sterne's tremendous social success is not immediately apparent. Assuredly, he was not what Swift called "a hedge parson"; but, in spite of his newly acquired sartorial elegance, his conversation did not always coruscate and he lacked many of the Chesterfieldian graces. He did not have the social instinct of "little Davy" Garrick. He was even said to be slightly shy in company; and, what with his emaciated frame and phthisic pallor, he was no male beauty. Nevertheless, he was widely regarded as a most agreeable companion.

Some years after his first great triumph Mrs. Montagu remarked of Laurence:

> He is full of the milk of human kindness, harmless as a child, but often a naughty boy, and a little apt to dirty his frock... He has a world of good nature, he never hurt anyone with his wit, he treats asses on two legs as well and gently as he does that four legged one in his book.

An encounter with a man whom many have considered an ass on two legs gives us a concrete example of the way in which Sterne acted under the stimulus. The story takes us back to the beginning of the London visit. On March 6 Sterne wrote to Garrick to deny the rumor that he had intended to introduce the character of the Bishop of Gloucester in his novel as the tutor of Tristram. The necessity for a denial is almost tantamount to an assurance that Sterne had had in his mind the notion of such a satirical portrait. He may even have dropped a hint in York, a hint that traveled rapidly by grapevine telegraph to a proud churchman whose mitre was still very new. It has been widely agreed, in spite of some valiant attempts in his defense, that the Right Reverend Dr. Warburton is a classic example of the heights a man can reach with only insolence, dullness, and superficial scholarship to propel him. Son of a town clerk of Newark, he had trained for the law and had gone into the Church because he saw there a better opportunity for indulging his bookish propensities. He was a voracious reader. Like Sterne himself, he could ride past a house on fire without taking any notice. (During a domestic dispute his wife is said at one time to have thrown a book at him, exclaiming, "If you will not listen to *me*, perhaps you will listen to a book.") From the publication of the first part of his *Divine Legation of Moses* in 1737 almost to the end of his life he had a disagreeable record of arrogant controversy in which he persisted (to quote himself) in hanging those who dared to disagree with him "as they do vermin in a warren," leaving them "to posterity to stink and blacken in the wind." So much for his spirit of Christian charity! After having lambasted Pope vigorously and even coarsely, he suddenly changed tack and wrote a defense of the *Essay on Man* against the attack of Crousaz, winning the noted poet's friendship ("You understand my work better than I do myself," remarked Pope) and laying a foundation for his own fortune. He ultimately became Pope's literary executor. His edition of Shakespeare was severely criticized for its inexact scholarship. He continued to answer attacks with verbal bludgeonings and brow-beatings, winning for himself some respectable friends, some toadies, and a fairly general reputation of a pompous bully.

If Sterne had considered using Tristram's "pretended tutor" as an instrument of satire on pedantry in the manner of *Martinus Scriblerus*, he could not have found a readier target. Pseudo-scholarship in Dr. Burton had provoked his contempt. He had lampooned a legal pedant in Didius. Here was a fine chance to extend his satire to a nationally known figure. If Bathurst recognized the power of his satire, Dr. Warburton may also have done so. At any rate, the Bishop of Gloucester apparently did not treat the rumor with the contempt with which a great and blameless prince of the Church might have treated it.

Sterne's own idea about the lampoon apparently underwent some change when he arrived in London. There was, after all, no need to promote an antagonism that might make his visit unpleasant and that might work to his disadvantage in his search for preferment in the Church. He, therefore, sought an introduction through Garrick in order to scotch the rumor in person and to reap whatever reward the new contact might offer. The Bishop received Sterne with friendliness enough, but also with a fatal touch of ineptness. He took the opportunity to bestow on the new author "a purse of guineas"; moreover, he presented several books (as Croft reported) "to improve his style, with proper and salutary advice for his future conduct in life and pursuits of literature." The purse of guineas gave rise to a story that Warburton sought to bribe Sterne. Since Warburton was a notoriously able controversialist, one can hardly assume that he was quite so crass or so cowardly. However, he might have realized that a satirical portrait in the most popular novel of the day would be infinitely more difficult to dissipate than the attacks on his *The Divine Legation of Moses* or on his edition of Shakespeare, and that an ounce of prevention in the form of patronage might be worth several pounds of cure after the damage was done. His future attitude toward Sterne lends credence to the assumption.

The experience certainly did not foster a warm and lasting friendship between the two men. A little over a year after Warburton's meeting with Sterne, the Bishop was to exclaim, "The fellow . . . is an irrecoverable scoundrel." Five years later he was writing to the poet William Mason:

> All you say I *know*, and all you think I believe of that egregious Puppy who has received of me the most friendly services and has repaid them as all such men do. Not but that I deserved as much, for 'tho Nature sowed in him the seeds of *Puppybility*, yet I cultivated them when I brought him out into the world.

This statement sounds very much as if Warburton had failed in his attempt to escape unscathed. Indeed, he had not escaped from ridicule in *Tristram Shandy*. "Don't fear," Sterne replies to an imaginary critic in Volume IV, "I'll not hurt the poorest jack-ass upon the king's highway." "But," rejoins the critic, "your horse throws dirt; see you've splashed a bishop." And in the ninth volume the author inquires: ". . . for what has this book done more than the Legation of Moses, or the Tale of a Tub, that it may not swim down the gutter of Time along with them?"

But this is a matter of later months. While Sterne was in London on his first triumphant visit, Warburton was boasting that he had recommended *Tristram* to all the best company in town; and he even busied himself about swelling the subscription list of the sermons.

Whatever may have been the Bishop's feeling, there were others who for less obvious reasons were inclined to dislike Sterne and his book. Since most of the dissenters were among literary men, professional jealousy may have played some part. Aristocratic Horace Walpole was not amused, although his friend Thomas Gray was favorably impressed. Dr. Goldsmith wrote deprecatingly in the *Citizen of the World*. Almost the whole story of the antipathy is reflected in the title of Goldsmith's article: "The Absurd Taste for Obscene and Pert Novels, Such as 'Tristram Shandy,' Ridiculed."

> . . . a prurient jest [he wrote] has always been found to give most pleasure to a few very old gentlemen, who, being in some measure dead to other sensations, feel the force of the allusion with double violence on the organs of risibility.

But, alas, continues the moralizer, the work is read not only by old men but by "pretty innocents" who discuss the most scandalous parts in their politest conversation. The attack is reflected in the next century in Thackeray's thoroughly Victorian pronouncement: "There is not a page in Sterne's writing but has something that were better away, a latent corruption—a hint of an impure presence." Both the seeming chaos of the book and the immorality mitigated against the approval of Dr. Johnson, although the lexicographer regarded the author as socially acceptable.

Sterne's own defense against charges of immorality is enshrined in a story told by Sir Walter Scott. When Sterne asked a Yorkshire lady whether she had read *Tristram*, she replied, "I have not, Mr. Sterne; and, to be plain with you, I am informed it is not proper for female perusal." To which Sterne replied, losing no aplomb, "My dear good lady, do not be gulled by such stories; the book is like your young heir there (pointing to a child of three years old, who was rolling on the carpet in his white tunics); he shows at times a good deal that is usually concealed, but it is all in perfect innocence."

CHAPTER VII

KITTY

WHILE STERNE was enjoying the second week of limelight in the capital, another Yorkshire clergyman (once Yorick's curate) lay dying in the obscurity of Coxwold. The demise of the Reverend Richard Wilkinson in a little village just north of York left vacant a living for whose award Laurence had unsuccessfully sought some years previously. Immediately upon receiving the news, Squire Croft waited on the Earl Fauconberg to suggest Sterne's appointment. The Earl, who was an old friend of Laurence, did not hesitate. Since the Archbishop of York was conveniently in residence in Grosvenor Square, the appointment was completed in record time. Thus the *London Chronicle* for March 29, 1760, recorded under a York dateline:

> Last week the Right Hon. the Earl Fauconberg presented the Rev. Mr. Sterne, one of the prebendaries of this Cathedral, to the curacy of Coxwold, worth 140 *l.* a year, void by the death of the Rev. Mr. Wilkinson.

Kitty had been among the first to get the news by letter (with a slightly different valuation of the curacy's worth):

> 'Tho I have but a moment's time to spare, I would not omit writing you an account of my good fortune. My Lord Fauconberg has this day given me a hundred and sixty pounds a year, which I hold with all my preferment; so that all or the most part of my sorrows and tears are going to be wiped away —I have but one obstacle to my happiness now left—and what that is, you know as well as I.

The obstacle was, plainly enough, his wife, who was still an invalid in a house in the Cathedral Yard. "God will open a door," he wrote a few weeks later, apparently on the sanguine assumption that the Deity could be counted on to promote ideal and sentimental attachments. Sterne seems to have been blissfully unconscious of any guilt. A legend runs that one day Garrick caught him in the midst of fulminations against a man who had neglected his wife and who, Laurence was saying, deserved hanging. "Sterne," remarked the suave little actor, "you live *in lodgings.*"

At any rate, it was Kitty with whom he wished at the moment to share not only his present glories but also the permanent benefits of the new preferment. And it was Kitty who could inspire him to express the desire that Mrs. Sterne were conveniently out of the way.

Early in his visit to London he had determined to enveigle the pretty concert singer down from York. What he would do with her when she came, he did not bother to consider. He was riding the crest of a wave, and in his giddiness he thought that the only thing now necessary for his happiness was the warm and "sentimental" adulation of a charming young lady. The whole procedure of bringing Kitty to London is ample proof of Sterne's persistent adolescence in matters of the heart. He had forgotten that the world had changed for him since the day he climbed into Squire Croft's coach in York. Not once did it occur that the diamond of a provincial capital might appear to be a rhinestone in London. Kitty had represented to him everything that the sick and querulous Elizabeth Sterne was not. He had seen her first as a glamorous concert artist from a great city, and his attachment had been nourished by the music and by the specious Oriental splendor of the Assembly Rooms. He had not yet seen the glitter of fashionable London drawing-rooms or the beauties that flowered in the alcoves at Ranelagh and the boxes at the Drury Lane. Moreover, when he was urging Kitty to come to London, he forgot that his being the cynosure of all eyes would make any sort of affair very difficult to keep discreet.

Kitty arrived in town in the last weeks of April and established herself in Soho. Only her actual presence was needed to show Sterne his mistake. Perhaps the process of disillusionment had actually begun, however, before she came—for example, when he learned that she had applied for an engagement to sing at Ranelagh and had been rejected. Consciously or unconsciously he may have weighed the fact that his Kitty was not deemed worthy to sing in a pleasure resort where the great Mr. Sterne was pointed out by duchesses and ladies of the bedchamber and eagerly sought by the great of the realm. The glamour of the little singer may have begun to evaporate, and a gulf may have begun to yawn between the sentimental friends. One should not like to press the matter too far. But it is clear that when Kitty did arrive in London her "lover" did not know what to do with her. Naturally, she got in the way of his social schedule; and she had to suffer, not the dukes and earls whom he reckoned by the dozens:

> As I cannot propose the pleasure of your company longer than till four o'clock this afternoon [he wrote on one occasion], I have sent you a ticket for the play, and hope you will go there that I may have the satisfaction of hoping [*sic*] you are entertained—when I am not. You are a most engaging creature; and I never spend an evening with you, but I leave a fresh part of my heart behind me.—You will get me all, piece by piece, I find, before all is over—and yet I cannot think how I can be ever more than what I am at present
>
> Your affectionate friend
>
> Laurence Sterne

Alone in the stalls of the Drury Lane, Kitty may have reflected that she was hardly sharing her famous friend's triumph as he had suggested she would.

In spite of all the protestations of devotion there is a foreboding tone in another letter:

> I was so intent upon drinking my tea with you this afternoon that I forgot I had been engaged all this week to visit a gentleman's family on this day.–I think I mentioned it in the beginning of the week, but your dear company put that with many other things out of my head. I will, however, contrive to give my dear friend a call at four o'clock–tho', by the by, I think it not quite prudent–but what has prudence, my dear girl, to do with love? In this I have no government, at least not half so much as I ought–

When Sterne begins talking of prudence, the inevitable conclusion is that his sentimental affair is heading swiftly for the rocks. As a matter of fact, the end was not distant.

As days went by, Sterne's visits were separated by longer intervals, with only the lame excuse of the rush of engagements to fill the breach. "I am as much a prisoner as if I was in jail," he wrote. "I beg, dear girl, you will believe I do not spend an hour where I wish–for I wish to be with you always: but fate orders my steps, God knows how for the present." Prudence and fate! It could have taken little more than womanly intuition for Kitty to know that real love knows no such barriers, and that a man usually does what he *wants* to do.

The shelving of Kitty a few weeks after she had arrived in London hardly represents a tragic history. In fact, she drops out of sight as easily and gracefully as she enters the picture. If we first saw her under the great chandelier of the Assembly Rooms in York, she fades away from view in the candleglow of Ranelagh. There is no evidence that she took the sentimental attachment more seriously than her middle-aged lover did; and perhaps, after all, she got all out of the affair that a decent lady of the concert stage could ask. In some way Sterne arranged for her the coveted engagement to sing at Ranelagh, offering as an inducement to the management a song from his own pen. This song Miss Fourmantelle is singing with Mr. John Beard when the darkness closes round her and we lose her from our narrative.

It has been discovered in recent years that the house in Bond Street in which Sterne died was occupied by a Mrs. Mary Fourmantel. The name causes one to wonder whether the lady might have been the mother of Kitty and whether Sterne might have possibly preserved some strain of his love affair throughout the remaining years of his life. But more evidence is necessary before any conclusions can be reached. From what we now know, it seems that the parting came amiably, naturally, and inevitably, and there is no conclusive evidence that the thread was ever picked up again. *Sic transit Kitty!*

Again, amid the bustle of his social life Sterne did not neglect his real love—his art. A second edition of the initial volumes of *Tristram* came out on April 2, bearing a dedication to William Pitt written before Sterne had left Yorkshire, and the process of bringing out the first of the sermons went on.

The dedication to Pitt was timely. Indeed, it was all but inescapable, for *Tristram* was supposed to glorify military valor, and the recent brilliant successes of British arms were all redounding to the glory of the great Prime Minister. The year 1759 had brought more far-reaching triumphs for England and a more important rôle in world affairs than the nation had ever had before. In September had come the decisive battle of Minden, and in the following month came the great victory at Quebec. In November there was the French defeat at Quiberon. So amazing was the winning streak that Walpole remarked, "We are forced to ask every morning what victory there is for fear of missing one." And of all these victories Pitt ultimately became the hero. Hence, the man of the hour and the book of the hour were happily linked.

By the first of May Stephen Croft had returned home to Yorkshire, and Sterne was writing to thank him for news of Bess and Lydia and to request his replenishing of Mrs. Sterne's purse in the event of her needing a few extra guineas. "There is a shilling pamphlet wrote against Tristram," he asserted. "I wish they would write a hundred such." If he had uttered the wish while rubbing the lamp of a bad genie, he could not have been more promptly or balefully answered. "Cousin" John Hall-Stevenson had already entered the arena on April 17 with two scandalous verse epistles: "To My Cousin Shandy, On His Coming to Town" and "An Epistle to the Grown Gentlewomen the Misses of ****." These were the beginning of what was destined to be a flood of pamphlets containing continuations, burlesques, epistles, replies, explanatory remarks, and a variety of other things better unprinted. The extent of the vogue is demonstrated by the fact that several race horses were named Tristram, and the name was borrowed for a game of cards and for a salad. It was not unusual to see in the *London Chronicle* such an item as: "Lord Bolingbroke's Tristram Shandy beat the Duke of Grafton's Cocker for 200 guineas." There was no stopping the stream once it had started; and the novelist was soon to suffer some of the pangs of those who either court publicity or have publicity thrust upon them.

One of the greatest single objects of embarrassment was a sketch written about Laurence in the *Royal Female Magazine* by the notorious Dr. John Hill—actor, editor, botanist, apothecary. Dr. Hill did not let his readers forget that the elegant author, the Reverend Mr. Sterne, was "born in the barracks," and it was he who intimated that Dr. Warburton had sought to bribe Sterne into silence. He also perpetrated a devilishly clever bit of skulduggery by reporting that upon receiving the living of Coxwold, Sterne—wealthy on account of the success of his novel—had magnanimously promised the widow of the former incumbent the sum of one hundred pounds, not to mention some sort of relief in perpetuity. The story became widespread, for practically every London newspaper copied the article.—Finally, as if to add insult to injury, the article was published in pamphlet form, with a sheaf of scurrilous anecdotes attached, under the title of *Tristram Shandy's Bon Mots, Repartees, Odd Adventures, and Humourous Stories.*

Methodism, too, had its inning:

> O *Sterne* [ran a pamphlet called *A Letter from the Rev. George Whitefield, B. A.*] thou art scabby, and such is the leprosy of thy mind that it is not to be cured like the leprosy of the body, by dipping nine times in the river Jordan. Thy prophane history of *Tristram Shandy* is as it were an anti-gospel, and seems to have been penned by the hand of Anti-christ himself... Thou hast studied prophane plays more than the word of God, and thy text is generally taken from the writings of Shakespear, an author who never had any idea of the new birth, and yet without the new birth it will be vain for you to hope for salvation.

Well did Sterne have cause to regret his wish. "The scribblers use me ill," he was soon to exclaim in distress.

On May 22, in the midst of this unfortunate wave of notoriety and condemnation came the publication of the first two volumes of the *Sermons of Mr. Yorick.* It is remarkable that only the *Monthly Review* resented the fact that the work was brought out under the name of a character "in an obscene romance." Almost everywhere else the book was greeted with acclaim. Truly, the subscription list looked like a roll-call of the peerage, with a generous sprinkling of names from the world of arts and sciences.

For an edition of the sermons Sterne had cleverly prepared. It has already been mentioned that he had inserted in the second book of *Tristram* a sermon that he had preached as a young prebendary and that he had published in pamphlet form as "The Abuses of Conscience." This warmly anti-Catholic homily Dr. Slop, the papist, is forced to listen to while Trim renders it with great feeling and even tears, especially in the parts depicting the sufferings of victims of the Inquisition. Finally, pity for his brother, who had been a victim of the vicious Catholics, gets the best of the Corporal. Filled with indignation and passion, Mr. Shandy takes the sermon from the faltering Trim and carries on. Throughout, the rendition is punctuated with comments and sentimental by-play. For example, Trim has been reading of the unfortunates in the Inquisition—

> Here's a crown for thee, Trim, to drink with Obadiah to-night, quoth my uncle Toby, and I'll give Obadiah another too.—God bless Your Honour, replied Trim,—I had rather these poor women and children had it.—Thou art an honest fellow, quoth my uncle Toby.—My father nodded his head,—as much as to say,—and so he is.

At the end of the sermon there is the statement that more of these discourses are in the possession of the Shandy family and that they will be published in a "handsome volume" if the sample is well received. Obviously, Sterne was putting his best foot forward. In spite of the charm of the other sermons, one may feel that prospective readers were tempted with the dessert of the feast.

Swift, with all his classical instincts in regard to religion, felt that the greatest of all pulpit evils was the attempt to move the passions of the congregation. "A plain convincing reason," he wrote, "may possibly operate upon the mind both of a learned and ignorant hearer as long as they live and will edify a thousand times more than the art of wetting the handkerchiefs of a whole congregation." Sterne was manifestly of the opposing school:

> To preach, to show the extent of our reading, or the subtleties of our wit [he was to write in Book IV of *Tristram*]—to parade in the eyes of the vulgar with the beggarly accounts of a little learning, tinselled over with a few words which glitter, but convey little light and less warmth—is a dishonest use of the poor single half hour in a week which is put into our hands—'Tis not preaching the gospel—but ourselves—For my own part, continued Yorick, I had rather direct five words point-blank to the heart.—

The dramatic and the sentimental were always to him legitimate devices for the pulpit. Two years after his first London success, the Reverend Mr. Sterne, former papist-baiter, might have been seen standing rapt under the histrionics of Abbé Clément, who preached the damnation of heretics in the church of St. Roch in Paris. In Sterne's own England the period was one of great pulpit acting, especially among the Evangelicals or Methodists. Whitefield and John Wesley in the chapel of the Countess of Huntingdon and in the tabernacle in Moorfields ("theatre" it was actually called by the scoffers) were openly accused of being in competition with Garrick and Macklin and Barry, who held forth at the Drury Lane and at Covent Garden. Although the devout Evangelicals did not approve of the "heteroclite parson" of Yorkshire, at least in his return to emotionalism he stood with them against the cold intellectuality that in the first half of the century had all but dominated the Church.

But aside from all their drama and sentimentality, Sterne's sermons at times seem like the graceful Saturday essays of Addison. In them one hardly looks for originality of thought. Borrowings from Tillotson, Hall, and other easily accessible divines sometimes turn up in thin disguises. Laurence tells us that he jotted down comments on the first leaf of every sermon directly after he had preached it, recording the time, place, and occasion and making frank critical comments on the sermon's virtues and vices. For example, on one he scribbled: "This sermon upon the Jewish dispensation—I don't like it at all." On another: "The excellency of this text is, that it will suit any sermon,—and of this sermon,—that it will suit any text.—" And finally, "For this sermon I shall be hanged,—for I have stolen the greatest part of it. Doctor Paidagunes found me out. ☛ Set a thief to catch a thief.—"

The sermons propound an easy and comfortable morality. In the homilies of benevolence and charity one may easily recognize the strain widely popularized in the early decades of the century by Lord Shaftesbury's *Characteristics*. A passage from the third sermon reads like Shaftesbury's treatment of the "moral sense" and suggests his "virtuoso" identification of the Beautiful and the Good:

> In benevolent natures the impulse to pity is so sudden that, like instruments of music which obey the touch, the objects which are fitted to excite such impressions work so instantaneous an effect, that you would think the will was scarce concerned, and that the mind was altogether passive in the sympathy which her own goodness has excited.

The theme of another sermon runs: "Great and inexpressible may be the happiness which a moderate fortune and moderate desires, with a consciousness of virtues, will secure." The same sort of theme had been worked to death in scores of "retirement" essays and poems headed by Cowley's "Of Myself" and Pomfret's "The Choice."

The way in which Sterne can turn on the tremolo for the sentimental passages is exquisitely illustrated by his rendition of the parable of the Good Samaritan, also in Sermon III:

As he approached the place where the unfortunate man lay, the instant he beheld him, no doubt some such train of reflections as these would rise in his mind:—"Good God! what a spectacle of misery do I behold!—a man stripped of his raiment, —wounded,—lying languishing before me upon the ground, just ready to expire,—without the comfort of a friend to support him in his last agonies, or the prospect of a hand to close his eyes when his pains are over! But perhaps my concern should lessen when I reflect on the relations in which we stand to each other,—that he is a Jew, and I a Samaritan.—But are we not still both men? partakers of the same nature,—and subject to the same evils?—Let me change conditions with him for a moment, and consider, had his lot befallen me as I journeyed in the way, what measure I should have expected at his hand.—Should I wish when he beheld me wounded and half dead, that he should shut up his bowels of compassion from me, and double the weight of my miseries by passing by and leaving them unpitied?—But I am a stranger to the man;—be it so;—but I am no stranger to his condition;—misfortunes are of no particular tribe or nation... Had I known him, possibly I should have had cause to love and pity him the more;—for aught I know, he is some one of uncommon merit, whose life is rendered still more precious as the lives and happiness of others may be involved in it: perhaps at this instant that he lies here forsaken in all this misery, a whole virtuous family is joyfully looking for his return, and affectionately counting the hours of his delay! Oh! did they know what evil had befallen him,—how would they fly to succor him!—Let me then hasten to supply those tender offices of binding up his wounds, and carrying him to a place of safety;—or if that assistance comes too late, I shall comfort him at least in his last hours;—and if I can do nothing else,—I shall soften his misfortunes by dropping a tear of pity over them!"

The dashes and the final tear trickling down the exclamation point are typically Shandean, as also is the stream-of-consciousness method by which Sterne with consummate skill analyzes not only Biblical characters in his sermons but also fictitious characters in his novels.

One does not get very far in arguing that Sterne's morality has any real depth; but there is a charm about it. William Cowper, who never read *Tristram* and who read the early volumes of sermons before his great religious and mental crisis, acclaimed Sterne a "great master of the pathetic" and expressed the belief that no writer was "better qualified to make proselytes to the cause of virtue" than he. Gray felt that the sermons were in a proper style for the pulpit and that they showed a strong imagination and a "sensible" heart; "but," he continued, "you see him [Sterne] often tottering on the verge of laughter, and ready to throw his periwig in the face of the audience." Actually, the morality of the sermons differs little from that which shines through *Tristram,* in spite of the novel's surface levity. Coleridge, with keener perception than the Victorian critics were to have, asked his hearers to note "Sterne's assertion of, and faith in a moral good in the characters of Trim, Toby, etc., as contrasted with the cold skepticism of motives which is the stamp of the Jacobin spirit." Indeed, Sterne himself insisted upon his mission as a moralist in fiction. But it is always difficult to tell what in Sterne is sincerity and what is pose. As for the morality of the sermons, there will doubtless continue to be many who will preserve the skepticism of Dr. Johnson. On a visit to Lichfield, the Doctor was given a volume of the sermons by an old friend and asked for an opinion. Upon being asked as a counter question whether he ever read other sermons, the friend replied, "Yes, Doctor, I read Sherlock, Tillotson, Beveridge, and others." "Aye, Sir," said Johnson, "*there* you drink the cup of Salvation to the bottom; here you have merely the froth from the surface."

CHAPTER VIII

"LAUGH, MY LORD, I WILL"

ON THE AFTERNOON of Thursday, March 29, 1760, a carriage entered briskly through York's Micklegate and drove toward the towering Minster, now rapidly being engulfed in the gathering mist. Its portmanteau contained the fashionable London clothes of Yorkshire's most illustrious son, a man who but a few weeks ago had hurriedly packed his "best breeches" for a departure without fanfare.

What went on in Laurence's head during the triumphant return journey one can only conjecture. Certainly his brain seethed with memories of his remarkable weeks in the capital and with ideas for forthcoming volumes of *Tristram.* Eagerness to plunge into writing again made the long miles seem longer. As he neared York, he could not have escaped feeling a warm glow at the thought of being able to bask—if for only a brief space—in the admiration of his friends, as well as of being able to command the envy of his enemies both in the Chapter and in the city. And, most of all, he thought tenderly of seeing his daughter again. The prospect of seeing his wife, now much improved in health, could have caused no great elation.

And Kitty. Did he spare a thought for the young singer who had once been a pensioner at Mrs. Joliffe's in the parish of St. Helen, Stonegate? One cannot say. At least there were no bottles of Lisbon wine or packages of sweetmeats to be dropped discreetly before he drew up before the house in the Minster Yard. So there is every reason to believe that Sterne proceeded directly home.

Happy is the man who can carry his triumphs into his own household. Once inside his door, Laurence felt much of the ebullience of his success vanish into the mist that laid feathery fingers on the panes. He had hardly done more than plant a husbandly peck on the brow of Mrs. Sterne before that lady began an account of Lydia's disgraceful conduct in her father's absence. Apparently, the backwash of Sterne's fame had not been long in reaching York; and Lydia had considered herself the chief sufferer, especially when her school friends accosted her as "Miss Shandy." Her little head got busy to plot revenge. Pretty soon the parents of several young ladies of York were properly horrified to discover that their daughters were carrying on correspondence with players in a local stock company. Wrath fell not only on the daughters but also on the actors, who took it upon themselves to ferret out the culprit. In short, Lydia had been forging in a high-handed way.

If Mrs. Sterne had taunted Lydia with the commonplace "I shall tell your father," she was undoubtedly disappointed by her husband's reaction. The prank could not have failed to amuse him. The damage, he saw immediately, might be embarrassing but it was not irreparable. Furthermore, he was too glad to see Lydia to reprimand her; and there were too many important things in his mind to cause him to concern himself with trivialities.

One does not change a residence of over twenty years without bother. So much was entailed in taking over the living of Coxwold that several weeks were necessary to get affairs in order. Not only had matters of moving to be attended to, but a curate had to be established in the old parishes. Upon his moving to York in the preceding winter, Sterne had secured a curate for Sutton and Stillington; but since the appointment had not been official, Laurence now had to get the necessary licenses. The curate was one

Marmaduke Callis, a pedestrian time-server of the Lord whose appointment was happy neither for Sterne nor for himself. In the first place, Sterne underpaid him. As a consequence, his dissatisfaction grew with the passing months. The unfortunate story is climaxed by the burning of the Sutton parsonage five years later and the departure of Mr. Callis for two parishes in Nottinghamshire. Ultimate disaster Sterne was, of course, unable to foresee. He was now concerned with settling the curacy as quickly as possible so that he could begin writing once again.

The new living was some seven miles north of York and was, according to Laurence, "a sweet retirement in comparison to Sutton." Like Sutton, Coxwold was a small village. One of its chief landmarks was a low-eaved inn with a green beside it. On a gentle hill beyond was the church, with an octagonal tower and a generally attractive exterior of perpendicular Gothic. However, like many English churches that everywhere make the landscape picturesque, it had a disappointing interior. Its ceiling was low, the beams were grotesquely bossed, and the walls were drab and plain. The effigied tombs of the Fauconbergs were in the chancel. Beyond the church and near the highroad was the house that Sterne was to occupy for the rest of his life, calling it Shandy Castle or Shandy Hall. It was a rambling gabled house on a hillside overlooking the moors. In Laurence's day no parsonage was attached to the living; therefore, this already "ancient house" had to be rented from the Fauconbergs at £12 a year.

At Coxwold, Sterne was removed from his friends both at York and at Stillington. But the daemon of writing possessed him. He had tasted fame, and he wanted more. Thus he was glad to establish himself in a little study with a deal table cluttered with writing materials. Here he could put on his old slippers and dressing gown, push his wig askew, grow a beard, and take his pen on countless flights from the inkhorn to the curling sheets. He lived, he wrote, he walked like one possessed:

> It is not half an hour ago [he confessed at one point in *Tristram Shandy*], when (in the great hurry and precipitation of a poor devil's writing for daily bread) I threw a fair sheet, which I had just finished, and carefully wrote out, slap into the fire, instead of the foul one.
>
> Instantly I snatched off my wig, and threw it perpendicularly, with all imaginable violence, up to the top of the room.

He would sally forth from the house and down the hill only to turn suddenly and hurry back to jot down something to be used in *Tristram.*

In spite of his retirement, the exasperating spirit of Dr. Warburton hung over Sterne's study. This fact determined not a little of the color of the next two volumes of *Tristram.*

Before Sterne left London he sent the Bishop two sets of his sermons by the hand of Richard Berenger. Slightly over a week after his return to York, Sterne wrote to Warburton to thank him for "the generosity of your protection, and advice to me." Dr. Warburton replied, telling of the scurrilous odes of Hall-Stevenson and giving more of his smug admonition: "You have it in your power to make that, which is an amusement to yourself and others, useful to both: at least you should above all things, beware of its becoming hurtful to either, by any violations of decency and good manners." This advice was not only more of the same sort that the Bishop had given before; but it was also more of the kind included in the *Letter from Whitefield,* which had counseled: "Learn to chew the cud of piety, make a hearty meal upon faith; and you'll find it very different from Dr. Slop's wafer." We do not wonder that momentarily Sterne had the feeling that he would like to give up *Tristram Shandy* forever. A matter of greater amazement is that he did not make a *hearty meal* of his gratuitous advisers. What he actually did was to pull himself together for a retort courteous:

> Be assured, my lord, that willingly and knowingly I will give no offence to any mortal by anything which I think can look like the least violation either of decency or good manners; and yet, with all the caution of a heart void of offence or intention of giving it, I may find it very hard, in writing such a book as 'Tristram Shandy,' to mutilate everything in it down to the prudish humour of every particular. I will, however, do my best; though laugh, my lord, I will, and as loud as I can too.

The *caveat* seems too plain to miss. How a man so intelligent as Warburton could have failed to see defiance behind the seeming acquiescence it is difficult to fathom. At any rate, he should have seen that it was time to let the whole matter drop. Unfortunately, he was foolhardy enough to write Sterne again, this time admonishing him to "laugh in good company, where priests and virgins may be present" and further warning that "a man was never writ out of the reputation he had once fairly won, but by himself." At the same time, Warburton was writing Garrick to say that he had done his best to keep Sterne from playing the fool.

Laurence's rage is only thinly concealed in a letter that he wrote to Miss Mary Macartney, later Lady Lyttleton:

> 'God forgive me, for the volumes of ribaldry I've been the cause of'–now I say, God forgive them–and 'tis the prayer I constantly put up for those who use me most unhandsomely–the Bishop of Gloucester, who (to be sure) bears evils of this kind–so as no man ever bore 'em, has wrote me a congratulatory letter thereupon–the sum total of which is–That we bear the sufferings of other people with great philosophy–I only wish one could bear the excellencies of some people with the same indifference–

Defiance of the Bishop is one of the motivating forces of Sterne's third and fourth volumes. Out of nothing less than sheer perversity, these volumes become increasingly scatological; and Laurence leers and thumbs his nose at Warburton from behind every "Your reverence" or "Your worship" that punctuates the narrative. And if there is need for a final answer, the "preface"—placed in the middle of Book III—gives it: "All I know of the matter is—when I sat down, my intent was to write a good book. . . I detest and abjure either great wigs or long beards. . . I write not for them." That was *that* for the Bishop, who might consider himself sufficiently "splashed."

If it is interesting to see the influence of the Bishop on the pen of the heteroclite parson at Coxwold, it is also interesting to see how his recent weeks in London influenced his writing. There are some obvious evidences like the references to Reynolds and Garrick, replies to the *Monthly* reviewers and other adverse critics, and compliments to Pitt, to the young King, and to the Duke of York. The influence of the theatre is subtle and pervasive, intensifying the dramatic effect of a talent that was already instinctively dramatic. There is every evidence that Sterne had watched Garrick closely and that he returned to the "stage business" of *Tristram* with added skill for gesture, pantomime, and pause.

The local satire is again prominent. Didius keeps popping in and out, and the character of Dr. Slop increases in importance. The anti-Catholic feeling continues strong. The lengthiest treatment of a local situation is the scurrilous tale of Phutatorious and the hot chestnut. Appearing in the fourth volume, this story returns to the circumstances that gave rise to *The Good Warm Watch-Coat*. Here is the final pay-off for Dr. Topham.

The increased richness and bawdiness of the comedy are under the guidance of "dear Rabelais and dearer Cervantes."

In the series of "misfortunes" upon Tristram's birth, in Mr. Shandy's desolation over his son's mashed nose, in the circumstances of the christening, Sterne's comic genius is at its height. In the *double-entendres* of Slawkenbergius's Tale it is frequently at its most obscene. The tale itself is an ironic answer to Warburton's advice about laughter in the company of priests and virgins. Even such a warm friend as Squire Croft of Stillington seemed scandalized by its ribaldry. Sterne's own explanation—that it was a satire on pedantry—appeared to be hardly sufficient to justify it.

The eccentricities continue. As we have seen, the "preface" is placed midway in Book III. The same book contains a marbled page. In Book IV a whole chapter is "torn out" and ten pages are dropped from the pagination. An entire chapter is needed to give an explanation. In Book IV there are also a Chapter on Chapters (aping Swift's Digression on Digressions) and a chapter Of Things.

ii

Although we have little positive evidence concerning the relations of Mr. and Mrs. Sterne at this time, there are a few significant straws in the wind. Apparently, after Kitty was disposed of, the parson contracted no other binding sentimental attachments. With Miss Macartney his friendship showed no signs of extraordinary warmth; and he manifested no greater commitment to the elusive "witty widow, Mrs. F." than the exclamation written from Shandy Hall, "Now I wish to God I was at your elbow!" But the fact that no other sentimental diversion was in immediate prospect by no means argues that Sterne turned his affections toward his wife. His impatience with the hypochondriac Bess may be reflected (if somewhat indirectly) in Mr. Shandy's complaint about his pregnant spouse: "What a teazing life she did lead herself, and consequently her foetus too. . ." It was a teazing life that Mrs. Sterne constantly led; and so great seems to have been the annoyance when Laurence himself was keyed up to a fever pitch of composition that he wrote "Cousin" John Hall-Stevenson in dog Latin: ". . . nescio quid est materia cum me, sed sum fatigatus & aegrotus de meâ uxore plus quam unquam." (I do not know what is the matter with me but I am more tired and sick of my wife than ever.)

"& sum possessus cum diabolo qui pellet me in urbem" runs the next line. Indeed, there is every reason to believe that Laurence was eager to get back to London with more manuscript pages under his arm for the press. His eagerness was accelerated by the publication in September of a forged volume of *Tristram* by one John Carr. Sterne hurriedly inserted in the *York Courant* a notice that the authentic third and fourth volumes would be on the shelves of the Dodsleys in Pall Mall and of Hinxman in Stonegate about the following Christmas.

Book III had been finished in August. The last sheet of Volume IV lay on the deal table in November; and Sterne was off to plunge once more into the exciting whirl of London and to enjoy the blandishments of society.

In 1760-61 London's winter social season was colored by important political developments in which the newly arrived novelist soon found a lively interest. Everybody was talking about the new and young monarch, George III; about the rising Scottish statesman, the Earl of Bute; and about the progress of the war in Germany. With the support of Pitt, Frederick II of Prussia had been carrying on a valiant but uneven struggle against France and Austria. Without additional support from England, the war now had every prospect of turning into a disaster. Unfortunately, Pitt was tottering to his fall. As Head of the King's Household the crafty Earl of Bute was working assiduously to bring about a peace with France and to make the

King supreme over Parliament. Although only a few months previously Sterne had dedicated the first volumes of *Tristram Shandy* to his great hero, Pitt, he now discovered himself among the King's friends and his opinion of the Great Commoner underwent some change:

> I wish you was here [he wrote to Squire Croft] to see what changes of looks and political reasoning, have taken place in every company, and coffee house since last year; we shall soon be Prussians and Anti-Prussians, Butes and Anti-Butes, and those distinctions will just do as well as Whig and Tory...

Sterne was most favorably impressed by the business-like and energetic appearance of the young King, who rose at six, rode out at 7:30 or 8, at nine gave "himself up to his people," and who later in the day appeared at the play—"but at no opera." "George," the Monarch's mother had admonished him, "George, be king." And George was *being* king as fast as he could, imparting by the appearance of piety and assiduity the conviction that, as Sterne put it, he was going to "bring all things back to their original principles, and to stop the torrent of corruption and laziness." Sterne did not choose to see that corruption and laziness were the hallmark of such of the King's supporters as Sir Francis Dashwood, George Bubb Dodington, and Robert Vansittart—who took up the Yorkshire parson and led him into gaieties unsuited to the cloth.

In February Sterne was sitting in the packed gallery of the House of Commons, hoping to see Pitt "throw down the gauntlet in defence of the German war." Unfortunately, however, on this particular occasion a fit of gout prevented the great man's appearance; and the gallery was forced to hear as a substitute for Pitt's eloquence a "long, passionate, incoherent speech" of William Beckford, soon to be Lord Mayor of London and a prominent supporter of John Wilkes. Although a long day of speeches ensued, Sterne had enough interest to stick to the gallery.

In the middle of March Laurence was writing, "The court is turning topsy-turvy." It was a triumphant period for Bute and the King's supporters. Dashwood, the Medmenham *doyen* and Sterne's friend, was elevated to the post of Treasurer of the Chamber. This event doubtless gave the parson a feeling of contact with the inner circle. Moreover, he could also look upon such an important personage as Charles Townshend as a warm friend.

But, curiously enough, in the midst of all this triumph for Sterne's friends, the rumor got back to York that he himself was *persona non grata* at court; and years later a story was told to suggest the offence that George's piety had taken at Sterne's license. According to the account of Jonas Dennis published in 1820, Cruden, the author of a famous biblical concordance, and Sterne were received at Court on the same day. The King having treated Cruden with great deference bowed so slightly to Sterne as to make the novelist feel that His Majesty had not caught his name. When at Sterne's request the sponsoring nobleman pronounced the name a second time, the King is alleged to have replied, "My Lord, you have told me so already." So the indelicate and shameless Shandy is supposed to have been squelched and His Majesty's piety, attested. But like many of the stories about Sterne, this one is difficult to authenticate. Sterne himself assured Stephen Croft that he had incurred no royal displeasure.

So much for politics. It is remarkable that at this time so much political discussion gets into Sterne's letters, which in the main reflect little of the stirring times in which the author lived. But it is well to remember that to Sterne the outcome of the German war was by no means so important as his dinner engagements or the success of his next two volumes.

These volumes were published not about Christmas time, as promised, but on January 29. There were several laudatory reviews, but there were also attacks. The *Monthly Review* made the charge not only of immorality but of dullness. "One half of the town abuse my work as bitterly, as the other half cry it up to the skies—the best is, they abuse and buy it," wrote Sterne. The very popular novelist Samuel Richardson—a knight *sans peur et sans reproche*—could not stomach the immorality. The Bishop of Sodor and Man concurred, admitting that he had read "accidentally" some of "Shameless Shandy" and had found the author "hardly capable of any sort of defense." Walpole found that the new volumes were "the dregs of nonsense" and reported that they had "universally met the contempt they deserved." The Bishop of Gloucester managed to maintain silence behind his now inhospitable door in Grosvenor Square.

The kind of social life that the provincial parson had learned to love continued. He attended routs at Northumberland House, presided over by Elizabeth, Countess of Northumberland. Among the Bluestockings he had important entrée. His trump card was his relationship to Mrs. Montagu, the "Madame du Deffand of England," who glittered with diamonds and with literary criticism and who was to win renown for ability to entertain seven hundred people at breakfast in her fabulous room with feathered hangings. Besides being of social value, the great lady took a motherly interest in her half cousin-in-law, censuring him when she felt it necessary and advising him to mend his ways. Sterne's response to her censure could not but win her heart. "I used to talk in this severe manner to him," she confessed, "and he would shed penitent tears." Another Bluestocking, the dainty Mrs. Vesey (called the "Sylph" in her coterie) succeeded at this time in setting Sterne a-twitter. Upon very short acquaintance with the attractive lady, Laurence burst into rhapsody:

> ...that you are sensible, and gentle and tender—and from [one] end to the other of you full of the sweetest tones and modulations, requires a connoisseur of more taste and feeling—in honest truth you are a system of harmonic vibrations—You are the sweetest and best tuned of all instruments—O Lord! I would give away my other cassock to touch you—but in giving this last rag of my priesthood for this pleasure you perceive I should be left naked if not quite dis-Ordered.

("You are always letting puns," an old clergyman once said to Sterne; "it deserves punishment." "That," replied Sterne to his everlasting discredit "is—as the pun is meant.")

Back in Coxwold sat Mrs. Sterne, often getting messages only as they were relayed through Squire Croft and frequently fuming because Mrs. Montagu was lavishing on her husband social attentions that she herself had been denied from her fashionable relatives.

If Sterne's reputation of indelicacy did not imperil his social life, it also did not prevent his being asked to mount the pulpit for charity. On May 3 he preached in the Chapel of the Foundling Hospital, a charity of the day fashionable for reasons perhaps not too difficult to fathom. A large crowd gathered to hear the famous Mr. Yorick on one of his few appearances in the pulpit. There were ladies and gentlemen of distinction. For the occasion he chose a sermon called "The Parable of the Rich Man and Lazarus Considered." The discourse was short, but it was admirably adapted to its purpose. It began with an exposition of the difficulties encountered in attempting to convert the skeptical, modulated into a discussion of the dangers of riches, presented the "moral delight arising in the mind from the conscience of a humane action," and ended with a magnificently sentimental appeal for "your alms-giving in behalf of those who know not how to ask it for themselves." No doubt here and there a fine linen or cambric handkerchief dried away a tear. At any rate, the ultimate success of the sermon was recorded in *Lloyd's Evening Post* on the following day: "a handsome collection was made."

CHAPTER IX

INTERLUDE AT COXWOLD

> He flew like lightning–there was a slope of three miles and a half–we scarce touched the ground–the motion was most rapid–most impetuous–'twas communicated to my brain–my heart partook of it... I made my vow, 'I will lock up my study-door the moment I get home, and throw the key of it ninety feet below the surface of the earth, into the draw-well at the back of my house.'

THE TIME WAS June, and the place was a rolling stretch between Stilton and Stamford. Again Laurence found himself on the road to York, jogged almost out of his senses by a madcap of a postillion. The adventure was hardly well timed to fill him with exuberance. He needed rest and quiet rather than discomfort and excitement. His body was giving way under the strain of dissipation and his nerves were beginning to fray. He had drunk deeply of the cup of fame and notoriety, and he knew that the draught was not all sweet. At least temporarily, the prospect of withdrawing to the quiet retreat of Coxwold looked pleasant to him. Not even York could hold him. Through the city he hurried, and on to Shandy Hall.

Of course, he was soon ready to admit that the transition had been a little too abrupt and that a few days in York might have better prepared him for rural seclusion. Unfortunately, at the moment Coxwold did not wear its most pleasant aspect, being in the grip of a bleak, cold, and "churlish" spell of weather that made December of June. "Here 'tis the devil," Sterne wrote to Hall-Stevenson, who had remained in London. And at least half seriously he wished himself back amid the warmth and gaiety of Ranelagh.

For the time being the domestic situation had improved. The continued assurance that Kitty was definitely shelved and that nobody had taken her place was at least part of the explanation:

I return you thanks for the interest you took in my wife [Sterne had confided to Mrs. Montagu in the spring]—and there is not an honest man who will not do me the justice to say, I have ever given her the character of as moral and virtuous a woman as ever God made—what occasioned discontent ever betwixt us, is now no more.—We have settled accounts to each other's satisfaction and honour—and I am persuaded shall end our days without one word of reproach or even incivility.

The same rash optimism, suggesting a sort of domestic non-aggression pact, is found in the letter to Hall-Stevenson just cited:

As to matrimony, I should be a beast to rail at it, for my wife is easy—but the world is not—and had I stayed from her a second longer, it would have been a burning shame—else she declares herself happier without me—but not in anger is this declaration—but in pure sober good sense, built on sound experience—She hopes you will be able to strike a bargain for me before this time twelvemonth to lead a bear around Europe.

In September, Sterne gave to a titled female friend a little vignette of the halcyon homelife of the famous author at Coxwold:

'Tis within a mile of his Lordship's [Fauconberg] seat and park. 'Tis a very agreeable ride out in the chaise, I purchased for my wife.—Lyd has a pony which she delights in.—Whilst they take these diversions, I am scribbling away at my

Tristram... My Lydia helps to copy for me—and my wife knits and listens as I read her chapters...

The picture is a little too ideal to be convincing.

Since the daemon of writing no longer possessed Sterne so completely as it had formerly done and since he found his materials wearing thin, he experienced some difficulty in settling down to work. But when the next book was definitely under way, he began writing at a rapid clip, reaching Chapter XVII of the fifth book on August 10 and beginning the next book not many weeks afterward.

His writing did not stand in the way of his determination to fulfill some of his parish duties. Therefore, he took up preaching with fair regularity. When he did so, he recognized the disagreeable arrangement of the pews in his little church—an arrangement whereby many parishioners were forced to sit with their backs to the minister. For this reason the Vicar busied himself in devising an arrangement similar to that of a cathedral so that all the congregation could see and be seen. How conscientious he was in performing his pastoral duties there is no actual record. A local tradition preserved in the *Yorkshire Notes and Queries* has it that about this time he was called to the bedside of a poor widow of his parish to administer the last sacrament. Upon the Vicar's asking what the widow would bequeath him, the dying woman replied that she had nothing to leave even to her relatives. "That excuse shall not serve me," Sterne is supposed to have replied. "I insist upon inheriting your two children." The story would have brought tears to the eyes of Uncle Toby. Whether it is true we have no way of determining. If Sterne did contribute to the support of the children, he did not manifest the same generosity toward his curates, whom he paid in a manner that was, to say the least, niggardly.

We can see him more vividly in character as he moved

among his parishioners on that gay and great occasion for Coxwold, Coronation Day, on September 22, 1761. As a staunch admirer of the new king and as a new incumbent who desired to ingratiate himself with his parish, the Vicar felt called upon to do something handsome. Thus he contributed an ox with "gilt horns" to be roasted whole outside the village inn and provided two barrels of ale to whet appetites and to promote good cheer. All the morning the delicious aroma of roasting meat and of glowing coals filled the green and caused the villagers to lick their chops in anticipation. When the ox was roasted, the church bells rang and in crowded the throng, packing the little building to the doors.

After the proper prayers were said, the Vicar mounted the pulpit and delivered a brief but eloquent thanksgiving sermon, taking as his text 2 Chronicles xv. 14: "And they sware unto the Lord with a loud voice, and with shouting, and with trumpets, and with cornets.–And all the men of Judah rejoiced at the oath." With the familiar homiletic trick of drawing an almost exact biblical parallel to a contemporary occasion, the minister presented George III under the guise of Asa, who "succeeded, in the room of Abijah his father, with the truest notions of religion and government that could be fetched either from reason or experience." The King's desire to end the Continental war found expression in a bit of anti-war sentiment that would have had more force had it not been political rather than humanitarian:

His experience told him, that the most successful wars, instead of invigorating, more generally drained away the vitals of government,–and at the best, ended but in a brighter and more ostentatious kind of poverty and desolation:–therefore he laid aside his sword, and he studied the arts of ruling Judah with peace.–Conscience would not suffer Asa to sacrifice his subjects to private views of ambition, and wisdom forbade he should suffer them to offer up themselves to the pretence of public ones;—since enlargement of empire, by the destruction of its people... was a dishonest and miserable exchange.

With assurances that the Lord would strike down the enemies of Judah and with exhortations to loyalty to the new king, Sterne ushered on the stage the prince of "just and gentle spirit." It remained, too many years later, for Southey in his *Vision of Judgment* to usher off a mad old monarch who had forfeited England's brightest gem, the American colonies.

About three o'clock a large crowd numbering several thousand assembled on the green, and the ox and the ale were distributed presumably on the principle of first come, first served. Surely, the food and drink could not have gone very far among as many as the reported three thousand people. At any rate, everybody seems to have had a good time. Firecrackers were shot, bonfires were built, and bells were rung. In the evening a ball ended a truly gala day; and the Vicar could retire to his bed with a sense of duty convivially done.

With the celebration off his hands, Sterne resumed writing. By November, the sixth book was completed, and Yorick was ready to set out once again for London. Whether the household maintained its halcyon calm throughout the Vicar's labors is a matter worthy of doubt. If we remember that Sterne had caricatured his wife before, we cannot help feeling that something of the domestic situation is reflected in the new books of *Tristram*. For example, Mrs. Sterne's continued jealousy and curiosity may be reflected in the chapters in which Mrs. Shandy, ignorant of the calamity that has befallen the family, is left eavesdropping while Mr. Shandy goes into a lengthy philosophical descant on the death of their son Master Bobby. Mr. Shandy rises to a climax—

–'I have friends,–I have relations,–I have three desolate children,'–says Socrates.–

–Then, cried my mother, opening the door,–you have one more, Mr. Shandy, than I know of.

By heaven! I have one less,–said my father, getting up and walking out of the room.

Further along we find Sterne writing, this time using the Protean Jenny:

This is the true reason, that my dear Jenny and I, as well as all the world besides us, have such eternal squabbles about nothing.–She looks at her outside,–I at her in–. How is it possible we should agree about her value?

Then there is the amusing "bed of justice" scene in which Mrs. Shandy exasperates her husband by failing to distinguish "betwixt a point of pleasure and a point of convenience." And, finally, there is the famous injunction in regard to the blank page left for the reader's own description of the Widow Wadman: "Sit down, Sir, paint her to your own mind–as much like your mistress as you can–as unlike your wife as your conscience will let you–" This kind of evidence is dangerous; but when it is cumulative, as it is in this case, it seems less likely to mislead. Important corroborative evidence that Mrs. Sterne had again become querulous and resentful is found in a letter that she wrote to Mrs. Montagu just after Sterne had left Coxwold for his third visit to London:

Cou'd Mrs Montagu think this the way to make a bad Husband better, she might indeed have found a better, which I have often Urgd, though to little purpose, namely, shewing some little mark of kindness or regard to me as a Kinswoman, I meant not such as would have cost her money but indeed this neither she or any one of the Robinsons vouchsafed to do though they have seen Mr Sterne frequently these two last winters & will the next. so that surely never poor Girl who had done no one thing to to [*sic*] merit such neglect—was ever so cast off by her Relations as I have been.

I writ 3 posts ago to inform M[rs] Montagu of the sorrow her indiferition had brought upon me, & beg'd she wou'd do all that was in her power to undo the mischeif, though I can't for my soul see which way & must expect to the last hour of my Life to be reproach'd as the blaster of his fortunes

And so the letter continues with bad spelling and bad punctuation. The whole suggests a sick mind that deserves pity. On the other hand, one cannot help feeling some sympathy for the "bad Husband," blameless though he most assuredly was not. Mrs. Montagu, at least, understood what he had to contend with:

Mrs. Sterne is a woman of great integrity [she once wrote] and has many virtues, but they stand like quills upon the fretful porcupine, ready to go forth in sharp arrows on the least supposed offence; she would not do a wrong thing, but she does right things in a very unpleasing manner, and the only way to avoid a quarrel with her is to keep a due distance.

Sterne's third visit to London was far less triumphant than the two preceding visits. There had been increasing imitations and forgeries, accompanied by decreasing sales of the original and growing hostility of the critics. For example, in the preceding spring had appeared *The Life and Opinions of Bertram Montfichet*, a weak imitation that William Cowper read and promptly burned in disgust. The fact that Cowper never read the original may possibly be explained by his violent reaction to the imitation; and thus other readers may have been affected. An index of critical opinion had also been suggested in the review appearing in the *Annual Register for 1760*, the famous resumé of events and literature. Whereas the reviewer could see some merit in the book and was forced to admit its popularity, he found the digressions tiresome and asserted that the book was "a perpetual series of disappointments." In October there had appeared a shilling pamphlet, *A Funeral Discourse occasioned by the much lamented Death of Mr. Yorick*, arguing in a manner faintly similar to Swift's on the astrologer Partridge that although the animal Sterne might still be alive his wit and fancy had died with "Slawkenbergius's Tale."

Such unfavorable publicity, coupled with declining sales of his books, may have caused the very real blow that came to Sterne on this trip—the loss of Dodsley as a publisher. And a rebuff from the Great Cham of literature was not the least of the wounds to his pride.

The only encounter of the authors of *Tristram Shandy* and *Rasselas* occurred at Sir Joshua Reynolds'. With *Tristram Shandy* Dr. Johnson had had little patience. When on an evening at Sir Joshua's Sterne had the brashness to produce the dedication to Lord Spencer that had been designed for the fifth volume, the lexicographer's disapproval was unequivocal. "Sir, it is not English," he growled. Thus he probably summed up not only his disapproval of the dedication but also of the novel itself.

As a climax to his ill fortune Sterne burst a vessel in his lung. The hemorrhage was the most serious since the night many years before in Cambridge when he was startled out of sleep by a "bed full of blood," and it was the beginning of a series of hemorrhages destined to redden his handkerchiefs and pillowcases at intervals for the rest of his life.

To the readers of the fifth and sixth volumes—now published by T. Becket and P. A. Dehondt and autographed by the author to forestall forgers—the opening pages probably suggested the drying up of inspiration that Sterne himself felt when he was writing them. There is a despairing cry in the exclamation in the initial chapter of Book V: "Shall we for ever make new books, as apothecaries make new mixtures, by pouring only out of one vessel into another?" Indeed, there seems at first to be nothing new and refreshing.

The Chapter on Whiskers is merely another tale of *double-entendre*, in no way very subtle. Mr. Shandy's philosophical disquisition on the death of his son is not brilliant. The general tone of the humor seems to be set by the barn-yard flavor of the story of Mr. Shandy's favorite mare, consigned for breeding to a most beautiful Arabian horse. When a mule was the alarming result (the story runs), Mr. Shandy vented his wrath on the handy-man Obadiah:

> See here! you rascal, cried my father, pointing to the mule, what you have done!–It was not me, said Obadiah.–How do I know that? replied my father.

But in spite of the disappointing beginning, the artistry immeasurably improves with the chapter involving the association of ideas among the servants when Master Bobby's death is announced, especially in the section dealing with Susannah's anticipation of acquiring her mistress' wardrobe:

> –My young master in London is dead! said Obadiah.–
>
> –A green satin night-gown of my mother's, which had been twice scoured, was the first idea which Obadiah's exclamation brought into Susannah's head...
>
> –O! 'twill be the death of my poor mistress, cried Susannah. –My mother's whole wardrobe followed.–What a procession! her red damask,–her orange tawney.–her white and yellow lute-strings,–her brown taffeta,–her bone-laced caps, her bed-gowns, and comfortable under-petticoats.–Not a rag was left behind.

As for Obadiah and the dropsical scullion:

> –He is dead, said Obadiah,–he is certainly dead!–So am not I, said the foolish scullion.

The accidental circumcision of Tristram is as delightful a bit of off-color humor as one can find in any language. The book is then completed with Mr. Shandy's plan for a *Tristra-paedia* (after Xenophon) and his device for a "northwest passage to the intellectual world" in a system of auxiliary verbs through the juggling of which one might talk on any possible subject.

If as a whole the fifth book is not up to standard, a stroke of genius gave the sixth book a real importance. That stroke was the highly sentimental story of Le Fever, a retired officer whose mortal illness gave a magnificent chance for the display of Uncle Toby's tender-heartedness. The climax comes in Captain Shandy's determination to see his brother in arms restored to health again:

> –He will march, said my uncle Toby, rising up from the side of the bed, with one shoe off:–An' please your honour, said the corporal, he will never march but to his grave...He shall not die, by G–, cried my uncle Toby.
>
> –The Accusing Spirit, which flew up to heaven's chancery with the oath, blushed as he gave it in;–and the Recording Angel, as he wrote it down, dropped a tear upon the word, and blotted it out for ever.

This peak of sentiment was never transcended. The whole story was a complete and immediate success. In fact, it was the object of so much acclaim that it gave to the author himself new ideas of his sentimental potentialities.

PART THREE: CE MONSIEUR STERNE

CHAPTER X

WHEN DEATH KNOCKED AT THE DOOR

I will lead him a dance he little thinks of—for I will gallop, quoth I, without looking once behind me, to the banks of the Garonne; and if I hear him clattering at my heels—I'll scamper away to mount Vesuvius—from thence to Joppa, and from Joppa to the world's end; where, if he follows me, I pray God he may break his neck...

THE PURSUER is Death; and the occasion—so charmingly metamorphosed into literary material for the first pages of *Tristram Shandy*, Book VII—is the burst vessel in Laurence's lungs. According to the novel, the summons came while the author was in the midst of a "tawdry" story to Eugenius; whereupon that artisan of the obscene tale "led me to my chase—Allons! said I, the postboy gave a crack with his whip—off I went like a cannon, and in half a dozen bounds got into Dover."

The suggestion of a precipitant decision to go to France somewhat belies the facts. As early as June, 1761, Sterne was toying with the idea and was even suggesting the thought of his serving as "bear-leader" or tutor-companion to some rich or noble young gentleman making the Grand Tour. His efforts to establish Marmaduke Callis officially as curate for Stillington and Sutton and to provide a curate for Coxwold suggest preparations against a possible decision to go abroad in the winter. The burst blood vessel provided either a reason or an excuse, or both. But even then he could not set out, bag and baggage, on a moment's notice. First, he had to arrange with the Archbishop for a leave; then he had to attend to the matter of safe conduct. Although hostilities between England and France had ended, a treaty had not yet been signed; thus a regular passport was not available. Pitt's aid had to be sought. In spite of the fact that the Reverend Mr. Sterne had consorted much in previous months with Mr. Pitt's political enemies, the statesman behaved like a man "of good breeding, and good nature," giving Sterne a letter which provided ample assurance of safety.

Two other matters of some seriousness remained: one was getting a twenty-pound loan from Garrick to augment his traveling fund (a loan that seems never to have been repaid) and the other was preparing a memorandum—"In case I should die abroad"—to be left in the hands of Mrs. Montagu for ultimate delivery to his wife. ("I leave this in the hands of our cousin Mrs. Montagu," he explained, "—not because she is our cousin—but because I am sure she has a good heart.") The memorandum, directing the disposition of his property, is a most interesting and revelatory document. According to the writer's expressed wishes, sermons and letters left in a trunk and a bureau in Coxwold and in garrets in York were to be utilized for the benefit of his wife and daughter. However sadly the neurotic Elizabeth Sterne may have vexed her husband, in the shadow of death he thought with tenderness of her future. Another woman who had caused her share of vexation also appears in the document—the only will that he ever made. "If Lydia should die before you," he directs his wife, "leave my sister something worthy of yourself." This curious resurgence of fraternal feeling emphasizes the seriousness of Sterne's state of mind; and it also reminds us that while Laurence was being toasted by the politically great and socially elect, the former Catherine Sterne may have been drawing beer in her husband's pub in less elegant quarters of the great city. Sterne's desire to straighten a muddle that had played too large a part in his life appears in another section of the memorandum. In this "death-bed" confession he is ready to admit that his dislike for the much abused Dr. Topham had been too readily colored by his friendship for Dean Fountayne and his own ambitions. His bitter disillusionment in regard to Fountayne he cannot repress. Thus Sterne asserts apropos of the Latin sermon that he wrote for the occasion of Fountayne's receiving his doctorate from Cambridge: "He got honour by it—What got I?—Nothing in my life time. Then let me not (I charge you Mrs. Sterne) be robbed of it after my death."—If indeed the stains on the manuscript (at present in the Morgan Library in New York) are tear drops, Laurence, who had wept when Mrs. Montagu admonished him for his indelicacy, now wept for better reason.

It was a sick man who set out for Dover. Upon him the interesting scenery along the way was wasted. "I never gave a peep into Rochester church," he wrote, "or took notice of the dock of Chatham, or visited St. Thomas at Canterbury, though they all three laid in my way." The fever of his body and the throbbing of his pulse produced a delirium that might easily have made the trip seem merely "half a dozen bounds."

For the weakened traveler passage across a choppy channel had more than the usual discomforts:

...I am sick as a horse, quoth I, already—what a brain!—upside down!—hey-day! the cells are broke loose one into another, and the blood and the lymph, and the nervous juices, with the fixed and volatile salts, are all jumbled into one mass

–good G–d! everything turns round in it like a thousand whirlpools. . ."

"Sick! sick! sick! sick!" he reiterated.

The little channel boat docked at Calais in the gathering dusk, and before sunrise the next morning Sterne was off to Paris by way of Boulogne, Montreuil, Abbéville, Amiens, Chantilly. The effects of the trying passage did not wear off easily. As a result, the fagged Laurence was glad to snatch *en route* a few minutes of dozing whenever he could. His attempts to sleep, however, met with difficulties. There was always something out of commission with a French post-chaise at the start of a journey:

> What's wrong now?–Diable!–a rope's broke!–a knot has slipt!–a staple's drawn!–a bolt's to whittle!–a tag, a rag, a jag, a strap, a buckle, or a buckle's tongue, want altering.

Even after getting started, the traveler could manage only about six miles of dozing on a stretch. There was the nuisance of paying for the horses at each stage. The popping in of the postboy and the uncertainty of the tariff tried Sterne's patience. Thus the fictional account has it.

But the traveler was not too sick or too fatigued to keep an amiably lecherous eye open for the young ladies. During the stop at Boulogne there was the *chère fille* who dropped a curtsy as she tripped from her matins and who was blown a kiss in return. And in Montreuil there was Janatone, daughter of the innkeeper and mistress of "the little coquetries." Her curves inspired Laurence both as a man and as an artist. "May I never draw more . . ." he resolved, "if I do not draw her in all her proportions, and with as determined a pencil, as if I had her in the wettest drapery."

Since the inn at Abbéville was insufferably bad ("infested" is the word), he was glad to get away at four o'clock in the morning:

Hollo! Ho!—the whole world's asleep!—bring out the horses —grease the wheels—tie on the mail—and drive a nail into that moulding—I'll not lose a moment—

Soon the postboy had cracked his whip and "with the thill-horse trotting, and a sort of an up and down of the other, we danced it along to Ailly-au-clochers":

And so making all possible speed, from
Ailly-au-clochers, I got to Hixcourt,
from Hixcourt, I got to Pequignay, and
from Pequignay, I got to Amiens,
concerning which town I have nothing to inform you...

So roll on both the *vers libre* of the travelogue and Sterne's postchaise toward Paris!

At nine o'clock in the evening of January 16 or 17, 1762, Sterne entered the French capital, his arrival heralded by the cracking whip of a postillion clad in a tawny yellow jerkin. "So this is Paris!" exclaimed the traveler with historic triteness. His first impressions of the City of Light were anything but romantic: the place smelled, its streets were dirty and "villainously narrow," and it was filled with cook's shops, barbers, and hotels. One might fear that the English author would be an unwelcome guest. But Laurence was not to develop into such a disagreeable tourist as Smollett, whom he aptly dubbed "Smelfungus." To the end he maintained the ability to be candid about France and the French without being offensive.

As a matter of fact, it is a great wonder that he was able to observe anything, pleasant or unpleasant, when he arrived in the city; for his trip had been rigorous and there was little life left in his frail body. Indeed, there was so little life left that the physicians whom he soon consulted shook their heads gravely and allotted him a few months to live. An immediate sojourn in southern France was recommended as a slender hope. A few weeks after his arrival in Paris, the *London Chronicle* for February 2-4—apparently expecting him to obey the doctors—announced news of his death that had come *via* private correspondence; and his parishioners in Yorkshire prematurely went into mourning for him. But Sterne's disease was unpredictable and the man himself was even more so. From now until the end of his life, days of deathly illness were to be followed by periods of astounding vivacity and activity. Consequently, by the time the somewhat "exaggerated" report was making the rounds in London and stimulating readers of the journals to say the best about the "departed" author (*de mortuis nihil nisi bonum*), Laurence was presenting to Parisians the aspect of a very lively corpse; and, enshrined as one of the premier lions of the season, he had already gone a long way toward duplicating on the Continent the brilliant success of his first visit to London. Plans to go south were already temporarily shelved.

With pride not entirely pardonable, Sterne had written to Garrick on January 31 to tell his friend of his quick triumph and of his taking his place among sixteen or seventeen English gentlemen of distinction who lived in the Faubourg St. Germain in luxury becoming *milords Anglois.* "Tristram was almost as much known here as in London," he boasted. "... I have just now a fortnight's dinners and suppers on my hands." Among the young Englishmen was George Macartney (later Sir George and a diplomatist of ability) who took Laurence in hand, showing him the theatres and in general introducing him to the gaieties of Parisian life. Sterne also had as a companion one of the sons of fabulous Lord Holland—the youthful Stephen Fox.

His reception by his compatriots was flattering enough; but vastly more flattering and important was his reception by the French themselves. His most fortunate single triumph was his being welcomed by the brilliant and rich Baron d'Holbach, Maecenas of the Encyclopedists and one of the most influential literary figures in all France. Like Mme. Geoffrin, Mlle. de Lespinasse, and Mme. d'Epinay, the Baron drew about him a coruscating coterie of *philosophes* –those intellectual revolutionaries who wanted to replace the monarchy by the rule of humanity and to supplant the priesthood of God by that of science, and who by their independence of thought did much in laying the groundwork of the Revolution. Entrance to the Baron's *salon*–which was graced at different times by Diderot, d'Alembert, Franklin, Jean-Jacques Rousseau, Hume, and Grimm–was guarantee of literary or intellectual celebrity. Sterne was lucky enough to ride in on a wave of Anglomania. ("C'était le beau moment de l'anglomanie," remarked the nineteenth-century critic, M. Stapfer.) Not many of the great Parisian intellectuals had read in its entirety and understood a work so unFrench as *Tristram*. As M. Stapfer has observed, the normal reaction of any Frenchman who reads the book is astonishment and boredom. How much truer this circumstance must have been in the eighteenth century than it was in M. Stapfer's day. But whether or not they had read the book, practically all the well-known French literary figures had heard of the furore that it had caused in London, and they seemed determined not to fall short of their English contemporaries in appreciation of the author. Such an attitude seems crystal clear in an obviously but charmingly flattering bit of "business" arranged by one of the local grandees who later provided Sterne with delightful company. The Count de Bissie, having expressed the desire to meet the famous author, managed to have at hand an open copy of *Tristram* when Sterne was introduced. Acting of this sort the French do well. Sterne's complete delight is attested in the fanciful use he makes of the incident in *A Sentimental Journey*.

Baron d'Holbach's patronage extended to his agreement to stand surety for Sterne's behavior in France. Thus with reason could Laurence exclaim: "The Baron is one of the most learned noblemen here, the great protector of wits, and the Sçavans who are no wits." The pursuit of Death was pleasantly forgotten in the company of a man whose atheism was so violent that even Voltaire could not approve of it. However, the spectacle of the Anglican priest in the *salon* of the godless is not so shocking when one remembers that the Catholic priesthood had furnished many of the shining lights among the *philosophes:* Abbé Bonnot de Condillac and his brother Abbé de Mably, Abbé de Marmontel, Abbé Raynal—to mention only a few. Sterne salved his conscience with an occasional argument for "the necessity of a first cause" against an antagonist like Mme. de Vence or even against the Baron himself, who insisted that the principle of the universe was matter in spontaneous motion. "I declare I had the credit all over Paris of unperverting Madame de Vence," Laurence asserted. This lady had been good enough to affirm that in one hour Sterne had said more for revealed religion than the *Encyclopedia* had said against it. But if the truth be known, the religious and political tenets of the group concerned Laurence relatively little. What was more important was that he found himself at home in a group of philosophers who shared his profound admiration for John Locke. To those who could better have appreciated Sterne as a thinker than as a literary artist, he did not neglect to pose as something of a philosopher. The way he could fit his religious beliefs and his artistic theories rather neatly into the philosophical pattern of the deists is shown in his confession to Jean Baptiste Suard, the young journalist who for a time played Boswell to Sterne's Johnson. His originality Laurence attributed to three causes: first, to his own imagination linked with a delicate sensibility; second, to a daily reading of the Old and New Testament, a habit of preference and of profession; and finally to a life-long study of Locke, whose work he looked upon as a sacred philosophy without which a true universal religion, a true science of morals, or man's true mastery over nature could never be attained. The climax is significant.

Like most Englishmen, Sterne at first had difficulties with the language, and he naturally found some of the evenings among the intellectuals boring. When he had no opportunity to "Shandy it," he could easily come to the conclusion that the *sçavants* were no wits. But he set himself to the task of learning the language, and on March 17 he could write to Mrs. Sterne: "I speak it fast and fluent." He admitted, however, that his "accent and phrase" were still incorrect. The French themselves were polite enough to tell him that he was doing "surprisingly well," and he accepted the compliment at its face value. Once having the language somewhat in hand, he did not neglect to oil his discourse, repaying *politesse* with *politesse*. Finally, we are encouraged to know, his insincerity bothered his conscience:

> For three weeks together, I was of every man's opinion I met. *Pardi! ce Mons. Yorick a autant d'esprit que nos autres. Il raisonne bien*, said another. *C'est un bon enfant*, said a third. And at this price I could have eaten and drank and been merry all the days of my life at Paris. But 'twas a dishonest *reckoning* —I grew ashamed of it. It was the gain of a slave—every sentiment of honour revolted against it. The higher I got, the more I was forced upon my *beggarly system*....

That he went very high it is plain enough. He was privileged to have the attention of the powerful Duc de Choiseul, the Duc de Biron, and, highest of all, Louis Philippe, Duc d'Orléans. Louis Philippe's painter, Carmontelle, did a jaunty watercolor of Laurence dressed (under the guidance of M. le Comte de Fainéant) in the most fashionable ruffles of the moment. The Yorkshire parson might have been seen either in the drawing room of Prince de Conti, famous as a French generalissimo and as an enemy of Mme. de Pompadour, or at a soirée of the fabulously rich member of the farmers-general, M. Popelinière. He was also invited by the eccentric Baron Charles-Ernest de Bagge, whose "humour" led him to keep a staff of competent musicians "studying" with him, although he could barely scrape a violin. This touch of Shandyism could not have failed to appeal to Sterne, who was himself an amateur fiddler.

Two of the greatest Frenchmen among the intellectuals Sterne failed to meet: Voltaire and Rousseau. It is especially unfortunate that he could not know Voltaire, who was among the few who understood the English mind and language well enough to appreciate *Tristram.* With the licentious and voluptuous Crébillon *fils*, Laurence struck up what seemed to be a lively friendship. So lively was the acquaintance that the two conceived the notion of criticizing the morals of each other's work and publishing the results in a single volume. Unfortunately or fortunately, the plan never came to fruition.

Sterne's warmest literary friendship was that with Diderot, who was at the time deep at work on the *Encyclopedia.* Diderot had two important things in common with Sterne: he had indulged a sentimental vein—in bourgeois drama; and, like most of the *philosophes*, he was an admirer of Locke. Moreover, Diderot was also among the select few who could really appreciate *Tristram.* Calling the author "the Rabelais in English," he wrote enthusiastically in October, 1762, that it was impossible to give an idea of Sterne's "universal satire" to one who had not read it—so foolish, so wise, so gay it was. Laurence was pleased to help build up the learned Frenchman's library by ordering books from England for him: the works of Pope ("—the neatest and cheapest edition—therefore I suppose not Warburton's"!), the dramatic works and the life of Colley Cibber, the works of Chaucer, Tillotson's sermons, and Locke's works. The six volumes of *Tristram Shandy* Sterne presented as a gift. Diderot later showed his appreciation by subscribing to the third and fourth volumes of the sermons, and finally by imitating Sterne in the novel, *Jacques le Fataliste.*

Into every mood of Paris Laurence attempted to enter. By his own confession, he "Shandyed it" on every possible occasion, looking for the greatest part of the time through rose-colored glasses: "I laugh 'till I cry, and in the same tender moments *cry* 'till I laugh. I Shandy it more than ever. . ." Indeed, he could weep for fashionable or for sentimental reasons as occasion demanded. He put on mourning when the court put on mourning, and was moved when his barber told him how many people were deprived of their livelihood by a great fire at the St. Germain fair:

> *Oh! ces moments de malheur sont terribles,* said my barber to me, as he was shaving me this morning; and the good-natured fellow uttered it with so moving an accent, that I could have found in my heart to have cried over the perishable and uncertain tenure of every good in this life.

The apogee of his sentimental histrionics is recorded by the biographer of Suard. Stopping before the statue of Henry IV on the Pont Neuf one day, Sterne is said to have attracted by his movements a crowd of curious people. "Why are you all staring at me?" he suddenly exclaimed. "Do as I do, all of you!" He then fell down on his knees before the statue, and the crowd followed suit. In such a manner could an unorthodox English parson make those who came to scoff remain to pray.

Another story of Yorick in Paris has been told so often by biographers and commentators that it hardly needs retelling here. I include it, however, as an example of Shandyism in action. It concerns a dinner-party given by the youthful Lord Tavistock at which a French diplomatist, M. Dutens, found himself seated next to the famous novelist. The conversation turned to Turin, where Dutens had been representing the English government. Laurence, who for some reason had not established the identity of his table-companion, turned to the diplomatist with the question: "Do you know M. Dutens?" "Yes, very intimately," replied the diplomatist with characteristic poise. Upon perceiving the situation, the other dinner guests laughed; whereupon Sterne innocently assumed the laughter to mean that Dutens was a singular fellow. "Is he not a strange fellow?" asked Sterne, carrying on from his miscue. "Yes," replied Dutens, "an original." "I thought so; I've heard him spoken of," continued Laurence; and with that he proceeded to regale the guests with stories about the diplomatist. He was not allowed to discover his mistake until Dutens had withdrawn. The dinner guests then added further to Laurence's discomfiture by telling him that the gentleman who had been the butt of the jokes had kept his peace only out of respect to his host and that he could be expected to demand satisfaction for the raillery. The next morning found Sterne waiting on M. Dutens' doorstep to tender the necessary apologies. The diplomatist, who had been highly amused throughout the affair, acted with entirely proper graciousness, and the two parted friends.

Since Sterne was always up to his neck in acting of his own, it is remarkable that he had much time for the *legitimate* theatre. But from the first, as it has been already suggested, he seems to have felt it his duty to see what was to be seen on the Parisian stage and to give a report to Garrick back in London, rarely neglecting an occasion to flatter his friend and the English theatre. He could check off Mlle. Clairon, the popular tragedienne, playing in de la Touche's *Iphigénie en Tauride;* Préville, the comedian and the friend of Garrick, in Boissy's *Le Français à Londres;* and Mlle. Marie-Françoise Dumesnil, another leading tragedienne, in her current piece. He went with the brilliant throng to hear comic opera at the hôtel de Bourgogne. To green rooms he went to meet "half of their best Goddesses," and he was invited to one of la Clairon's receptions. Clairon he found to be "great" and Dumesnil "greater"; but he was soon bored by the Comedie Française, which–belying its title–presented too many tragedies. French tragedies, Sterne contended, preached too much. To him the union of drama and preaching found its natural home in the pulpit, not on the stage. Therefore, he preferred to satisfy his appetite for drama by going on three Lenten mornings in succession to the Rue St. Honoré to hear the pulpit oratory of Abbé Clement, preacher to Stanislas I of Poland:

> ...he has infinite variety [the admiring Sterne wrote], and keeps up the attention by it wonderfully; his pulpit, oblong, with three seats in it, into which he occasionally casts himself; goes on, then rises, by a graduation of four steps, each of which he profits by, as his discourse inclines him: in short, 'tis a stage, and the variety of his tones would make you imagine there were no less than five or six actors on it together.

Here, undeniably, was drama after Laurence's own heart.

So proceeds the story of the first lap in the race between Death and *ce Mons. Yorick*–a story to be continued, as Yorick himself would say, in my next chapter.

CHAPTER XI

THE CHAISE BREAKS DOWN

On April 10 Sterne seized the occasion of Mr. Joseph Wilcock's return to England to dispatch a gay letter to Garrick. "I am recovered greatly," he wrote, "and if I could spend one whole winter in Toulouse, I should be fortified, in my inner man, beyond all danger of relapsing." On the same day he wrote more soberly to his patron, Lord Fauconberg, that he had intended to remain in Paris only until the end of May and then to return to England by way of Holland, but that he had been advised by his physicians to avoid foggy English weather for another winter. It seemed evident that he had little notion of returning to England so long as he could find a good excuse for pursuing his purpose in France.

As a matter of fact, an excellent excuse had already presented itself. Word had come from Mrs. Sterne that Lydia was again suffering with a "vile asthma," an affliction of three years' duration that, the doting father was ready to believe, threatened her very existence. Both Nice and Toulouse had been considered as possible winter resorts for the family; but Toulouse had been selected because it was cheaper and because Sterne's friends, the Abbé Macarthy and the Hodges, offered help and advice in getting accommodations there. Already some arrangements had been made toward bringing mother and daughter to France with the idea of establishing them on the banks of the Garonne. "In case I find myself very well when I have fixed them there," Sterne wrote to Lord Fauconberg, "[I] shall return

–if not, stay the winter through, and come back in May following."

Having made a good effort to convince his patron that it was necessary for him to forego Yorkshire for some additional months, Laurence set out to Versailles to seek of the Duc de Choiseul passports for bringing the family to France and securing their safe transit southward. The quest was entirely successful. "A man who laughs can never be dangerous," commented the Duke on the risk he was taking in giving a passport to such an enemy alien as Mr. Yorick. So away the suppliant came from Versailles bearing a solemn document directing "all lieutenant-governors, governors, and commandants of cities, generals of armies, judiciaries, and all officers of justice, to let Mr. Yorick, the king's jester, and his baggage, travel quietly along."

Continued social activity and whatever additional running about he did in connection with getting his family to France proved more overtaxing than he suspected. Thus when he wrote on May 10 to his new Archbishop, the Rt. Reverend Dr. Drummond, he could report a *defluxion Poitrine* constituting such a serious set-back that he had lost in ten days all that he had gained in France. "This evil sends me directly to Toulouse," he wrote, "for which I set out from this place the moment my family arrives." Just exactly what a *defluxion Poitrine* was, His Grace may not have known. Indeed, Sterne's editors and biographers have been uncertain. But the term (perhaps best taken to indicate a kind of pleurisy and not a hemorrhage) served its purpose to justify comfortably Laurence's neglect of ecclesiastical duties back in England.

Though the effects of the set-back may have been exaggerated, it *was* another reminder that Death had not abandoned pursuit. This fact, coupled with sincere anxiety concerning his daughter, caused Sterne to be all but consumed with tenderness toward his family. With letter after letter he plied the post, dispatching to the house in the Minster Yard at York minute directions for the journey to France. He neglected nothing from advice regarding the ladies' travel-wardrobe to concern for the wayside refreshments of the journey. "For God's sake rise early and gallop away in the cool," he cautioned, "—and always see that you have not forgot your baggage in changing postchaises... drink small Rhenish to keep you cool... Lydia must have two slight negligees—you will want a new gown or two... They have bad pins, and vile needles here—bring for yourself, and some for presents—as also a strong bottle screw... Buy a chain at Calais strong enough not to be cut off, and let your portmanteau be tied on the forepart of your chaise for fear of a dog's trick... Bring your silver coffee-pot, 'twill serve both to give water, lemonade, and orjead—to say nothing of coffee and chocolate... You must be cautious about Scotch snuff—take half a pound in your pocket, and make Lyd do the same." So ran the directions. Addressing his wife as "Dear Bess," Laurence rises to a high pitch of sentimentalism in a letter written about the middle of June:

> I wish I was with you... to strew roses on your way—but I shall have time and occasion to show you I am not wanting —Now, my dears, once more pluck up your spirits—trust in God—in me—and in yourselves... Dear Bess, I have a thousand wishes, but have a hope for every one of them—You shall chant the same *jubilate*, my dears, so God bless you. My duty to Lydia, which implies my love too. Adieu, believe me
>
> Your affectionate, *etc.*

How Mrs. Sterne responded to all this we do not know. It is safe to assume that not since she was a young lady on a visit to Staffordshire and Sterne was a pining lover in Little Alice Lane had she been privileged to read more succulent discourse. We can only trust that in her satisfaction in this proof of her triumph over her husband's mercurial affections she failed to see that her intelligence was seriously impugned.

When his wife and daughter were actually on their way to join him, Sterne found himself faced with a serious problem, that of transportation. The end of the war had brought a great demand for vehicles of every sort to bring army officers home, and almost every chaise in Paris had been requisitioned for that purpose. Fortunately, into the picture came a young friend, Thomas Thornhill, who was willing to sell his chaise at a bargain. The offer had only to be made to be taken. Thus a splendid vehicle worth "at least forty guineas" was to be waiting at Calais to convey "Dear Bess" and Lyd to Paris; and the same conveyance would take them southward:

> You will wonder all the way [Sterne wrote concerning its capacities], how I am to find room in it for a third—to ease you of this wonder, 'tis by what the coach-makers here call a cave, which is a second bottom added to that you set your feet upon which lets the person (who sits over-against you) down with his knees to your ankles, and by which you have all more room...Lyd and I will enjoy this by turns; sometimes I shall take a bidet—(a little post horse) and scamper before...

But, alas, Sterne was a little too optimistic about Mr. Thornhill's bargain.

A week or ten days before Mrs. Sterne's arrival, Laurence had another hemorrhage. One night he awoke to discover once again that the bed was full of blood. In the morning he sent for a surgeon, who immediately bled him. That he did not succumb to the illogical but orthodox treatment of his day is a great wonder. The additional bleeding probably did much toward keeping him flat on his back and speechless for three days. But in a week he was out again, convinced that he had been saved by the surgeon.

Early in a torrid July Mrs. Sterne and Lydia arrived in Calais, stopping by prearrangement at an inn well known to English travelers, the Lyon d'Argent. The inn had been leased from Hogarth's acquaintance, M. Grandsire, by one Pierre Quillacq—better known as Dessein—who later purchased the handsome Hotel d'Angleterre and won immortality in *A Sentimental Journey*.

Acting on sound advice, the ladies took the journey to Paris in easy stages, arriving without mishap on July 8. They had few complaints to make about the trip; but the heat wave that gripped Paris was most unpleasant to them. Fourteen-year-old Lydia refused to become excited about being in the gayest of European capitals, resigning herself to looking out of the window of their apartments and to complaining of being "frizled." ("I wish she may ever remain a child of nature," commented Sterne with typical indulgence; "I hate children of art.") Laurence himself admitted that France was like "Nebuchadnezzar's oven." How much more thoroughly "frizled" the family would all be when they began their southward journey we hope that they did not guess.

The Sternes did not set out immediately for Toulouse. A break in the heat wave was awaited; then, too, Mrs. Sterne certainly wanted to see the shops. So a few days were spent in resting and shopping. Among other things, an Indian "taffety" was purchased and dispatched to London for Mrs. Edmunds, who had entertained mother and daughter before they sailed.

On July 19 the party set out on their long, adventuresome, and uncomfortable journey. As they rode out into the open country on a dusty, scorching morning, the chaise —piled with portmanteaus, drawn by four horses, and piloted by two postillions—must already have begun to take on some of the aspects of a desert stage-coach.

Valiantly Laurence made notes along the way:

> There's Fountainbleau, and Sens, and Joigny, and Auxerre, and Dijon the capital of Burgundy, and Chalons, and Mâcon...
>
> All you need to say of Fountainbleau... is, that it stands about forty miles (south something) from Paris, in the middle of a large forest—
>
> As for Sens—you may dispatch—in a word—' 'Tis an archepiscopal see.'
>
> —For Joigny—the less, I think, one says of it the better.
>
> But for Auxerre—I could go on forever.

In the eighteenth century a trip from Paris to Toulouse was no small undertaking, especially if one chose (as the Sternes did) a circuitous route through Dijon, Mâcon, Lyons, Avignon, and Montpellier. Down the valleys of the Seine and Yonne their itinerary led them, across into Burgundy, down the valley of the Saône to Lyons, down the Rhône to Avignon, and across a large part of Southern France, including the "rich plains of Langue d'Oc." The journey required three weeks.

Nuisances of travel in France, about which Sterne had learned previously, began repeating themselves early. Broken ropes, excessive tolls for the posts, and the general uncertainty of traveling expenses again plagued the travelers. But these were minor worries. Much worse was the fact that the roads were choked with dust and that a relentless sun beamed out of a cloudless sky. "I never saw a cloud from Paris to Nismes half as broad as a twenty-four sols piece," exclaimed Sterne. "Good God! we were toasted, roasted, grill'd, stew'd, and carbonaded on one side or the other all the way." And the inns! The hostelry at Abbéville (of infamous memory) had counterparts *ad nauseam.* "... being all done enough (*assez cuits*) in the day," Laurence complained, "we were eat up at night by bugs, and other unswept out vermin, the legal inhabitants (if length of possession gives right) of every inn we lay at."

Then there was at least one major accident: the breaking down of the chaise. On the details of this uncomfortable experience the letters and Book VII of *Tristram Shandy* disagree. On August 14 Sterne, then safe in Toulouse, wrote to his banker, Robert Foley:

> Can you conceive a worse accident than that in such a journey, in the hottest day and hour of it, four miles from either tree or shrub which could cast a shade of the size of one of Eve's fig leaves—that we should break a hind wheel into ten thousand pieces, and be obliged in consequence to sit five hours on a gravelly road, without one drop of water or possibility of getting any—To mend the matter, my two postillions were two dough-hearted fools, and fell a crying—Nothing was to be done! By heaven, quoth I, pulling off my coat and waistcoat, something shall be done, for I'll thrash you both within an inch of your lives—and then make you take each of you a horse, and ride like two devils to the next post for a cart to carry my baggage, and a wheel to carry ourselves—Our luggage weighed ten quintals—'twas the fair of Baucaire—all the world was going, or returning—we were ask'd by every soul who pass'd by us, if we were going to the fair of Baucaire—No wonder, quoth I, we have goods enough! *vous avez raison mes amis*—

The account in *Tristram* places the upset much earlier in the journey; and since it is treated in a strikingly different manner, there has been the assumption that two such accidents, rather than one, marred the journey. Yet against the assumption of two accidents the letter to Foley seems plainly to argue. If, indeed, there were two and if the first occurred as it is described in *Tristram*, then Sterne himself would have been able to conceive of a "worse accident," which he logically would have included in his account to Foley. It is entirely in keeping with the novelist's manner to violate chronology for the sake of his narrative and to place the incident of the broken chaise before the arrival in Lyons.

Although we can accept the itinerary of the account in *Tristram*, we shall have to realize that the incidents themselves are embellished with Sterne's own variety of fancy and that he was writing a comic rather than a serious account. With such a *caveat*, we—for lack of better authority—shall have to accept Book VII as the chief source of information about the delights and miseries of the journey.

Sterne's own amusing story introduces us with some suddenness to a scene of an upset chaise just outside Lyons, and the author pictures himself (Bess and Lyd are missing from the narrative) walking into the city behind a slow-moving cart in which his baggage was laid "higgledy-piggledy." As he neared Lyons a "pert vamping chaise-undertaker" presented himself and offered repairs. His services were rejected. However, when he offered to buy, the ill-fated coach was sold to him at once at a price of four louis. The disgusted traveler could breathe a sigh of relief at the thought of proceeding by river boat the next day to Avignon. In such a way, he believed, he could escape hot, dusty roads and, at the same time, economize. The deal disposing of the chaise was made so quickly that Laurence cleanly forgot that he had left his travel notes in it.

As the traveler sallied forth on the following morning to see the sights, he encountered at the inn gate an ass—Old Honesty—loaded with panniers "to collect eleemosynary turnip-tops and cabbage leaves." The animal, munching the stem of an artichoke which in the process he dropped a half dozen times, provoked one of the most delightful pieces of Shandean musing extant:

God help thee, Jack! said I, thou hast a bitter breakfast on't—and many a bitter day's labour,—and many a bitter blow, I fear for its wages–'tis all–all bitterness to thee, whatever life is to others.–And now thy mouth, if one knew the truth of it, is as bitter, I dare say as soot–(for he had cast aside the stem) and thou hast not a friend perhaps in all this world, that will give thee a macaroon.–In saying this, I pulled out a paper of 'em which I had just purchased, and gave him one–and at this moment that I am telling it, my heart smites me, that there was more of pleasantry in the conceit, of seeing how an ass would eat a macaroon–than benevolence in giving him one, which presided in the act.

Then ensued a scene that will appeal to anybody who has suffered antilogies peculiar to foreign travel. A commissary from the postoffice arrived to present the traveler with a bill for six livres and some odd sous. To the astonished Laurence the commissary explained that the fee covered the next post between Lyons and Fons:

–But I don't go by land; said I.
–You may if you please; replied the commissary...

. . . .

–Sir, said I, collecting myself–it is not my intention to take post–
–But you may–said he, persisting in his first reply–you may take post if you choose–
–And I may take salt to my pickled herring, said I, if I choose–
–But I do not choose–
–But you must pay for it, whether you do or no.
Aye! for the salt; said I (I know)–
–And for the post too; added he. Defend me! cried I–
I travel by water–I am going down the Rhône this very afternoon–my baggage is in the boat–and I have actually paid nine livres for my passage–
C'est tout égal–'tis all one; said he.
Bon Dieu! what, pay for the way I go! and for the way I do not go!
–*C'est tout égal;* replied the commissary.

Thus Laurence was acquainted with an ordinance ruling that "if you set out with an intention of running post from Paris to Avignon, etc., you shall not change that intention or mode of travelling, without first satisfying the fermiers for two posts further than the place you repent at–" There was nothing to do but pay. Seeing his inexorable fate, the traveler was determined to get his money's worth in protests. With the thought of jotting down remarks on the incident, he reached into his pocket for his notes. But, to his horror, they were not there. Soon he remembered that they had been left in the pocket of the chaise. Off he rushed to the purchaser. Since it was a holiday, the shop was closed. Finally (not to spoil the story, which should be read as Sterne wrote it), he found that the notes had been used as curlpapers by the chaisemaker's wife. When this lady learned what she was carrying in her hair, she removed the papers and gravely put them in Sterne's hat. Thus twisted, the author warns, how could they help being distorted in the published account?

When Laurence at last got around to his sight-seeing (under the stimulus of Piganiol de la Force's famous French guidebook) he was singularly unsuccessful. At the Cathedral of St. Jean he was disillusioned to find that the wonderful clock of Lippius of Basil (a curiosity that he had longed to see) was "out of joints" and had not been in operation for years. The Jesuits' library was closed on account of illness in the order; hence the traveler was unable to see the thirty volumes of a monumental history of China done in Chinese characters. And, to cap the climax, he found that another object of great interest–the Tomb of the Two Lovers–no longer existed.

Without frustration, however, he took the noon boat; and ere he had sailed a hundred yards, "the Rhône and the Saone met together, and carried me down merrily betwixt them."

So the narrative runs. But concerning what was ordinarily an interesting boat trip, Laurence has nothing to say —so completely omitting details, in fact, that it is possible to doubt that he took the trip at all. When he complained to Foley about the trials of the journey by chaise, he implied that the terrific heat and unpleasant dust dogged him all the way between Paris and Nîmes, making no mention of the surcease provided by a river journey. Although the highroad from Lyons to Avignon ran along the riverside, the rapidity of travel by water made the boat trip desirable. Smollett, who definitely traveled by water, made an amusing account:

> Travellers bound to the Southern parts of France [he wrote], generally embark in the *coche d'eau* at Lyons, and glide down this river with great velocity, passing a number of towns and villages on each side, where they find ordinaries every day at dinner and supper. In good weather there is no danger in this method of travelling, till you come to the Pont St. Esprit, where the stream runs through the arches with such rapidity that the boat is sometimes overset. But those passengers who are under any apprehension are landed above bridge, and taken in again after the boat has passed... The boats that go up the river are drawn against the stream by oxen, which swim through one of the arches of this bridge, the driver sitting between the horns of the foremost beast.

It is a wonder that such a fascinating circumstance could have been omitted from Laurence's narrative, if he actually experienced it. —But when we are unable to settle such a point, we are forced to follow the narrator.

"So now I am at Avignon," Laurence remarks abruptly, expecting his readers to follow him at a bound. Here his hat was blown off, and he was given an opportunity to remark (*double entendre* intended) on the windiness of Avignon. Here, too, desiring somebody to hold his mount while he adjusted a jack-boot, he accosted a man standing at the door of an inn ("Prithee, friend... take hold of my mule for a second") only to discover that the person he was treating so familiarly was a marquis.

Provided with new equipment, Laurence set out for his journey across Southern France. Establishing Mrs. Sterne and Lyd in a chaise (we are to assume), he himself chose the mount just mentioned:

> ...you will see me crossing the bridge upon a mule, with François upon a horse with my portmanteau behind him, and the owner of both striding the way before us, with a long gun upon his shoulder, and a sword under his arm, lest peradventure we should run away with his cattle.

If we can accept Sterne's own intimation, he was unconscionably dilatory, getting behind the party and stopping to chat whenever the mood struck him—as he did, for example, with a drum-maker, who attempted to explain the principles of his art, and with two Franciscans who actually succeeded in carrying him backward in his journey.

After Avignon the account moves swiftly (without mention of an accident to the wheel of the chaise). There was gaiety enough—

> ...for I had left Death, the Lord knows—and He only—how far behind me—'I have followed many a man thro' France, quoth he—but never at this mettlesome rate.'—Still he followed, —and still I fled him... but, like one who pursued his prey without hope—as he lagged, every step he lost softened his looks—

On went Sterne from Nîmes to Lunel, where he was set aflame by Muscatto wine and by the singing and dancing of the peasant maid, Nanette. "Vive la joia! was in her lips —*Vive la joia!* was in her eyes," and Laurence's pen in describing her received the electric charge of real poetry.

Thus intoxicated—

I danced it away [wrote Sterne] from Lunel to Montpellier —from thence to Pesçnas, Beziers—I danced it along through Narbonne, Carcasson, and Castle Naudairy, till at last I danced myself into Perdrillo's [*sic*] pavilion.

CHAPTER XII

PERDRILLO'S PAVILION

THE LONG JOURNEY ended, Sterne was able to settle in Toulouse amid elegance appropriate to his renown. Through the good offices of his friend the Abbé Macarthy, he was immediately established on the edge of town in "the prettiest situation" that the provincial capital afforded. The comfortably large house was built around a court, and a two-acre garden laid out in serpentining walks extended behind it. So large and so fine was the garden that, to quote the proud lessee, "the company in our quarter usually come to walk there in the evenings, for which they have my consent—'the more the merrier.'" A prospect of the distant Pyrenees added to the grandeur. Above stairs the house had a respectable dining room and a fine drawing room commodious enough for private theatricals. Three handsomely furnished bedrooms also provided ample comfort for the tenants. Below stairs were a study for the master of the house and a sitting room where he could receive informally. The little "estate" was adequately staffed with a good cook, a chamber maid, and an impressive lackey. A gardener was provided by the landlord. For all this comfort and even magnificence there was an absurdly small annual rental of thirty pounds.

So deceptive was the prospect of cheap luxury that the landlord had no trouble in renting Laurence in addition, a summer house in the country. Apparently, the new place appeared in the novel as "Perdrillo's Pavilion" in a flippant and ironic play on Pringello, the "celebrated Spanish architect" who had appeared in Hall-Stevenson's recently published *Crazy Tales.* At any rate, the little house is a convenient symbol of Sterne's insouciance in matters of money. Before his stay in Toulouse was out he had occasion to regret his expansiveness.

Since it was the end of summer, there was not a whirl of social activity in the city; therefore the parson could devote himself to his two objects of chief concern: his health and his writing. For his health, he had a diet of ass' milk three times a day and cow's milk as often. For his literary labors, he maintained some sort of schedule at his rural pavilion.

On August 12 he wrote Hall-Stevenson that he was engaged on a "crazy chapter." Once more he had turned to the amour of Uncle Toby and the Widow Wadman. The new book was begun beneath a "genial sun" when all flesh was "running out piping, fiddling, and dancing to the vintage." But Sterne had not gone very far when he fell ill of an epidemic that a contemporary diarist explained as resulting from the eating of certain sorts of fruit in a period of excessive heat. For six weeks he was held prisoner by a fever that killed many people in the vicinity. But once again he made an amazing recovery, and he was soon able to write that he was as "stout and foolish again as a happy man can wish to be." No wonder he had come to believe that he was leading a charmed life. "... one or two more escapes," he asserted, "will make me believe I shall leave you all at last by translation, and not by fair death."

But in spite of the pleasure that he got from "playing the fool with my Uncle Toby" and from basking in the luxury of his position as *Monsieur Sterne gentilhomme Anglois,* the charm of Toulouse at length began to wear thin. He felt his isolation from the brilliant and witty society that he had come to demand. "I believe, the groundwork of my *ennui,*" he explained, "is more to the eternal platitude of the French characters—little variety, no originality in it at all—than to any other cause—for they are very civil—but civility itself, in that uniform, wearies and bodders one to death." The truer explanation is that he needed an audience. The good people of Toulouse treated him with the deference due a rich Englishman, not with the attention deserved by a witty and distinguished literary artist. Who in Toulouse could appreciate *Tristram?*

Unfortunately, Bess and Lydia did not share his boredom. Lydia was getting along nicely with her music, her dancing, and her French; and Mrs. Sterne was so exasperatingly pleased with the whole scheme of things that she was urging another year just when her husband was looking forward to getting away. "...this opposition of wishes," Laurence remarked dryly, "tho' it will not be as sour as lemon, yet 'twill not be as sweet as sugar candy."

Nevertheless, circumstances could alter cases. As soon as the winter gaieties of the city began, Sterne was "fiddling, laughing and singing, and cracking jokes again." The social life of the provincial capital was not like that of Paris; but there were the levées of M. Bonrepos, M. le Baron d'Orbessan, and Mme. la Comtesse de Fumel, as well as the less formal society of English residents like the Hodges and young Mr. Woodhouse (or Wodehouse). Sterne might even have had an opportunity to develop a sentimental affair, this time with a lady whose name Lydia struck out of her father's letters but who has been identified as a Mrs. Meadows. But Bess did not give him much chance to philander. If the testimony of one of Laurence's friends is correct, she had developed the habit of following her husband everywhere he went and of wanting a part in everything he did—all of which Laurence had learned to support with "une patience d'ange."

Among his English friends Sterne introduced the idea of amateur theatricals, and gay evenings of rehearsals were spent at the Hodges'. The arrival of a troupe of English actors turned the project into something considerable. A fusion of talent was effected, and Sterne's own drawing room now hummed with activity as a theatrical center, with the parson himself gaily functioning as adapter and manager. Mrs. Centlivre's *The Busy Body* and Sterne's adaptation of Vanbrugh and Cibber's *The Provoked Husband* were the fare. For the first time Laurence had a real opportunity to exercise his dramatic talents. There is evidence of an exciting Christmas season.

In the spring of 1763 Sterne was in serious financial straits. Back in December he was beginning to see how fast money could go, even though on the surface living expenses were low. To his Parisian banker, Foley, he had written, asking for an advance:

> When a man has no more than half a dozen guineas in his pocket—and a thousand miles from home—and in a country where he can as soon raise the Devil, as a six livre piece to go to market with—in case he has changed his last guinea—you will not envy my situation.

His Yorkshire income was not enough to afford a great amount of luxury, however cheap, and the bad news from Becket was that *Tristram* could no longer be called a best-seller.

> Is it not enough thou art in debt [Laurence complained in Book VIII], and that thou hast ten cartloads of thy fifth and sixth volumes still—still unsold, and art almost at thy wit's ends, how to get them off thy hands?

Worse still was the fact that his creative impulse had petered out, and his productivity was lagging.

Moreover, by spring Sterne had concluded that Toulouse was a failure as a health resort. The climate was too moist, and agues afflicted him. A move into the rarer atmosphere of the Pyrenees seemed necessary. But before Sterne could make definite plans, he had to face two problems. The first was a matter of obtaining from his Archbishop an extension of his leave from clerical duties. The letter to his lord spiritual is designed with his careful art for eliciting sympathy. Not one word is suggested of any pleasant aspects of the winter. Rather does Laurence write, "...since the first day of my arrival here [I have] been in a continual warfare with agues, fevers, and physicians–the first brought my blood to so poor a state, that the physicians found it necessary to enrich it with strong bouillons, and strong bouillons and soups a santé threw me into fevers, and fevers brought on loss of blood, and loss of blood agues–." After reading such a pitiful account of a vicious circle, the Archbishop could hardly have failed to accept the harassed parson as a "*Miles emeritus*" and to see the necessity of his encamping "like a patriarch with my whole household upon the side of the Pyreneans."

The second problem was slightly more difficult–that of raising additional money. In this attempt he for a time seemed perilously near failure. On May 21 he wrote to Foley:

> I took the liberty three weeks ago to desire you would be so kind as to send me fourscore pounds, having received a letter the same post from my Agent, that he would order the money to be paid to your correspondent in London in a fortnight.–It is some disappointment to me that you have taken no notice of my letter, especially as I told you we waited for the money before we set out for Bagnères,–and so little distrust had I that such a civility would be refused me, that we have actually had all our things pack'd up these eight days, in hourly expectation of receiving a letter.–Perhaps my good friend has waited till he heard the money was paid in London –but you might have trusted to my honour–that all the cash in your iron box (and all the bankers in Europe put together) could not have tempted me to say the thing *that is not*...

But the necessary cash finally arrived, and the Sternes set out for Bagnères.

Unhappily, Laurence's expectation of finding the higher altitude salubrious was disappointed. His disease continued to plague him, and the thinness of the air "brought on continual breeches of the vessels" in his lungs.

At the end of the summer he was trying to make up his mind about a proper wintering place. He describes himself as having traversed the South of France so often, in his effort to decide, that he ran "the risk of being taken up for a spy." Montpellier, Aix, and Marseilles presented themselves as possibilities. Marseilles was too expensive, a small apartment renting for the preposterous sum of nine guineas. Aix Laurence rejected for the somewhat tenuous reason that it was a parliament town and that he had had enough of provincial parliaments in Toulouse. Montpellier (itself a parliament town) was the final choice. Although it was dearer than Toulouse, it was cheaper than Marseilles; and its English residents offered promise of interesting company. Another reason for the choice of Montpellier may have been the fact that it was the home of a Mr. Ray, an English merchant and banker, who a few months previously had, without having seen Sterne, given him a letter of credit at a time when his need was acute.

Instead of a house with a garden, an apartment on a hill served the need of the Sternes. Laurence was easily able to see the need for retrenching. All through the fall and winter money was to be a serious concern. Pleas went out to Becket, to Foley, and even to John Mill, a London merchant with whom he was not personally acquainted, as well as to Lord Grosvenor, who very generously sent a hundred pounds instead of the fifty requested.

Among the English arrivals in Montpellier in the fall of 1763 the most distinguished was Tobias Smollett, who had detoured on his way to Nice for the purpose of picking up his baggage and of making banking arrangements. Although his ill health had caused him to be a disgruntled traveler, his first impressions of Montpellier were pleasant:

> We entered Montpellier on a Sunday, when the people were all dressed in their best apparel. The streets were crowded; and a great number of the better sort of both sexes sat upon stone seats at their doors, conversing with great mirth and familiarity. These conversations lasted the greatest part of the night; and many of them were improved with music both vocal and instrumental. Next day we were visited by the English residing in the place, who always pay this mark of respect to new-comers. They consist of four or five families, among whom I could pass the winter very agreeably, if the state of my health and other reasons did not call me away.

Among the English people in Montpellier meeting Smollett's approval were a "sensible" physician, Dr. Fitzmaurice, and the affable Lieutenant Colonel Tents of the Irish Regiment of Berwick, then garrisoned in the French city. The inhabitants in general, the novelist found, were gay, sociable, and industrious. The markets were well supplied with fish, poultry, butcher's meat, and game. And there were enough Protestants in the vicinity to give comfort to a papist-hating Englishman. But all could not be well for the splenetic traveler. The weather began treating him scurvily, bringing on an outbreak of his asthmatic disorder attended by fever, coughing, spitting, and lowness of spirits.

Sterne must have seen the redoubtable Tobias in his worst mood, for he was apparently irritated by the complaints and the bad humor of his compatriot. In spite of the fact that they both shared hearty contempt for the French medical profession, they seem to have found little else in common. When Laurence ultimately read Smollett's account of his travels, his irritation returned and increased. "I was most disappointed at sight of the Pantheon," Smollett wrote of his Italian journey, "which, after all that has been said of it, looks like a huge cockpit, open at top...I cannot help thinking that there is no beauty in the features of Venus, and that the attitude is awkward and out of character..." Such amazing observations, coupled with his generally disagreeable account of his travels in France, caused Sterne to lash out at him in *A Sentimental Journey:*

> I pity the man who can travel from *Dan* to *Beersheba*, and cry, 'Tis all barren. And so it is; and so is all the world to him, who will not cultivate the fruits it offers. . . The learned SMELFUNGUS travelled from Boulogne to Paris, from Paris to Rome, and so on, but he set out with spleen and jaundice, and every object he pass'd by was discoloured or distorted. He wrote an account of them, but 'twas nothing but the account of his miserable feelings.
>
> I met Smelfungus in the grand portico of the pantheon–he was just coming out of it–'*Tis nothing but a huge cockpit*, said he. I wish you had said nothing worse of the Venus of Medicis, replied I, for in passing through Florence, I had heard he had fallen foul upon the goddess, and used her worse than a common strumpet, without the least provocation in nature.

And so on!

Greater personal interest Sterne surely had in other visitors of the fall and winter: for example, the remarkable William Hewett, "Demoniac" and friend of both Hall-Stevenson and Smollett. His extraordinary thinness and his habit of riding a pale gray horse ("like Death in the Revelations," said Smollett) drew from the Italians among whom he lived and traveled the nickname of Cavallo Bianco. Smollett's description of his death I have quoted elsewhere. An incident showing his classic indifference as a traveler is one of the most delicious bits in *Humphrey Clinker:*

> When he was going abroad the last time, he took his passage in a ship bound for Leghorn, and his baggage was actually embarked. In going down the river by water, he was by mistake put on board of another vessel under sail; and, upon in-

quiry, understood she was bound to Petersburgh. 'Petersburgh! Petersburgh!' said he, 'I don't care if I go along with you.' He forthwith struck a bargain with the captain, bought a couple of shirts of the mate, and was safe conveyed to the court of Muscovy, from whence he travelled by land to receive his baggage at Leghorn.

To Montpellier also came Thomas and George Thornhill and J.-B. Tollot. Tollot—a native of Geneva—was a strange combination of master-apothecary, poet, traveller, and bear-leader. He had served as an escort for Hall-Stevenson, through whom he had met Sterne in Paris in 1762. Tollot reported to the master of "Crazy Castle" early in January, 1764, that the "agreeable Tristram" was in good spirits. It was also he who reported that Mrs. Sterne was too insistent in keeping her husband under her eye and thumb.

When Tollot arrived Laurence's health was so deceptively good that he was telling his friends of plans to return to England. But scarcely had the Genevan written his report to Hall-Stevenson than a circumstance occurred that put Sterne once again on the mat in a struggle with death. Shortly after January 5 he attempted a trip to Pezenas, a little village near Montpellier where several English families resided. The beast that was conveying him proved obstinate, and after a time he stopped on the way, refusing to be budged. In the situation, Laurence did not prove the philosopher that his sentimental passages on asses cause us to expect. In fact, he whipped so zealously that he half dislocated his arm. Of course, he was not without twinges of conscience:

> This quoth I is inhuman—No, says a peasant on foot behind me, I'll drive him home—so he laid on his posteriors, but 'twas needless—as his face was turn'd towards Montpellier he began to trot.

When Sterne reached home again he was in a "shivering fit," and his fever raged for ten days. In the ensuing "scuffle with death" he assures us that his suffering was considerable. Again, his physicians prescribed the French cure-all: *bouillons refraichissants.*

> A *bouillon* [wrote Smollett, who had also been "poisoned" with the dose] is an universal remedy among the good people of France; insomuch, that they have no idea of any person's dying, after having swallowed *un bon bouillon.* One of the English gentlemen, who were robbed and murdered about thirty years ago, between Calais and Boulogne, being brought to the post-house of Boulogne, with some signs of life, this remedy was immediately administered. "What surprises me greatly," said the postmaster, speaking of this melancholy story to a friend of mine, two years after it happened, "I made an excellent *bouillon,* and poured it down his throat with my own hands, and yet he did not recover." Now, in all probability, this *bouillon* it was that stopped his breath.

Sterne would have contended that his dose had practically the same effect. ". . . 'tis a cock flead alive," he remarked wryly, "and boiled with poppy seeds, then pounded in a mortar, afterwards pass'd thro' a sieve.—There is to be one crawfish in it, and I was gravely told it must be a male one —a female would do me more hurt than good."

Not only their therapeutics but everything else about the French was growing tedious. Again, Sterne complained of the insipidity of their character. And he had become convinced that the air of Montpellier had become too sharp and that there might be fatal results. The Sternes had heard an alarming story (which Mrs. Sterne told to Smollett) of a young consumptive who had been killed by the climate. Laurence's thoughts now turned once again to England. Back in Coxwold he could live quietly without being forever plagued with the complicated business of getting advances of money from international bankers. The dampness of Yorkshire, he felt, could not be a great deal worse than that which he had encountered in France. But "dear Bess" was still of a different mind. Lydia was continuing to make progress in French and in dancing. The young lady, she argued, should not be deprived of the advantages of a continental education. Besides, she herself had fewer twinges of rheumatism in France than she had in Yorkshire. Her attitude could not have been too encouraging to her husband. One cannot very well economize if one must support a family abroad. But there was no use in trying to outargue a lady who felt that she had been kept on a shelf in Yorkshire long enough. "My system is to let her please herself," Laurence remarked stoically.

So with a tear in his eye only for his "little slut"—as he affectionately called Lydia—he left Montpellier for Paris, ultimately to join his "other wife" the Church, in Yorkshire. He had originally planned to make the homeward journey by way of Geneva and Holland, but Tollot and the Thornhills were in the French capital. These friends offered hospitality at the Hôtel d'Entragues near the Luxembourg Palace. A round of gaieties began immediately upon Laurence's arrival. John Wilkes, then in "exile," provided opportunity for carousing, and the "goddesses of the theatre" contributed the necessary sex appeal. The brilliant and dissolute politician shared his wide acquaintance among lively, young, and handsome actresses with the gaunt and witty parson. What a pair the two must have made! So often were they seen together that a report got abroad that they were planning a tour of Italy in each other's company. Stephen Fox was also on hand to cast the weight of his father's fabulous fortune on the side of the English rakes. No wonder Sterne could call Paris the "city of seductions" and remark of his two merry months: ". . . we have lived (shag, rag, and bobtail), all of us, a most jolly nonsensical life of it."

On the more respectable side of his social life were the magnificent levees of the Earl of Hertford at the Embassy, and dinner engagements with the ambassador's young son, Viscount Beauchamp, and with another of his aristocratic young friends, the Marquess of Tavistock. One of the most remarkable aspects of Sterne's charm was his ability to draw around him socially attractive youths. The Thornhills, the Foxes, Woodhouse, Boswell, William Combe, Lord Beauchamp, and Lord Tavistock formed only a partial roll-call of his young admirers.

A sentimental affair once again occupied his emotions:

> I have been for eight weeks smitten [he wrote in May] with the tenderest passion that ever tender wight underwent... how deliciously I cantered away with it the first month, two up, two down, always upon my hânches along the street from my hôtel to hers, at first once—then twice, then three times a day, till at length I was within an ace of setting up my hobby horse in her stable for good and all. I might as well considering how the enemies of the Lord have blasphemed thereupon; the last three weeks we were every hour upon the doleful ditty of parting—and thou mayst conceive... how it alter'd my gait and air—for I went and came like any loaden'd carl, and did nothing but mix tears and *Jouer des sentiments* with her from sunrising even to the setting of the same...

The lady left for the South of France and another beautiful friendship came to an end. Whether the object of his sentimentality was one of Wilkes's actresses or a lady in Embassy circles there is no record. At any rate, when he was winding up this attachment, he was at the same time writing to express solicitous interest in the welfare of Bess and Lyd at Montaubon and to warn his daughter against developing coquetry by associating with French women.

From sentimental love affairs and unorthodox night life Laurence could find time to make a public appearance *in propria persona*. Lord Hertford, the ambassador, had just taken and furnished a new hôtel, sumptuous in every respect. When the ambassador's messenger delivered to the parson an invitation to preach in the elegant chapel of the embassy, he was engaged in a "sober game of whist" with the Thornhills. Naturally he accepted, and performed in fine style. However, the abruptness of the invitation (Laurence explained) caused him to choose for the performance an unfortunate text—a paraphrase of II Kings XX 13, 15, 17:

> And Hezekiah said unto the Prophet, I have shewn them my vessels of gold, and my vessels of silver, and my wives and my concubines and my boxes of ointment, and whatever I have in my house, have I shewn unto them: and the prophet said unto Hezekiah, thou hast done very foolishly.

One could trust to Laurence to make the best of the situation and to boast that a "concourse of all nations and religions" heard the sermon with interest.

There was at least one listener who appreciated the humor of the occasion. He was David Hume, Tory and infidel, who had paradoxically become secretary to the Whiggish and notoriously pious ambassador. When Sterne returned to the city from the South of France, he found that the brilliant historian and philosopher had become the leading English lion of the capital. To Hume, Paris was the same sort of literary Paradise as it had been earlier to Sterne. Never had talent been given more homage. Immediately upon Hume's arrival he had been received by the aging but beautiful Duchesse de la Vallière and the Duc d'Orléans, and he had been flattered by a reception by the whole royal family, even down to the five-year-old Comte d'Artois, who (though scarcely intelligible) presented a memorized eulogium. With Hume, Sterne was forced to share the spotlight. But in spite of stories to the contrary, the rivalry that developed was friendly.

At the dinner given in the Embassy after Yorick's sermon, it is true, "*David* was disposed to make a little merry with the *Parson;* and, in return, the Parson was equally disposed to make a little mirth with the Infidel." A debate on miracles resulted, much to the delight of the other guests. Later this merry tilt was interpreted as a quarrel, and it was even said that Lord Hertford had been offended by Sterne's sermon. These reports Laurence himself vigorously denied, protesting his friendship for the philosopher. On his part, Hume was slightly less demonstrative. It was he who remarked of *Tristram*, "The best book that has been writ by any Englishman these thirty years . . . bad as it is"!

PART FOUR: ALAS, YORICK

CHAPTER XIII

PHILANDER IN ENGLAND

HE END of Laurence's "shag, rag, and bobtail" spree in Paris would be perfectly predictable even if he himself had not written the conclusion with his usual pithiness: "I fell ill, and broke a vessel in my lungs and half bled to death." Thus his return to England was somewhat delayed. But in June he was back in London again.

The homecoming of the eminent English novelist after more than two years on the Continent was in no sense triumphant. Shortly after he had left for France, as we have seen, he had been reported dead by one of London's leading newspapers, and there were doubtless many who still thought him so. He had published nothing; and public interest in his novel had dwindled sadly. Besides, many of his friends were out of town. Garrick, whose presence was always a guarantee of social activity, was abroad trying to regain his health. Mrs. Montagu, it is true, was in residence, but she apparently had little to offer the parson but her own gracious company. A visit to Becket was enough to convince him that he must soon begin writing again in order to recoup both his fortune and his reputation.

But all was not drab and cheerless; for Tollot and the Thornhills had returned to town with him. And before he returned to Yorkshire and the "world of Nonsense" that he had promised to write, he had the satisfaction of having his portrait "taken" once again by Reynolds. Moreover, he went to Surrey for a visit to a famous old man whose connection with the world of the fictitious Uncle Toby and the real Roger Sterne made him of fascinating interest. The host was Lord Ligonier, who bore among his titles the Irish one of Viscount Ligonier of Clonmel. This long-lived veteran had been associated with the Duke of Marlborough, had fought at Ramillies and Oudenarde, and, like Roger Sterne, had served in the Vigo expedition. Few men could have had memories of greater value to the author of *Tristram Shandy*.

The short visit in London concluded, Laurence turned homeward. His friends and his business affairs in York undoubtedly kept him from going directly to Coxwold. When he did arrive there, he did not stay long enough to make much progress with his writing. Although he took time to make a report to the Archbishop on the state of the parish, he did not bother to appear in the pulpit of his little church, having convinced himself that the sermon in Lord Hertford's chapel was his last. In August he was back in York for the racing season and for the concerts and assemblies. The city was full of distinguished people, including the Marquis and Marchioness of Rockingham, Lord Effingham, and those heroes of Minden and Kloster Kampen, Lords Granby and Shelburne. Moreover, there was, of course, the company of the still gay and reckless Hall-Stevenson, not to mention that of Miss Sally Tuting—who engaged, though briefly, the generous Yorick's heart.

Miss Tuting, whom Laurence had met several years previously, came of a racing breed; but the poor dear was a fragile flower whose nourishment of sentiment could not keep her from wasting away in the Yorkshire air. The doctors had prescribed Italy for the winter. Laurence with heady gallantry rushed off a letter to Foley to recommend the lady to his kind offices in Paris. Then he dipped his pen into a gushing heart to write a farewell:

—Well! once more adieu!—farewell! God be with you! in this long journey may no thorn grow near the path you tread; and when you lie down, may your pillow, gentle Sally, be soft as your own breast... The gentle Sally T—— is made up of too fine a texture for the rough wearing of the world—some gentle Brother, or some one who sticks closer than a Brother, should now take her by the hand, and lead her tenderly along her way—pick carefully out the smoothest tracks for her—scatter roses on them—and when the lax'd and weary fibre tells him she is weary—take her up in his arms—

The fraternal note suggests the confused ingredients of Laurence's affairs; and the fact that he carefully copied the letter in his letter book is evidence enough that his sentiments were highly self-conscious.

After the gaieties at York, Sterne found it impossible to settle down to a sober life at Shandy Hall. Some of the pleasure-seeking celebrities of the racing set had decamped to Scarborough, the coastal resort, for the salt air and the waters there. When Laurence sat down at his deal table and tried to cudgel his brain with the story of Uncle Toby, the bright sunshine and the thought of the good company at Scarborough taunted him. There would be many dull winter months, he rationalized, when he would be confined to the house. Then he could do his writing. It was little short of a crime to waste bright September weather. He recorded his decision in a note to Hall-Stevenson:

I am going to leave a few poor sheep here in the wilderness for fourteen days—and from pride and naughtiness of heart to go see what is doing at Scarborough—steadfastly meaning afterwards to lead a new life and strengthen my faith.

Surely, the poor sheep could not have missed their pastor, who for so long had relegated them to the dull shepherding of the downtrodden curate, Mr. Kilner. One hardly has to remark that Sterne's "other wife the Church" had little more hold on him than did the lady whom he had left in Southern France. But the really dangerous matter was the neglect of his writing. Mrs. Sterne was drawing on Foley, and money was needed to meet various obligations. With remarkable self-confidence he had advised Foley to honor his wife's drafts and had assured the banker: "You shall always have money before hand of mine." Such unstable optimism spurred him off to the seaside resort to dissipate money and energy that he did not have.

Three weeks later he was back in his "Philosophical Hut" writing a characteristic report to Hall-Stevenson, who had been disporting himself at the bleak but popular inland spa of Harrogate:

> I am but this moment return'd from Scarborough where I have been drinking the waters ever since the races, and have received marvelous strength, had I not debilitated it as fast as I got it, by playing the good fellow with Lord G[ranb]y and Co. too much.

In the meantime a sobering letter had come from Mrs. Sterne at Montaubon. Her purse was empty again; and a rumor that she and Sterne were permanently separated mitigated against her drawing money from her agent. Immediately, Laurence had to send a letter to Foley to scotch the rumor and, incidentally, to reassure the banker that he was a good risk. Sterne's exaggerated profession of affection and friendship for Foley—who was, after all, more of a business man than a sentimentalist—at this time perilously approaches wheedling. Since he had already had one experience in which the banker had delayed forwarding funds until his professional conscience could be satisfied, Laurence could not be entirely assured that Foley's friendship would be sufficient to save embarrassment. In the crisis he knew that he must produce something tangible. So now in all good faith he promised his banker to finish the work on

Tristram and to have it "ready for the world about Christmas."

Beyond doubt he proved that he could rise to the occasion. With a will, he returned to his purple jerkin, his yellow slippers, his foolscap, and his quills. Part of one volume he had written. But he needed two. The travel notes that he had made in France with the original idea of a separate volume enabled him to meet the demand. The result was a happy one, for the idea perhaps seized upon in some desperation gave him zest for the completion of the book that he had previously begun; and it provided the opportunity for writing one of the most charming travel accounts in the language. Also, as a light imitation of Piganiol de la Force's *Nouvelle Description de la France* it paved the way for *A Sentimental Journey:*

> You will read as odd a tour through France [Laurence wrote as additional assurance to Foley], as ever was projected or executed by traveler or travel writer, since the world began—'Tis a laughing good-tempered satire against traveling (as puppies travel)...

Surely enough, at the end of November Sterne could write Foley that he had finished the two volumes and that he expected to be in London for Christmas.

A gap in the letters draws a veil over this visit to the great city. We do know, however, that in January, 1765, two more volumes, almost as thin as their author, were added to the six already published volumes of *Tristram.* Again, charges of indecency were brought against Sterne; but the public bought his books and his reputation once more swung upward. In March he wrote to Garrick, still abroad, that he was planning to consolidate his gains by issuing two more volumes of sermons; and he gaily boasted that the subscription list would be dazzling: "a prancing list of *de toute la noblesse*—" Already he was overestimating the income from the project and planning to spend some of his new wealth on a tour of Italy, "where I shall spring game, or the deuce is in the dice." There was every reason for his believing that travel would give him additional material that he could transmute into more wealth. Once more he wore rose-colored glasses.

But bad health was not long in changing the outlook. Mrs. Montagu suggested Bath for a cure. Of the famous resort Smollett wrote with his usual cynicism—

> There is always a great show of the clergy at Bath; none of your thin, puny, yellow, hectic figures, exhausted with abstinence and hard study, labouring under the *morbi eruditorum;* but great overgrown dignitaries and rectors, with rubicund noses and gouty ankles, or broad bloated faces, dragging along great swag bellies, the emblems of sloth and indigestion.

Laurence belonged to the thin and hectic, but not—as we have seen often enough—because he had allowed himself to be crucified on the cross of the Church. For him the other reverend gentlemen in Bath, fat or thin, offered no particular attraction; but since he never took recuperation seriously, there were other possibilities in the fashionable resort that made Mrs. Montagu's idea a happy one.

Prior to Queen Anne's visit to Bath in 1703 to mend her health, the city had been an unlovely one without elegant buildings and with no uniform squares. But an eccentric gambler had appeared on the scene and had wrought a profound change. The reign of Beau Nash not only brought improvements in architecture but also in amusements and manners. Before Nash's death in 1761—just four years previous to Sterne's visit—the former monarch of the city had become a doddering, boring old man; but he had left a fashionable health resort as his monument.

The place was unusually vibrant with activity in April. Its fine Palladian houses took on a new grandeur whether they were seen rising from the river in lovely terraces or providing for the streets and squares dignified scenery as if for a classic drama. A pageant of splendid equipage and rich apparel was daily enacted in the Circus, in the Square, and in the Parades. The noise of the coaches, chaises, and chairs and the merry sound of the Abbey bells filled the air. Around the Pump Room and the Assembly Rooms centered a continuous program of activity: music in the morning, cotillions in the forenoon, balls twice a week, concerts on alternating nights—not to mention countless other private affairs.

Into this maelstrom of social life Laurence went to mend his health. Mrs. Montagu wrote to commend him to the watchcare of her charming but gossipy sister—the novelist and historian Mrs. Sarah Scott, familiarly called "The Pea" because she and Elizabeth Montagu looked so much alike:

> Not knowing what temptations the town of Bath may offer, I have sent you the deepest divine, the profoundest casuist, the most serious (on paper) the reformed Church affords. I suppose from the description you will guess this grave and sage? personage can be no other than the Reverend Mr. Sterne. I will venture to say for him, that whatever he may want in seriousness he makes up in good nature.

Mrs. Montagu also suggested that Laurence would give news of "our cousins"—Elizabeth Sterne and Lydia. It is amusing that in a letter written some days later she herself gives a portrait of "Dear Bess" that might have elicited sympathy for any philandering that Laurence cared to do at Bath:

> She is certainly ill tempered. I have seen many letters of hers from York to him and she was always taking a frump at somebody and forever in quarrels and prabbles... In the South of France she met Miss Townshend and Captain Orme, and instead of avoiding them she entered into violent quarrels till

> she could not live in the place... All people at home and abroad say she is as rude as a bear to those she does not like, and indeed it was always her manner, at the same time she has many good qualities, but neither conscious virtue nor superior parts authorize people using their neighbors with haughty contempt or bitter sarcasm.

But along with this excoriation of Mrs. Sterne, the lady could remark of Laurence: "I cannot imagine he is of a sort to make a good husband, and I wish his wife may not often feel the want of money." Mrs. Montagu was well aware of Sterne's extravagance.

On April 6 Sterne wrote Garrick that he was "playing the devil" at Bath. Shortly after his arrival he had fallen in with the generous and amiable Irishman Francis Pierpont Burton of Buncraggy, County Clare—heir to the peerage of his uncle, Baron Conyngham of Mount Charles. This gentleman introduced Sterne to enough charming Irish "widows" to provide sentimental occupation to spare. In the delightful circle of compatriots in which he found himself he took pains to emphasize his Irish background—a fact that he had not always delighted to parade. And to make himself attractive to the ladies on another score he deliberately falsified his age, posing as forty-four when he was actually fifty-two. But the "widows" were a toothsome lot and well worth a little light perjury:

> ...there is the charming widow *Moor* [*sic*], where, if I had not a piece of legal meadow of my own, I should rejoice to batten the rest of my days;—and the gentle elegant *Gore*, with her fine form and Grecian face, and whose lot I trust it will be to make some man happy, who knows the value of a tender heart.

Outside the group of Irish ladies, Sterne found interesting society in Mrs. Scott, who had been separated from her husband for some years, and in her companion, Mrs. Cutts.

But most important of all was the dainty and sophisticated Mrs. Vesey, for whom several years before Laurence had conceived a sudden passion. "The Sylph" was hardly a widow. She had a perfectly good husband (her second) who was an Irish M. P. and who was later to belong to Dr. Johnson's select "Club." But at the moment Agmondesham Vesey was looking over his estate at Lucan, near Dublin, and his wife—who sought "to see everything and everybody"—was free to exert the charm of her voice, face, and figure wheresoever and on whomsoever she pleased. The attachment which she formed with Sterne at Bath was no mere passing phase but was to grow warmer in the remaining years of her friend's life. Her own greatest social success came after Sterne's death, her parties in London achieving their greatest fame between 1770 and 1784 when she was the chief rival of Mrs. Montagu as leader of the "Bluestockings."

All in all, Laurence had a brief but exciting field-day of *tendresse*—an amazing way to recover from a hemorrhage. How reckless he was in professions of affection one can only guess. But whatever his apparent recklessness, he actually risked little; for he always had his "legal meadow" to which he could retire for safety. When crucial issues were involved, he was careful not to overstep bounds, subtly using his marital status, his sensibility, his ill health, and his Shandyism as quadruple protection:

Good God! Is it you Mrs. F.—! [he wrote from London to an unidentified admirer in Bath] What a fire have you lighted up! 'Tis enough to set the whole house in a flame.

'*If Tristram Shandy was a single man.*' (O dear!)... Do you know I say to what a devil of a shadow of a tantalizing help-mate you must have fallen a victim on that supposition.—Why my most adorable! except that I am tolerably strait made, and near six feet high, and that my nose... is an inch at least longer than most of my neighbors'—except that— That I am a two footed animal without one lineament of hair of the beast upon me, totally spiritualized out of all form for connubial purposes ... that I am moreover of a thin, dry, hectic, unperspirable habit of body—so sublimated and rarified in all my parts that a lady of your wit would not give a brass farthing for a dozen such.... I have not an ounce and a half of carnality about me—and what is that for so long a journey.

In such a way he gave satisfaction to another "Dulcinea," and created an additional document to prove his contention that he loved "in the French way, sentimentally."

In Bath he cajoled and flattered the charming Irish ladies, "Shandying it" with them to their delight and his. But back in more sophisticated circles in London, he talked about them too gaily—"goblet in hand"—at the table of Lady Mary Lepell Hervey. What, Laurence contended, was innocent banter to amuse his hostess and her sister Lady Caroline Hervey, Lady Barrymore carried back to Francis Burton in Bath as unflattering mimicry. As soon as Sterne heard that Burton was offended he wrote immediately to his friend William Combe, denying any intention of ridicule and asking him to square the matter with Burton. We have seen before how Sterne's table conversation could get out of control. Although his guilt in this instance may not have been greater than that involved in the incident of M. Dutens, he may not have been entirely guiltless. His vanity, his indiscretion, and the wine might all have combined to create the unfortunate impression.

Another source of embarrassment upon his return to London was a change in the attitude of his social patroness, Mrs. Montagu. For a long time that literary lady had been tolerant of the obscenities in *Tristram Shandy*, even though a friend like Sir James Macdonald might write from Paris as he did in April, 1764:

Sterne's book has struck everyone with the utmost astonishment and horror—I have not yet seen it—I never believe anything I hear quoted out of a book till I see it, but I hope with all my heart for the sake of some of my friends that people have invented the things I hear cited from their letters.

It is true that Mrs. Montagu had admitted to Mrs. Scott shortly after Laurence had been packed off to Bath: "The age has graced him, he has disgraced the age... I like Tristram better than his book." But before he returned to London, the great lady had ostensibly read the two new volumes and had developed stronger feelings of revulsion. A story like that of the Abbess of Andoüillets might have shocked her sufficiently. Hence the "Queen of the Blues" became ashamed at the thought of having the author of "a tawdry book" in her immaculate drawing room; and when Sterne rang her doorbell, she was not at home to him.

Barred at one of the most respectable doors that had ever admitted him, Laurence turned to less respectable company, engaging in something of a passage at arms with the madcap and scandalous Anne Stuart Percy, variously styled Lady Warkworth and Countess Percy. Lord and Lady Warkworth belonged to the sporting crowd that attended the York races and subscribed to the concerts and assemblies. The lady's charm attracted so many admirers and involved her in so many sordid intrigues that her husband was ultimately driven to divorce her. From this point her history reads like that of one of Defoe's heroines. She married the Baron von Poellnitz with whom she came to America and whom she later deserted to follow a paramour, leaving her husband in ruin.

It was this gentle creature that caused our sentimental hero to pause at the Mount Coffee House on a balmy afternoon in late April. As he dallied on his way to dine with a friend in Wigmore Street, the thought of proximity to the siren made the idea of attempting an assignation irresistible. So into the coffee house he went, called for a sheet of gilt paper, quill and ink:

> O my dear lady [he wrote]—what a dishclout of a soul hast thou made of me? . . . I am a fool—the weakest, the most ductile, the most tender fool, that ever woman tried the weakness of—and the most unsettled in my purposes and resolutions of recovering my right mind.—It is but an hour ago that I kneeled down and swore I would never come near you—and after saying my Lord's Prayer for the sake of the close, of not being led into temptation—out I sallied like any Christian hero, ready to take the field against the world, the flesh, and the devil; not doubting but I should finally trample them all down under my feet—and now I am so near you—within this vile stone's cast of your house—I feel myself drawn into a vortex, that has turned my brain upside downwards, and though I had purchased a box ticket to carry me to Miss ******** benefit, yet I know very well, that was a single line directed to me, to let me know [Lady Warkworth] would be alone at seven, and suffer me to spend the evening with her, she would infallibly see every thing verified I have told her.

Whether or not the lady returned a favorable answer and whether Laurence spent the evening at the theatre or in Lady Warkworth's apartments we do not know. Nor do we know on what other occasions the parson had a chance to pursue his most perilous fancy. Apparently he soon realized that he had ventured out of his class and that his new inamorata, far from being like the gentle Sally Tuting or the dainty Mrs. Vesey, was a Circe or a Calypso of the first magnitude. At any rate, we next see him in "flight" to York in the company of Captain Sir George Savile, leaving behind a red leather pocket book with silver clasps, two sticks of sealing wax, his scissors, and his penknife—narrowly escaping, we are to assume, with his virtue and his reputation. He recorded the flight, it is true, in a jesting letter written to the enchantress herself; but we may be reasonably certain that he mingled truth with jest when he wrote—

> I fled with a militia-captain: it was not from principles of rebellion,—but of virtue, that we made our escapes: The Goddess of Prudence and Self-Denial bears witness to our motives. —We ran headlong like a Telemachus and a Mentor from a Calypso and her nymphs, hastening as fast as our members would let us, from the ensnaring favours of an enchanting court...

Again, Tristram was in true form. The ultimate risk he had managed to sidestep with a flattering jest. He may have seen his Calypso again when she appeared in York for the races in the following August. If he did, the presence also of Lord Warkworth he doubtless allowed to be protection enough—not for the lady but for himself.

At the present moment the only menace in York was the company of Hall-Stevenson. But whatever gaieties the two may have plotted were soon cut short by another broken vessel in Sterne's rebellious lungs. ("...the deuce take these bellows of mine.") It was high time to go to Coxwold and to retire for a period of restricted physical activity and of writing. Laurence also had the problem of building up for the projected volumes of sermons the dazzling subscription list about which he had already boasted excessively to Foley and others. This he intended to do by writing amusing and flattering notes to friends and even chance acquaintances in London, in Bath, or wherever else they might be. A splendid example of these "sales letters"—a form of which Sterne was a past-master—is seen in a note announcing the forthcoming publication to his friend Thomas Hesilrige, great-nephew of Lord Maynard:

> These [sermons] you must know are to keep up a kind of balance, in my Shandaic character, and are pushed into the world for that reason by my friends with as splendid and numerous a list of noblity, etc.—as ever pranced before a book

since subscriptions came into fashion—I should grieve not to have your name amongst those of my friends—and in so much good company as it has a right to be in—so tell me to set it down—and if you can—Lord Maynard's—I have no design, my dear Hesilrige, upon your purse—'tis but a crown—but I have a design up[on] the credit of Lord Maynard's name—and that of a person I love and esteem so much as I do you.

Hesilrige subscribed. Lord Maynard, however, did not fall for the bait.

A few domestic matters interrupted the composition of sermons and letters. For example, an elderly French gentleman had taken a fancy to Lyd as the daughter of *le fameux écrivain anglais* and had written with exquisite presumption to inquire concerning dowry. Sterne's reply is classic:

'Sir, I shall give her ten thousand pounds the day of marriage—my calculation is as follows—she is not eighteen, you are sixty-two—there goes five thousand pounds—then Sir, you at least think her not ugly—she has many accomplishments, speaks Italian, French, plays upon the guitar, and as I fear you play upon no instrument whatever, I think you will be happy to take her at my terms, for here finishes the account of the ten thousand pounds.'

Nothing more was heard of the gentleman.

Then there was tragedy at Sutton. On the afternoon of August 1 the parsonage caught fire, presumably on account of the carelessness of Mrs. Callis, wife of Sterne's underpaid and disgruntled curate. A bucket brigade made up of neighbors saved the house in which the Sternes had lived for two decades, and watchers sat up during the night to see that there was no further conflagration. The next day, however, fire broke out again, this time doing a thorough job.

As soon as I can I must rebuild it, I trow [wrote Laurence] —but I lack the means at present—yet I am never happier than when I have not a shilling in my pocket—for when I have I can never call it my own.

In this mood of insouciance he forgot his troubles amid the excitement of the August races at York. In fact, he never found opportunity to restore the ruined house, allowing the problem to remain for Mrs. Sterne and Lyd to solve after his death.

In September he was spitting blood again and finding it necessary to go to York to "recruit" himself.

> ... after I have published, [I] shall set my face, not toward Jerusalem [he wrote], but toward the Alps—I find I must once more fly from death whilst I have strength—I shall go to Naples and see whether the air of that place will not set this poor frame to rights—

So he passed the summer with hemorrhages, sermons, and trips to York to mark the intervals. In October, by the grace of God and the toughness of something in his frail body, he was back in London again with copy for twelve sermons ready for the press.

With two possible exceptions the sermons designed for the new volumes were not greatly different from the earlier sermons. They still showed that Sterne could write with grace and dignity whenever he chose, that his dramatic and imaginative powers still flourished, and that he had not veered far from his favorite themes. At least three of the sermons had been preached on notable occasions. "The Case of Hezekiah and His Messengers" had been delivered in Lord Hertford's chapel in Paris. "The Parable of the Rich Man and Lazarus" had been preached earlier as a charity sermon. For the third Sterne reached so far back into the past that he thought an apology necessary—as, indeed, it was, since "The Abuses of Conscience" had already appeared in pamphlet form and in *Tristram Shandy*. Several of the other sermons were drawn from his file and refurbished for publication. Everything considered, Laurence's turning his face toward Jerusalem seemed not to entail too much effort.

Especially concocted to add Shandaic dash to the new volumes were "The Levite and the Concubine" and "The Prodigal Son." The first is easily one of the most astonishing of Sterne's productions. Never had Laurence played more lightheartedly with Biblical commentary than he did in discussing the polygamy and concubinage of the patriarchs. Into his discourse he wove the obviously classic example of Solomon—

> ... whose excess became an insult on the privileges of mankind; for by the same plan of luxury, which made it necessary to have forty thousand stalls of horses,—he had unfortunately miscalculated his other wants, and so had seven hundred wives, and three hundred concubines.
>
> Wise,—deluded man! was it not that thou madest some amends for thy bad practice by thy good preaching, what would become of thee!—Three hundred!—But let us turn aside, I beseech you, from so bad a stumbling block.
>
> The Levite had but one...

The Biblical story on which the sermon is based is not carried to its horrible conclusion. Very characteristically, Sterne uses just enough of it to accomplish his purpose: "to discredit rash judgment" and to pose the question, "Must beauty for ever be trampled upon in the dirt for one—one false step?"

As a sermon, "The Prodigal Son" is as palpably ridiculous, turning as it does on a discussion of the proper kind of "bear leader" (the eighteenth-century term for tutor and traveling companion) to accompany a young man who has the urge to travel on the Continent.

It is inevitable that some of the sermons should suggest autobiographical material. Elsewhere, "The Levite and the Concubine" has been cited for its rationalization of Laurence's philandering on the basis of his need for companionship. "The History of Jacob," we have also seen, offers hints of the failure of his marriage because of his having been "mistaken in the person." The lover, the preacher warns, is naturally inclined to overestimate and over-idealize the beloved—with fatal result!

One sermon traces the providential course of Protestant succession in England; and another exalts Christianity over Paganism because Christianity offers a better guide for human conduct and "has a proper tendency to make us a virtuous and a happy people." But Sterne's favorite themes are still that of the dangers of great wealth and the complementary one of the "moral delight" arising from the consciousness of a humane deed. Avarice, he argues in the sermon on Felix, may stand between us and belief: ". . . it is some selfish consideration—some secret dirty engagement with some little appetite, which does us so much dishonour." But generosity in material things—though it may build schools, asylums, and hospitals—is not enough: "One honest tear shed in private over the unfortunate is worth it all."

In spite of its absurdity as a whole, "The Prodigal Son" is important for the enunciation of an idea near the core of Sterne's philosophy. "When the affections . . . kindly break loose," the preacher asserts, "Joy is another name for Religion." In "The History of Jacob" this theme is forcefully expanded:

> Grant me, gracious God to go cheerfully, on the road which thou hast marked out!
>
> . . . .
>
> I pity the men, whose natural pleasures are burdens, and who fly from Joy . . . as if it was really an evil in itself.
>
> If there is an evil in this world, 'tis sorrow and heaviness of heart.—The loss of goods,—of health—of coronets and mitres, are only evil as they occasion sorrow;—take that out,—the rest is fancy, and dwelleth only in the head of man.

Whether this philosophy is considered shallow or deep, it is consistent. It lay at the basis of Sterne's admirable gallantry in his struggle against very serious obstacles, and it offered the securest prop for what he could call with Alexander Pope "this long disease, my life."

The sermons were not published until January, 1766. When they appeared, the subscription list all but lived up to Sterne's extravagant promises. It bore not only the names of his fashionable acquaintances in Bath, Scarborough, York, and London and those of his Yorkshire neighbors, but also those of such brilliant lights of French intellect as Voltaire and Diderot and that of such an old friend as Baron d'Holbach. The campaign for subscriptions had worked well.

Moreover, the volumes were well received in the press. Periodicals continued to quote the sermons several weeks after their publication. On the distaff side, one dissenting vote requires recording. Mrs. Sarah Scott wrote to Mrs. Montagu:

> Have you read Sternes new sermons? Surely such stuff never was published. His Levite and his Concubine and the Prodigal Son are the quintessence of absurdity. I question whether any of our learned Commentators ever thought of the youths being cheated by a Ciceroni. The detail of articles in which he supposes his extravagance to have existed, the adapting it to present times, wou'd have the merit of originality, were it not for Mr. Montagu's friend's sermon, on Remember Lots wife. He has the most cavalier way of treating the Patriarchs that ever I met with, and his discovery that Solomon was guilty of the same foolish greediness with children when Nurses tell them of the unconscionable bigness of their eye, in no very delicate phrase, is curious. A mightier man than Sterne might indeed have the same sense of that wise man's folly in the article of women.

The lady must have known!

CHAPTER XIV

ITALIAN JOURNEY

LONDON DID not detain Sterne long. Once he had deposited his manuscript in the hands of the faithful Becket, he was ready to engage a place in the Dover stage. On October 7 he was writing to Foley requesting that a new periwig be made for him in Paris. In less than two weeks he was on hand to wear it.

Although Death was again in pursuit, Laurence's departure for France was by no means so grim as that of several years before. The celerity and ease of the journey were little short of marvelous. The traveler merely packed "half a dozen shirts and a pair of silk breeches," seated himself in the Dover machine one afternoon, and sailed on a packet for Calais at nine the next morning. By three o'clock in the afternoon of the second day he was sitting down to a fricasseed chicken, "incontestibly in France."

In the French port he descended for a short stay at the elegant new Hôtel d'Angleterre, which was now managed by M. Dessein and which was attracting most of the former custom of the older Lyon d'Argent. An angel could not have been a more propitious guest for the one-eyed hosteler whose shrewdness and swarthiness made him look "like a Jew, then a Turk." If M. Dessein had known that he was on the brink of literary immortality, he might have treated his distinguished guest with even more deference and affability than that with which he usually greeted his English clientèle.

Two sentimental adventures fixed the Hôtel d'Angleterre firmly in Laurence's memory. The first was an encounter with a mendicant friar to whom Sterne lectured on practical philanthropy instead of contributing to his cause, only to succumb later to the extent of giving the beggar his gold snuff-box. The friar had courtesy and sensibility enough to give Laurence his cheap horn snuff-box in return. Characteristically, the Yorkshire parson was able to make his charity pay dividends when he used the incident in *A Sentimental Journey*. The second, and vastly more important, experience was the meeting with the lovely Madame de L*** of Brussels:

> She had a black pair of silk gloves, open only at the thumb and two forefingers . . . a face of about six and twenty, of a clear transparent brown, simply set off without rouge or powder.

A "widow'd look" completed her charm. Both the lady and Laurence were on the point of purchasing chaises, and a delicious stroke of fate threw them both for a few minutes into the same vehicle from M. Dessein's collection. Alone with the lady in the chaise, the sentimental parson was quick but subtle in his gallantries. "Then I solemnly declare," said the lady finally, amid the most proper blushes, "you have been making love to me all the time." ". . . she suffered me to kiss her hand twice," the writer commented on the outcome. Unfortunately, the episode was cut short by the appearance of the fair one's brother. So exhilarated was the parson by his experience that he immediately bought a chaise at a price several guineas more than it was worth. Or so Yorick tells the story.

Whether he spent the night in Calais or in Boulogne it is not clear. At any rate, the next day he was driving through the rain to Montreuil. En route the weather and the portmanteau were the chief sources of trouble. Twice he had to get out in the rain and mud to tie on his misbehaving luggage.

In Montreuil he got another glimpse of Janatone; but,

what is more significant, he acquired La Fleur—who, though less of a gentleman and a scholar than the twentieth-century Jeeves, was destined to become one of the most famous valets in literature. This remarkable person—picked up because Laurence disliked tying on portmanteaus in the rain—had begun his career romantically as a drummerboy and had later deserted from the army. He was a perfect "find," for he could make the mud-guarding leggings called "spatterdashes," he could play a fiddle ("Why I play a bass, myself, said I; we shall do very well"), and he was almost as excellent a connoisseur of female face and figure as his master. The very gods had set him in Yorick's way.

With La Fleur in charge, the departure from Montreuil assumed the air of an event. While the postillion was leading out the horses, half a dozen girls encircled the new valet in the courtyard to bid him *bon voyage*. La Fleur gallantly "kissed all their hands round and round again, and thrice he wiped his eyes, and thrice he promised he would bring them all pardons from Rome." When the time for leaving came, the hero mounted and rode handsomely away, *avant-courier* for the chaise, "as happy and as perpendicular as a prince."

This noble picture, however, was shattered (happily, far beyond the gaze of the admiring fair) when near Namport La Fleur's horse shied at a dead ass, threw the rider, and galloped home. The discomfiture of the valet was quickly ameliorated by his being taken into the chaise with his master. The dead ass was tucked away in the writer's memory for a sentimental episode in his famous travel book.

The night was spent in Amiens, where Madame de L*** and her brother the Count again appeared. The Lady gave Yorick a letter of introduction to Madame de R——, one of her Parisian friends, and he in return sent the lady a *billet-doux* adapted from a letter provided by the adroit La Fleur from his collection (an ostensible missive from a drummer in La Fleur's regiment to a corporal's wife). The burden of the message was one of the most important tenets of Laurence's philosophy: "L'amour n'est *rien* sans sentiment."

After five days on the road, he arrived in Paris and installed himself at the Hôtel de Modène in the Rue Jacob, then a gay street in the fashionable Faubourg St. Germain and not the drab succession of small hotels, pensions, and shops that it now is:

> "I walked up gravely to the window in my dusty black coat [wrote Laurence], and looking through the glass saw all the world in yellow, blue, and green, running at the ring of pleasure.—Alas, poor Yorick! cried I, what art thou doing here? On the very first onset of all this glittering clatter thou art reduced to an atom.

But this first melancholy sentiment was probably due to fatigue or to the depressed mental state that often comes immediately after the cessation of a journey. It was soon to be dissipated. Near by in the Rue du Colombier was, again, John Wilkes, who had just returned from Italy; and also in town was the comedian Samuel Foote. The parson, the politician, and the actor were soon together, composing a veritable congress of wit—that is, for those who liked their wit. Horace Walpole, another visitor to Paris at the same time, affected not to. "You will think it odd," he wrote, "that I should want to laugh, when Wilkes, Sterne, and Foote are here; but the first does not make me laugh, the second never could, and for the third, I choose to pay five shillings when I have a mind he should divert me." But the antagonism of fashionable Mr. Walpole was no blight on Sterne's gaiety. There were many other aristocratic Englishmen to enjoy his Shandaic quibbles, and he had, of course, his French friends, not all of whom had accompanied the Court to Versailles. Again, the charm of the heteroclite parson attracted dazzling young

Etonians and Oxonians, drawing into his circle such twenty-year-old gentlemen as John Fitzpatrick, second Earl of Upper Ossory, and Lord William Gordon, son of the third Duke of Gordon and brother to the infamous and mad Lord George Gordon. Into the group also came the Scottish gambler, John ("Fish") Crauford of Errol–a lavish, witty, hypochondriac poseur who dashed through the streets of Paris in a fine carriage with liveried footmen and who enjoyed the esteem of one of the most brilliant and powerful of Parisian ladies, the blind Marquise du Deffand. To this extraordinary gentleman all readers of Sterne owe a debt of gratitude; for it was he who provided the story for "The Case of Delicacy," with which *A Sentimental Journey* ends.

From *A Sentimental Journey*, in fact, one must piece out the rest of the Parisian interlude. In so doing one must attempt to winnow fact from fiction and to separate details of a former visit from those of the present one. In neither task can there be hope of complete success.

Whether or not the incident happened even remotely as recorded, Laurence's most exquisite story is that of the "handsome" grissette into whose shop he wandered one day in search of the Opéra Comique. Engaging her in sentimental conversation–

> I am sure [he said] you must have one of the best pulses of any woman in the world. Feel it, said she, holding out her arm. So laying down my hat, I took hold of her fingers in one hand, and applied the two fore-fingers of my other to the artery.
>
> . . . .
>
> I had counted twenty pulsations, and was going on fast towards the fortieth, when her husband coming unexpected from a back parlour into the shop, put me a little out of my reckoning. 'Twas nobody but her husband, she said, so I began a fresh score. Monsieur is so good, quoth she, as he pass'd by

us, as to give himself the trouble of feeling my pulse. The husband took off his hat, and making me a bow, said, I did him too much honour; and having said that, he put on his hat and walk'd out.

Then there was the episode of Madame de R——'s maid, whom Sterne entertained, sentimentally, in his room, only to have his actions misunderstood by the *maître d'hotel:*

Voyez vous, Monsieur, said he, pointing to the foot of the bed we had been sitting upon. I own it had something of the appearance of an evidence; but my pride not suffering me to enter into any detail of the case, I exhorted him to let his soul sleep in peace, as I resolved to let mine do that night, and that I would discharge what I owed him at breakfast.

I should not have minded, *Monsieur*, said he, if you had had twenty girls—'Tis a score more, replied I, interrupting him, than I ever reckon'd upon—Provided, added he, it had been but in a morning. And does the difference of the time of the day at Paris make a difference in the sin? It made a difference, he said, in the scandal.

In the last week of October Sterne and La Fleur (the latter a flaming cockerel in a new scarlet coat) set out for Lyons. An agreeable journey it was in the mellow "hey day of the vintage," far different from the torrid trip of several summers before when Bess and Lyd were in tow. If we can accept Sterne's record, the adventures along the way perfectly befitted the high priest of sensibility. The proper amount of romantic melancholy was provided by an encounter near Moulins with the victim of a blighted romance, a gently demented maiden who piped the evening service to the Virgin. "Poor Maria," whose memory was perpetuated both in *A Sentimental Journey* and in the last book of *Tristram*, was destined for a place in the popular eighteenth-century galaxy of pathological females, of which Cowper's "Crazy Kate" was another distinguished member.

A thill-horse's losing two shoes necessitated a stop in a peasant's cottage. The picture that Sterne gave of the rustic family sitting down to their lentil soup, their wheaten loaf, and their flagon of wine ("—'twas a feast of love") is unexcelled in the literature of sensibility.

At Lyons Laurence found a hospitable commandant with whom he dined and supped every day for a whole joyous week. Including the commandant, about "a dozen English" were in the city. Among them could have been none more interesting than John Horne Tooke, as unorthodox a parson as Yorick himself—though in a rather different way. This gentleman was soon to take up the cudgel as a Wilkesite political agitator, was to serve a sentence in prison, and was to become the author of an eccentric philological work called *The Diversions of Purley*. Sterne's social connections with Wilkes gave the two immediate grounds for common understanding.

On November 7 Sterne had reached Pont de Beauvoisin (nine posts from Lyons) where he was held up by "the sudden swelling of two pitiful rivulets from the snows melting on the Alps." Over the mountain passes of Savoy, however, he soon made his way to Turin, where torrential rains again caused delays. In spite of the bad weather and the fact that the court at Turin was considered dull, the ebullient Laurence was undismayed. "I am very happy," he was soon writing, "—and have found my way into a dozen houses already." Naturally, so renowned and so attractive a visitor had no trouble in getting a presentation to the aging Charles Emmanuel III, King of Sardinia.

But his real catch was that "Marcellus of the North" (as Boswell called him) the twenty-three-year-old Sir James Macdonald. The young man had beauty of neither face nor figure; but he was a scion of one of Scotland's proudest families and his intellectual attainments were considered by all who knew him to earmark him for greatness. Unfortunately, however, he was ill-starred and he was destined to die tragically young. The ruddy ugliness of his face and his lack of the Chesterfieldian graces were to Sterne no deterrents to friendship, especially since the youth was rich and since he offered to Laurence the long-desired chance of being a "bear leader" to an affluent and noble young man. Sir James, on his part, seems to have been attracted to the famous author at first sight, in spite of Yorick's scandalous reputation (about which he had previously expressed concern to Mrs. Montagu). With Sir James enlisted as a companion, Sterne set out with great satisfaction for Milan.

The letters do not record the doings of the pair in the Lombard capital, but a passage in *A Sentimental Journey* records an episode with the Marchese Fagniani so slight and so delicate that only a great artist like Sterne could have used it with consummate perfection as literary material. As Laurence was entering a hall in Milan for a concert, he encountered the Marchesa, on her way out in some haste:

> ...she was almost upon me before I saw her; so I gave a spring to one side to let her pass. She had done the same, and on the same side too: so we ran our heads together: she instantly got to the other side to get out: I was just as unfortunate as she had been: for I had sprung to that side, and opposed her passage again. We both flew together to the other side, and then back, and so on. It was ridiculous. We both blush'd intolerably.

Laurence finally solved the problem by standing stock still. When he ran after the lady to apologize, she returned gallantry with graciousness, inviting him into her coach. "And what became of the concert, St. Cecilia, who, I suppose was at it, knows more than I." No evening in Italy, Sterne confided, gave him more pleasure.

On December 18 he wrote from Florence:

> I have been a month passing the plains of Lombardy, stopping in my way at Milan, Parma, Piacenza, Bologna with weather as delicious, as a kindly April in England—and have been three days in crossing a part of the Appenines covered with thick snow—sad transition.

The cold of Florence, in fact, was too much for him; so much so that he could not be detained even by the hospitality of "our Plenipo," Sir Horace Mann, or by the art treasures, or by the eccentric company of the Earl Cowper, who for years had not been able to tear himself away from the city (in spite of the fact that his trunks were packed) on account of his grand passion for the Marchesa de Corsi.

So on went Yorick to Rome, eager to see the Eternal City, to "tread the Vatican, and be introduced to all the Saints in the Pantheon." Once, when he wore the uncouth habit of a provincial prebendary, the parson had regarded Catholics as imps of the devil. Now his mental furniture matched the urbanity of his well-cut clothes, and his religious intolerance had disappeared. Of what he did and of whom and what he saw in Rome we have no record, save such a meager hint as his indignation at Smollett's scorn of the Pantheon. Although few Englishmen were in the city, he apparently did not want for company or amusement; for his visit was a leisurely one. He was successful in acquiring another traveling companion, young Henry Errington, who seemed willing enough to share expenses for the advantage of being in the party of the witty novelist. The company of two wealthy young men reduced Sterne's expenditures to a minimum, a fact of which he was very proud.

Naples he reached in fine fettle. It had been a long time since he had felt better. The climate was "heavenly" and there was plenty of gaiety to delight his heart. "We have a jolly carnival of it," he wrote, "—nothing but operas—punchinellos—festinos and masquerades." The British envoy, the Honorable William Hamilton, received his celebrated countryman with open arms. And the gentle Miss Tuting was on hand to provide fragile charm. But there was greater game. The first attraction of Naples was the consummate hostess and warm Anglophile, Eleonora Borghese, Princess Francavilla—who thought nothing of giving three balls in a week with a guest list of six to eight hundred for each and whose garden fêtes were paralleled in splendor only by the grand fireworks display of an erupting Vesuvius, a spectacle that at the time of Sterne's visit was in full progress. The Prince, who entertained at dinner each night, was as much of an Anglophile as his wife, sumptuously providing free board for English visitors of importance. The brilliant company, the epicurean fare, the lush growth and vivid colors of Southern Italy, the gentle air, the dramatic disgorgings of a picturesque volcano—all provided as fascinating an environment as a traveler could wish.

Although La Fleur testified that during these travels his master had periods of great dejection, we can see little but gaiety from Laurence's own account. At this time the only discernible shadow on his happiness was the knowledge that while he was growing "fat, sleek, and well-liking" in the salubrious Neapolitan sunshine, Lyd and her mother were plagued with agues in Tours. He wrote promising to join them in May and advising them to seek a less damp climate. Thinking ahead into the summer and fall, he ventured the plan of taking his wife and daughter back to England. "Your summers I will render as agreeable as I can at Coxwold," he promised, "—your winters at York—you know my publications call me to London." Obviously, this suggestion was an opening gun in a campaign to re-establish his family in Yorkshire. Thus far Laurence had been remarkably considerate and generous toward his wife —as generous, in fact, as Bess had been extravagant. One cannot blame him for wanting to put an end to a situation that kept him forever economizing and scraping around for money to meet her bank drafts. He knew that he could keep his family in Coxwold for a fraction of what it cost to keep them abroad—and that, for his part, whenever he chose he could be conveniently absent in London, on business. Unfortunately, however, he had no ordinary wife to reckon with.

Naturally, if one were in Italy during Holy Week, one would reluctantly miss the pomp and pageantry in the capital of Roman Christendom. So Laurence moved up with the fashionable English colony. Since Macdonald had been smitten with a "dreadful rheumatism," he was left behind. The hand of death was already on the promising young man, who died at Frascati in the following July. Errington accompanied Sterne. Beyond Rome, the two had made somewhat grandiose plans for travel. Contradictory to what Laurence had written Lydia, he wrote Hall-Stevenson early in February that he planned to go with Errington to Venice (presumably for the Ascension), thence to "Vienna, Saxony, Berlin, and so by the Spaw," and finally through Holland to England.

The two travelers made a gay trip to Rome by way of Capua and the impressive Benedictine Abbey of Monte Cassino, where they were received with great deference by "les religieux" and accommodated for the night in a guesthouse reserved for celebrated "voyageurs." Only a slight accident marred the journey: "a dromedary of a beast fell upon me in full gallop, and by rolling over me crushed me as flat as a pancake—but I am growing round again."

No record survives concerning what the Anglican parson did in Catholic Rome during Holy Week. But a letter written on Easter Sunday suggests not only that he found sufficient amusement during the solemn and impressive occasion but also that his whole observance involved little piety or sobriety: "We have pass'd a jolly laughing winter of it—and having changed the scene for Rome; we are passing as merry a spring as hearts could wish. I wish my friends no better fortune in this world, than to go at this rate—haec est vita dissolutorum. . ."

Since Errington was forced to abandon his plans for traveling, in May Laurence found himself free to keep his promise to Lydia and to embark on a "wild-goose chase" in search of his family whose whereabouts he did not exactly know. He finally found them in Upper Burgundy. He was delighted to see Lydia again. Mrs. Sterne received him cordially enough and showed some proper solicitude concerning his state of health; but she made no move toward falling in with his plan to take her back to Yorkshire. The record of Laurence's failure in suasion is succinctly put: "Poor woman! she was very cordial, etc. and begs to stay another year or so." Her obstinacy might have been a considerable blow had her husband not been in an exuberant mood. Unmindful of his rebuff, he was soon off to the "delicious chateau" of the Comtesse de Vair et de la Noüe near Dijon, where his customary resourcefulness and uncommon good luck had in some way produced an opportunity for "patriarching it" for a week among an assemblage of handsome ladies:

> This is a delicious part of the world [he wrote "Cousin Anthony"]; most celestial weather, and we lie all day, without damps upon the grass—and that is the whole of it, except the inner man (for her ladyship is not stingy of her wine) is inspired twice a day with the best Burgundy that grows upon the mountains, which terminate our lands here. . .

Prone on the greensward amid much feminine loveliness, elated with wine and with sensibility, in such a completely idyllic spot—Yorick might well have ended a sentimental journey.

But since he did not, I beg leave to conclude in another chapter.

CHAPTER XV

THE BELLE INDIAN

THE REST of the trip may be chronicled briefly. From Burgundy Laurence went to Paris, where he stayed such a short time that he did not have a chance to pay a congratulatory call on the newly married Foley. He proceeded to Montreuil, where he restored La Fleur to his "harem" and bade him a warm goodbye. At the end of June he was once more in Coxwold. His haste to return home was motivated by a desire to get back to his writing. He felt the need of striking while the iron of inspiration was hot; and he knew that there would be drafts from his Continental bankers to be met.

So deceptively good had been his health while he was abroad that he had boasted to Hall-Stevenson: "I shall live these ten years, my Anthony." But in Yorkshire his exhilaration and good spirits vanished with the summer showers. His bellows (deuce take them!) again rebelled, and he was again plagued with hemorrhages. To add to his miseries letters came from Lydia telling of her mother's ill health. In fact, as the summer grew on, Mrs. Sterne's condition appeared so serious that Laurence feared he might at any moment be called upon to make a hurried trip to France.

Aside from the concerns of his own health and that of his wife, "a thousand nothings, or worse than nothings" kept his pen inactive. "I take it up today in good earnest and shall not let it go until the York races," he wrote to Hall-Stevenson on July 15. At the same time, he hinted strongly that he might possibly be lured away from Coxwold for a week at Scarborough if "Cousin Anthony" should by any chance be interested. Whether or not he "laughed his miseries away" at the fashionable watering place, he records that he did not get into the first chapter of *Tristram Shandy*, Book IX, until August 12.

Over two weeks before that date, it is true, he had received a letter from Ignatius Sancho—ex-slave, protegé of the Duke of Montagu, and footling littérateur—requesting "half an hour's attention to slavery." Laurence had replied that by a strange coincidence he had just been writing "a tender tale of the sorrows of a friendless poor negro girl" and that his eyes "had scarce done smarting with it." He had continued expansively:

> I never look *Westward* (when I am in a pensive mood at least) but I think of the burdens which our brothers and sisters are *there* carrying—and could I ease their shoulders from one ounce of 'em, I declare I would set out this hour upon a pilgrimage to Mecca for their sakes—

As one might expect, Sterne's implied promise was far greater than his yield; hence his name is not enshrined in Thomas Clarkson's *History of the Abolition of the Slave Trade* as one of the "great coadjutors." But his direct promise—to weave the story into what he was writing—is at least partially carried out in the sixth chapter of Book IX when he introduces "a poor negro girl, with a bunch of white feathers slightly tied to the end of a long cane, flapping away flies—not killing them"—

> —'Tis a pretty picture! said my uncle Toby—she had suffered persecution, Trim, and had learnt mercy.
>
> . . . .
>
> A negro has a soul? an' please your honour, said the corporal (doubtingly).
>
> I am not much versed, corporal, quoth my uncle Toby, in things of that kind; but I suppose, God would not leave him without one, any more than thee or me—

...Why then, an' please your honour, is a black wench to be used worse than a white one?

I can give no reason, said my uncle Toby—

—Only, cried the corporal, shaking his head, because she has no one to stand up for her—

—'Tis that very thing, Trim, quoth my uncle Toby—which recommends her to protection—and her brethren with her...

If Sterne began his serious writing on August 12, he did not continue long at it; for on the eighteenth he was in York for the races. In all Yorkshire there was scarcely a more indefatigable attendant upon race-week festivities than the Vicar of Coxwold. Come weal, come woe, bad health or bad fortune, he could usually be found during the great August racing season either in the red brick grandstand of the county races or in the Assembly Rooms. In 1766 the season was given added brilliance by the presence of one of Sterne's acquaintances among the great, H. R. H. the Duke of York. It may have been at the Duke's suggestion that the merry Yorkshire parson was asked to preach before the fashionable congregation on Sunday, August 24. In spite of the fact that Laurence considered himself retired from the pulpit, the offer was too flattering to be refused. The occasion was one of great ceremony and pomp. Just before the service began the Duke appeared with his train at the West Porch of the great Cathedral, where he was received by the Residentiary and the Canons. A stately processional led the royal visitor to the Archbishop's throne, from which he listened to the service. Such was the magnificent occasion of Sterne's last sermon. What he preached about no one has yet discovered. But it is certain that the discourse was vastly different from the weird and triumphant one preached in St. Paul's Cathedral over a century before as the farewell message of the emaciated and pale Dean, John Donne. Nor is it likely that Laurence made the same mistake in text that he did when he preached in

Lord Hertford's chapel. Something sufficiently light and comfortable—tinctured as usual with sensibility and elegance of presentation—was doubtless offered the jaded palates of the race-week ladies and gentlemen, many of whom had dull pains of dissipation under their fine periwigs.

At the end of August Sterne was back at home, promising Becket that he would have the ninth and tenth books of *Tristram* ready for winter publication. Only a part of the promise was, of course, executed. But Laurence went seriously to work. Even a hemorrhage he utilized gamely:

> It is one comfort at least to me [he wrote in Chapter XXIV], that I lost some four-score ounces of blood this week in a most uncritical fever which attacked me at the beginning of this chapter; so that I have still some hopes remaining, it may be more in the serous or globular parts of the blood, than in the subtle *aura* of the brain. . . .

In spite of continual reminders of death, he made the ninth book in many respects the bawdiest of the lot, so full of innuendoes and phallic symbolism as to render Thackeray's charge of prurience nearly justifiable. Some of the writing is pedestrian, but much is in Sterne's best vein. The conversation between Uncle Toby and the Widow Wadman concerning the wound in the old soldier's groin has rarely been excelled in hilarious naughtiness. The stories of "Poor Maria" and the negro wench supply the appeal to sensibility. And the whole ends with "a cock and a bull" story rounding out the comedy of sexual begetting with which the novel began. Indeed, Laurence seemed to be taking little notice of the request of the *Monthly Review* in the previous year that he do something "innocently humourous."

While he was writing, Mrs. Sterne's health had grown alarmingly worse and had then improved. In November Lydia was asking for another hundred guineas in order to rent a "chateau" near Avignon for more or less permanent residence. As usual, she got what she requested and the two ladies were settled to their liking. Although the rental was only sixteen guineas the year (including permission to fish and to have game), the estate was a fairly pretentious one situated in a most romantic spot on the banks of the foaming Sorgue near the Fountain of Vaucluse, where Petrarch had composed his sonnets to Laura. The house (wrote Laurence, repeating Lydia's description) had "seven rooms of a floor, half furnished with tapestry, half with blue taffety." As neighbors and frequent visitors to their new home Mrs. Sterne and Lydia had the lively old Abbé de Sade, then still at work on his scholarly memoirs of Petrarch, and his nephew Donatien, Marquis (better known as Count) de Sade. The latter, at the age of twenty-six, was just out of military service and was not yet notorious for his unnatural sex life and for his obscene novels. Already, however, he was giving promise of future infamy. Although outwardly he might have been regarded as an eligible bachelor with titles and estates, his coarseness soon caused the Sternes to eye him askance. Nevertheless, they did not refuse invitations to his garden parties.

Mrs. Sterne and Lydia fished for trout in the romantic Sorgue. They apparently did their most serious fishing for a husband for Lyd in Marseilles, which was not too far away from their chateau for short visits. On one of these visits the young lady thought that she had hooked a highly desirable catch. Laurence reported immediately to Panchaud, associate of Foley in the Parisian banking house, doubtless to encourage him in the face of overdrafts:

> My daughter has an advantageous offer just now at Marseilles—he has 20,000 livres a year—and much at his ease—So I suppose Mademoiselle with Madame ma femme will negotiate the affair.

Unfortunately for Sterne's hard-pressed purse, Lydia did not land her man. The suitor may have cooled when he learned that the young lady possessed no fortune.

For Laurence back in Coxwold the progress of the fall and winter brought an increasing number of hemorrhages. In the first part of December he reported three. Many things were overtaxing his strength and patience. The Fauconbergs entertained him too much; and Stephen Croft's project to enclose Stillington Common (in which Sterne had interest as vicar and landowner) involved boring meetings and endless legal details. As a result of such distractions and of illness, he was able to get only one thin volume ready for the press. "I miscarried of my tenth volume," he wrote William Combe, "by the violence of a fever." But he could muster remarkable gaiety of spirit and could joke obscenely about his affliction.

On a Saturday in late December he braved a "terrible hurricane of wind and snow" to set out for London:

> –'twas one continued storm all the way, and many stages had we to plow through snow up to the horses' bellies, so that with utmost perseverance... we could get but to Barnet the third night–

By January 6 Sterne was comfortably installed in fashionable Old Bond Street, near Piccadilly, in apartments above the double-bow-fronted shop of Mrs. Mary Fourmantel, a respectable widow who described herself as "Hair Bag Maker to His Majesty."

For a short time the severity of the cold limited his activity. A terrible storm had all England in its grip, and there were many rumors of accidents and of suffering.

> When we got up yesterday morning [Sterne wrote on January 9], the streets were four inches deep in snow–it has set in, now, with the most intense cold–I could scarce lay in bed for it; and this morning more snow again...

But his social life could not be restricted long. *Cymon*, a "dramatic romance" by Garrick with music by Michael Arne, was easily the theatrical hit of the season, packing the Drury Lane to the eaves with aristocrats who applauded its scenes and went away to whistle its tunes. With tickets most likely provided by "little Davy" himself, Sterne timed his appearance at the play with that of the King, daring to share the spotlight with George III. All the people of importance, Laurence reported, went to see Garrick's newest work. So much so that Mrs. Centlivre's comedy *The Busy Body* at Covent Garden had to play to "citizen's children and apprentices." Aside from Garrick's success, theatrical small-talk among Sterne's friends centered in the Duke of York, who had developed dramatic aspirations to the extent of planning to appear in Rowe's *The Fair Penitent* in a "little theatre" of his own. The gossip concerning the project (including the King's disapproval) the parson got one night when he dined with the rakish Earl of March and Ruglen, later known as "Old Q," the infamous fourth Duke of Queensbury.

But overshadowing everything else was Mrs. Theresa Cornelys's first assembly of the season, scheduled for the evening of January 15. Little short of a national catastrophe could have prevented a traffic jam of hackney chairs and carriages in the snow and slush of Soho Square near Carlisle House, where an adventuress whose career makes that of Lady Roxana completely credible queened it over the smartest society that eighteenth-century London could boast. A cosmopolite of cosmopolites, the fabulous Theresa was born in Venice and had been mistress to an assortment of people including Senator Malipiero, the Margrave of Baireuth, and Casanova. She came to England as Mme. Pompeati, an opera singer with a masculine voice. In 1760 she purchased Carlisle House and began her assemblies.

Cards, dancings, and concerts amused her brilliantly dressed guests. In the winter of 1766-67, when Johann Christian Bach and Karl Friedrich Abel were alternating as conductors of her grand concerts, Carlisle House was more popular than ever. For the assemblies tickets admitting one gentleman and two ladies were a guinea each—if they were available. So great was the usual demand, that one was often forced to do wire-pulling of various sorts to get them. Balls began at nine and lasted all night. Thackeray allows the putative author of *Barry Lyndon* to describe the clientele:

> All the high and low demireps of the town gathered there, from his grace of Ancaster down to my countryman, Mr. Oliver Goldsmith the poet, and from the Duchess of Kingston down to the Bird of Paradise, or Kitty Fisher. Here I have met very queer characters, who came to queer ends too: poor Hackman, that afterwards was hanged for killing Miss Ray, and (on the sly) his reverence Dr. Simony, whom my friend Sam Foote, of the "Little Theatre," bade to live even after forgery and the rope cut short the unlucky parson's career.

Mrs. Cornelys herself came to a "queer" end, living obscurely during her last years as "Mrs. Smith," vendor of asses' milk at Knightsbridge, and finally dying in the Fleet Prison.

It was assuredly not "on the sly" that the Reverend Mr. Sterne appeared at the great January assembly. A thaw that filled the streets "knee deep" in mud brought out a record crowd. Thin and pale though he was, Laurence put on his best silk breeches and newest ruffles to brave the dampness. The evening was a complete success for him: "the best assembly, and the best concert I ever had the honour to be at." Among the great throng he recognized his Yorkshire neighbors Lady Anne and Lord Belasyse, children of his patron Lord Fauconberg. But more important were his sophisticated London friends among whom he gaily moved from group to group. To this brilliant and unmoral throng Sterne was indeed a merry jester. He recognized his power of charming them and he could feel confident that they would be regaled by the new book that he had in press. The society of Mrs. Cornelys's assemblies was as near an approach to Restoration society as the eighteenth century could boast; and for it, Sterne's astute bawdy, tempered with good humor and sensibility, fortunately took the place of Wycherley's more cynical and thorough-going licentiousness in the London of over half a century before.

Still the most important event of Sterne's season in London was yet to come. Not far from Carlisle House and also near Sterne's quarters in Bond Street lived Commodore (later Sir) William James, an adventurous sea-dog with a history like that of so many eighteenth-century Englishmen who went to sea as boys, performed brilliantly for the East India Company, and came home to buy fine houses, seats in Parliament, and, in some cases, titles. Commodore James's comfortable fortune—which enabled him to have a country villa at Eltham and a town house in Gerrard Street, Soho—had a particularly romantic origin in an expedition that he had led against the famous Malabar pirate Angria, the Indian equivalent of Blackbeard or Jean LaFitte. His wife, the former Anne Goddard, was a gracious but empty-headed lady. Her wealth and her mastery of the social amenities made her drawing-room the gathering place of a large circle of Anglo-Indians—or "nabobs," as they were scornfully called by the old gentry and aristocracy. Already, as *nouveaux riches* the successful Anglo-Indians were accused of overbearing manners; and often tales went the rounds that they had secured their wealth by extortion and tyranny of the worst sort. But not yet had the full measure of satirical venom fallen on their heads as it did in the next decade, and not yet had been directed against them such indignant lines as Cowper's in *The Task:*

> ... thieves at home must hang, but he that puts
> Into his overgorg'd and bloated purse
> The wealth of Indian provinces, escapes.

It is not surprising to find Sterne drifting into the group of the Jameses. Wherever he found an audience—especially if it were a wealthy and gay one—he was likely to be. And he had an unresisting nose for sensibility whether it existed among the Irish ladies in Bath or among the Anglo-Indian ones in Soho. At any rate, toward the end of January he appeared in Mrs. James's drawing-room in Gerrard Street, and there he met the heroine of his last great sentimental debauch, Eliza Draper.

Although the affair developed quickly, it was not a matter of love at first sight. In fact, when the fifty-four-year-old clergyman first saw the twenty-two-year-old matron his immediate impression was that she was plain and that, in spite of her modish clothes, she was unbecomingly dressed. Shortly afterward, he wrote the lady: "I'm half in love with you—I ought to be wholly so." The message accompanied a present of his books. "... the sermons came all hot from the heart," he asserted, with the same sort of sentimentality that he had used on Kitty Fourmantelle, "—I wish that could give 'em any title to be offered to yours—the others came from the head—I'm more indifferent about their reception—"

Sterne confessed that he was first drawn toward Mrs. Draper as an object of compassion. Certainly her story was one for which an aging sentimentalist might easily fall. She had been born at Anjengo—then a prosperous British factory on the Malabar Coast—where her father, May Sclater, was an employee of the East India Company. When she was little more than a babe, she lost both parents and was taken to live with her grandfather in Bombay. At ten she was sent to England and put in a boarding school. Here she spent three unhappy years. At thirteen she returned to Bombay after a wretched voyage of half a year. At fourteen she was married to Daniel Draper, a phlegmatic, morose, but efficient clerk of the East India Company who was twenty years her senior. From the beginning the match was ill-starred. In spite of her unhappy childhood, Eliza was a gay, fat, and rosy little girl who was mated with a man old enough to be her father and who was so conscientious in his attention to his ledgers that he actually developed writer's cramp. A son was born a year after her marriage, and a daughter two years later. Thus at seventeen Eliza was a matron with two babies. In 1764 she was in poor health; moreover, the spasmodic pains in her husband's arm were so annoying to him that he felt the need of taking the cure at some English spa. So the whole family set sail for the homeland. The first part of the visit was not too happy for Eliza, for the children were sick and her husband was still on hand to limit her activities. But after several months Draper returned to India, leaving his wife and children for a presumably indefinite stay. Then ensued the happiest weeks that the young wife had ever had. Having fixed her children with a maternal aunt, she spent her time visiting friends and relatives at country places in Hampshire and Shropshire, finally joining the brisk society of Anglo-Indian London as the guest of Mrs. James, whose husband and Draper were business associates. For Sterne there was appeal enough in this naïve, oval-faced girl—only slightly older than his own daughter—who after so many years of unhappiness and oppression was grasping eagerly for the good things of life and dreading the day when the gates of her old prison house would once again close on her.

While romance was ripening, the ninth volume of *Tristram Shandy* had come from the press on January 29. Sterne's fashionable friends accepted it flatteringly; but there was notable dissent among the general public and the periodical reviewers. The extent of the reprimands and protests is illustrated by a letter drafted by a group of "well-wishers" in which Archbishop Drummond was requested to "deter this wanton scandal to his cloth from proceeding in this lewd ludicrous manner as he has long done to the shame and disgrace of his sacred order and the detriment of society." The convivial prelate, whose dinners were famous both for champagne and wit, could hardly have been expected to take the matter too seriously. And there is no reason to believe that he did so. Several months later he was overwhelming the Vicar of Coxwold with kindness and asking "to stand godfather" for his next production. At this time Sterne himself gives little clue to his reaction to such vigorous public opinion. He merely writes to Panchaud in his usual formula for reporting future prospects to his banker:

> I am going to publish *A Sentimental Journey Through France and Italy*—the undertaking is protected and highly encouraged by all our *noblesse*.

Laurence's ardor for Eliza grew apace. Daily visits were interspersed with letters, constituting a sentimental correspondence that finally grew into the so-called *Journal to Eliza*. There was nothing secretive about the affair. Sterne chattered incessantly about Eliza wherever he went, drinking her health in many a toast and reading her letters to his friends. Even slight acquaintances he made "confidants" in his "Platonic" attachment. Eliza, on her part, was not so voluble as her admirer, but she sent at least one of Sterne's letters to her cousin, Thomas Limbrey Sclater, and she probably let other relatives and friends know of her sentimental conquest. She appeared with Sterne in the rotunda at Ranelagh and in the concert room at Carlisle House, with Anne James decorously in tow; she openly visited his apartments in Bond Street to dine on scalloped oysters; she drove with him "tête-à-tête" to see her children at Salt Hill. Moreover, the two exchanged pictures, Mrs. Draper sitting for a miniature very likely by the fashionable Richard Cosway, who painted her "simple as a vestal."

Few saw anything vicious in the attachment. Certainly Mrs. James, who connived at every stage, felt no pangs of conscience. Richard Griffith's opinion can be taken as reasonably typical of the way in which friends and acquaintances must have felt:

> ...in truth, there was nothing in the affair worth making a secret of—the world, that knew of their correspondence, knew the worst of it, which was merely a simple folly. Any other idea of the matter would be more than the most abandoned vice could render probable. To intrigue with a Vampire! To sink into the arms of *Death alive!*

However it must be recorded that some London friends of Eliza and the Jameses (perhaps members of the wealthy and numerous Newnham family) used all their power to break up the match, employing reasons that Laurence refused to commit to paper so bitterly did he resent them. And at least one purveyor of gossip thought the affair juicy enough to deliver to Mrs. Sterne in Marseilles scarcely a month after Laurence had met Eliza. For reasons all her own, Mrs. Sterne proved a model of *sang-froid*. "I do not care to be informed," she remarked icily to the tale-bearer, "and beg you to drop the matter." And so the matter was dropped—*there*. But Lydia took pains to record the incident for her father with motives that, I fear, were not of the highest sort. Laurence replied by way of reassurance:

> I do not wish to know who was the busy fool, who made your mother uneasy about Mrs. [Draper]. 'Tis true I have a friendship for her, but not to infatuation—I believe I have a judgment enough to discern hers, and every woman's faults.

Laurence was writing defensively to a wife and daughter who, in spite of superficial complacence, were beginning to be afraid that his philandering might affect their financial security. Hence we cannot rely upon the strict truth of the statement, especially since there is evidence of increasing sentimental extravagance in regard to Mrs. Draper. Of one thing there is certainty. Very soon, Sterne was in the clutches of an obsession so intense and so abnormal as to make him both pitiful and ridiculous. However absurd may have been the love-making of the middle-aged Yorick, his previous excesses of sentiment had been hardly excesses at all compared with his outpourings to his Indian. In the letters to Eliza and in the *Journal* we have hints almost for the first time that he is a lonely aging man physically and mentally debilitated.

Sterne's affection for Eliza is not so simple to analyze as it seems. Essentially, it was the product of a confusion that had long existed in Sterne's mind and that he never successfully resolved. Compassion we may accept (on his own word) as a kind of motivating force; and everywhere a paternal attitude is apparent. When his mind became clouded by disease and when his fevered dream-world and the actual world merged, he at times failed to distinguish between Eliza and the beloved Lyd whose affection had been kept from him by a disagreeable wife. Eliza is also associated with the ghostly maid Cordelia, who figures in the *Journal* partially as a creation of Sterne's eccentric fancy and partially as a reminder of Shakespeare's lovely paragon of filial devotion. The future union of himself and Eliza, Sterne at one point compared with the relationship between Fidelia and her father in Addison's *Spectator*, No. 449:

> Certain it is [wrote Addison], that there is no kind of affection so pure and angelic as that of a father to a daughter. He beholds her both with and without regard to her sex.

That no more real element of sex attraction entered into the matter it would be unsafe to say. Concerning Eliza, Sterne wrote to Lord Shelburne: "In some respects there is no difference between my wife and herself." Perhaps the statement is not too revelatory, since for years he had had no physical contact with his wife. But there can be little doubt that his attitude toward women was affected by the idea of a wife-daughter relationship, a constantly shifting balance that produced inevitable emotional confusion.

Sterne was emphatic in telling Eliza that her physical beauty was not her attraction.

> You are not handsome, Eliza [he wrote in an attempt to analyze her charm] nor is yours a face that will please the tenth part of your beholders,–but are something more; for I scruple not to tell you, I never saw so intelligent, so animated, so good a countenance... A something in your eyes, and voice, you possess in a degree more persuasive than any woman I ever saw, read, or heard of.

Beautiful she was not; but her bright eyes and her round face ("the most perfect oval I ever saw," once said Sterne in some contradiction of himself) were sufficient to enable her friends to call her the "belle Indian."

A "something" she undoubtedly had for Sterne, and also several years later for the Abbé Raynal, who succumbed to her "almost incomparable harmony of voluptuousness and decency." But Sterne was sadly misled if he seriously thought she had either real intelligence or strength of character.

As for Eliza's own point of view, there is no evidence that she had any genuine affection for Sterne. An obscure young matron who had led a thwarted life, she suddenly found herself admired by one of the most famous men in England. She was dainty, and she affected the sentimentality of the age in her rhetoric as well as in her ideas. Therefore, flattered by attention that a few months before meeting Sterne she could never have even dreamed of, she returned the sentimental parson's attention, enjoying not only his witty company and the limelight in which it placed her but also the adventure of indulging her own sensibilities. The two called each other Bramin and Bramine in allusion to Sterne's priesthood and Eliza's connections with India. In her dainty and winning way, Eliza informed her doting admirer that the Bramins were "easy, plain, unaffected sons of simple nature" and that there was something exceedingly touching in their conversation and manners. Beyond doubt, she could assume the rôle of old man's darling convincingly. But to Yorick all her gentle histrionics indicated genuine devotion.

William Combe—Sterne's unreliable literary friend—boasted to Samuel Rogers after Yorick's death that it was with him, not Sterne, that Mrs. Draper was in love; and there is evidence that Eliza may have shown him some of Sterne's sentimental letters. However, from Eliza's own letters it would seem that the most solid object of her affection in England was her cousin Tom Sclater, to whom she had been devoted from childhood. At any rate, her affection for her eccentric lover, the famous Yorkshire parson, did not outlast her voyage to India; and after his death her consuming passion was not one of grief for her departed friend but one of almost frantic desire to save herself from any scandal that her connections with Sterne might produce. The whole story of her life leads one to believe that her naïveté and sensibility were in a large measure sham and that beneath them she harbored vanity, flippancy, and a streak of calculating realism.—But we shall see more of the lady as we proceed.

CHAPTER XVI

"REMEMBER THEE! PALE GHOST"

THE CORONETED CHANDELIERS and the Doric arches of Ranelagh, the chintz-hung windows and the china tea cups of Mrs. James's sitting room in Gerrard Street were the *mise en scène* of a fool's paradise in which the sentimental lovers luxuriated for several weeks. Then suddenly tragedy descended. Eliza was summoned back to India. In order to return to a husband for whom she had no affection she was forced to give up her dear friends, the gayest life that she had ever known, and even her children—who were to be left in school at Salt Hill. Indeed, fate had struck with horrible grimness. Completely overcome, Eliza did the womanly thing: she took to her bed. Thus one day when Yorick paid his call the maid would not admit him.

The next morning he was writing impatiently, determined to see his Bramine at any cost:

> I cannot rest Eliza, though I shall call on you at half past twelve, till I know how you do... Remember, my dear, that a friend has the same right as a physician. The etiquettes of the town (you'll say) say otherwise.—No matter! Delicacy and propriety do not always consist in observing their frigid doctrines.

If he had not yet capitulated unreservedly, he certainly did so when he entered a darkened and scented room, saw a white tear-stained face against a pillow, and watched Anne James daub her nose with a cambric handkerchief in ready sympathy. Sterne suggested the situation in *A Sentimental Journey* when he described the "moral delight" that a man of sensibility gets from hearing a miserable tale of a fair sufferer:

> ...though I cannot dry up the fountain of her tears [he wrote], what an exquisite sensation is there still left in wiping them away off the cheeks of the first and fairest of women, as I'm sitting with my handkerchief in my hand in silence the whole night beside her.

Once before he had heard an inexpressibly touching story and had succumbed. His marriage had been the result. This time he was already tethered in a "legal meadow"; but he was not inhibited from folly.

For Eliza's delicate constitution and "alarming" indisposition he melted with tenderness. With his letters he attempted to buoy her sinking spirits. "Fear nothing my dear!" he counseled. "—Hope everything; and the balm of this passion will shed influence on thy health..." When Eliza continued to languish, his concern grew into a sick fear. To Lydia he confided:

> I am apprehensive the dear friend I mentioned in my last letter is going into a decline—I was with her two days ago, and I never beheld a being so alter'd—she has a tender frame and looks like a drooping lily, for the roses are fled from her cheeks —I can never see or talk to this incomparable woman without bursting into tears.

In her exaggerated anguish Eliza even talked of dying; and Yorick prematurely composed an epitaph whose neo-classical stiffness is unfortunately not mollified by its tender of eternally flowing tears.

Interestingly enough, in the depth of his melancholia Sterne turned to his wife and daughter for succor:

> Friendship is the balm and cordial of life [he wrote to Lydia in a highly illuminating passage], and without it, 'tis a heavy load not worth sustaining.—I am unhappy—thy mother and thyself at a distance from me, and what can compensate for

> such a destitution?—For God's sake persuade her to come and fix in England, for life is too short to waste in separation—and whilst she lives in one country, and I in another, many people will suppose it proceeds from choice—besides I want thee near me, thou child and darling of my heart.

But the tender mood toward Mrs. Sterne was not long sustained. As for that lady herself, we could not expect her to have returned much sympathy.

In the eighteenth century the matter of making a passage to India was far from that of merely consigning oneself for a month or more to the luxury of a great ocean liner. The voyage normally required over half a year; and shipboard comforts were few if they were not provided by the passengers themselves. The task of making proper arrangements sadly forced Mrs. Draper to leave London for Deal, the port of embarkation, at least ten days before the *Earl of Chatham* sailed out of the Downs. Somehow Eliza managed to mend her shattered nerves and to steel herself for the ordeal of parting. The distraught Yorick went to bid his Bramine goodbye in her chaise. The awful moment came and neither could find words to tell the other adieu. As the horses clattered away through Gerrard Street, Sterne turned with a constricted heart and Mrs. James dissolved in tears. Unless Sterne made a trip to Deal with Commodore and Mrs. James before the boat sailed, he never saw his oval-faced Eliza again.

The void in his life was painful. For consolation he haunted the Jameses' house, unable to stay away from the spot which had been the scene of so much sentimental pleasure. Mrs. James could be counted on to weep with him. When he was not at the Jameses' he was writing Eliza letters and busying himself about stocking her cabin with things that would bring amusement and comfort. He sent instructions to a pilot at Deal to provide the cabin with the best armchair that he could purchase; and he fulfilled Eliza's commission to provide from the London manufacturer, Zumpe, a hammer and pliers to tune her small pianoforte (not the large instrument of today, but a small rectangular affair easily installed in a cabin). Besides, he provided her with ten brass screws to hang her "necessaries" on.—He had purchased twelve, but he had sentimentally kept two for his own "cabin" at Coxwold. "I shall never hang, or take my hat off one of them," he promised, "but I shall think of you."—A celestial and a terrestrial globe completed the equipment.

Before she left London Eliza had been fortunate in securing as a traveling companion the vivacious Miss Hester Light, who was on her way to join her fiancé in India. Her first letter from Deal told of other people who were making the voyage, among whom she mentioned a young soldier whose eyes seemed to be on her companion. In his reply Yorick turned the compliment to his Bramine. Surely, the young man's eyes must be on her, who was "a thousand times more amiable." Further, he exclaimed in flattering envy of the soldier's rare fortune: "Five months with Eliza; and in the same room; and an amorous son of Mars besides!" Admittedly there was danger; but Eliza could be counted on to use her discretion. For the moment Yorick pretended that he was more concerned about the fresh paint in her cabin than about the rivalry of a lusty young man.—Paint, he wrote, might have a pernicious effect on the nerves and lungs of his delicate friend.—But in the last paragraph of his letter he subtly warned against shipboard intimacies of the deceptive sort.

When Eliza wrote telling of her continued illness, Sterne lapsed into incredibly extravagant pity. He begged her to stay another year. "Write to your husband," he urged; "—tell him the truth of your case." Mr. Draper's only reason for calling his wife back to India, suggested

Yorick, was the fear of her running him into debt. And if this were the only difficulty her Bramin himself would indemnify Mr. Draper:

> With joy would I give my whole subsistence—nay, sequester my livings, and trust the treasures Heaven has furnished my head with, for a future subsistence.

Such folly could have arisen only from a fevered and disordered brain, for the expenses of supporting his own wife abroad were all but unbearable. He had already offered to be a father to Eliza's children—a proposal that was foolish enough.—But the meridian of his madness came in another proposal:

> I will send for my wife and daughter, and they shall carry you, in pursuit of health, to Montpellier, the wells of Bancois, the Spa, or whither thou wilt. Thou shalt direct them, and make parties of pleasure in what corner of the world fancy points out to thee.

Never was there a wilder orgy of presumption. One can imagine Bess playing nurse and maid to Yorick's pale flower.—Consistency in thought, however extravagant, hardly outlasts the paragraph. In the next paragraph Laurence is writing:

> Talking of widows—pray, Eliza, if ever you are such, do not think of giving yourself to some wealthy nabob—because I shall design to marry you myself.—My wife cannot live long.... No Swift so loved his Stella, Scarron his Maintenon, or Waller his Sacharissa, as I will love, and sing thee, my wife elect!

But what he was offering, he hinted in the final sentence, was not conjugal joys of the usual kind but the opportunity for Eliza to be the reincarnation of Addison's Fidelia, who performed "the duty of a nurse with all the devotion of a bride" and whose highest joy and glory was "helping on an old man's slipper"! This kind of delirium was to impregnate the *Journal.*

The melancholy state into which Sterne had worked himself is pitifully apparent. Again, the strain was too great for his "poor, fine spun frame." He had no sooner finished dispatching the letter to Eliza than a vessel broke in his lungs and bleeding continued until four o'clock in the morning. All the India handkerchiefs that his friend had given him were soaked in blood. ("It came, I think, from my heart!") Finally, a fevered sleep brought a vision of Eliza flying from the Downs to comfort him—or, rather, it was a confused vision of Lydia and Eliza.

Well might he conclude that he was "within the verge of the gates of death." But serious though the attack was, with the end of the bleeding came a sense of renewed strength and hope characteristic of the disease. And Yorick summoned up all his energy for an impassioned farewell letter.

The *Earl of Chatham* sailed from the Downs on April 3. Now Sterne could no longer dispatch daily letters. But before Eliza had left London, the two had contracted to keep a journal for each other in which they would record their thoughts and meditations. The obvious model was Swift's *Journal to Stella.* Sterne began the first part of his journal when Eliza left London and sent it to her at Deal before she sailed. The second part he dispatched on April 13 by a merchant who was leaving for Bombay. The third and only extant part he still had in his possession at his death. Eliza's counterpart has never come to light.

In spite of the fact that throughout the affair with Mrs. Draper Sterne expressed in his letters and his journal a great deal of genuine—though abortive—feeling, much of the time he was inescapably the poseur and the literary artist, dramatizing himself with an eye on the public and even contemplating the pecuniary value of his recorded intimacies. "I shall print your letters," he wrote to Eliza, "as finished essays, 'by an unfortunate Indian lady.'" He believed that they would sell well, and he regarded them as a possible means of producing ready cash if he should need it. He admitted that he read them to "half the literati in town," wringing from his auditors compliments for the dainty author. At the beginning of the extant portion of the *Journal to Eliza* he wrote, ostensibly for some future publisher:

> This Journal wrote under the fictitious names of Yorick and Draper—and sometimes of the Bramin and Bramine—but 'tis a diary of the miserable feelings of a person separated from a Lady for whose society he languished—
>
> The real names are foreign—and the account a copy from a French manuscript—in Mr. S[terne']s hands—but wrote as it is to cast a veil over them....

The *Journal* contains much that is mawkish and morbid. Some of the mawkishness was engendered by disease; some was deliberate. Like Byron in the next century, Sterne was not infrequently a delighted spectator at the pageant of his own bleeding heart. Anything was his quarry when he wanted to produce an effect. Although the evidence is not completely clear, it is possible that he paraphrased in the *Journal* at least one letter written to Elizabeth Lumley a quarter of a century before. The classic example of this ingenious lifting (if lifting it was) is this easily recognizable passage concerning the forlorn lover, in which there is little more than a shifting of names:

> —I have just been eating my chicken, sitting over my repast upon it, with tears—a bitter sauce—Eliza! but I could eat it with no other—when Molly spread the table cloth, my heart fainted within me—one solitary plate—one knife—one fork—one glass!

But whatever may be the extent of Yorick's posing, one must take the false starts in his journal, the erasures, the repetition, the erratic spelling, the incoherence, and the incorrect dating as evidences of real tortures of body, mind, and soul.

While Yorick was well enough to dine out, he and Mrs. James continued to talk and weep together, and to despise the cruel Mr. Draper. As an appropriately sentimental gesture the distressed lover ordered a map of the Atlantic Ocean so that he could follow the *Earl of Chatham* day by day. He was increasingly plagued by loss of blood and by evil dreams "of things terrible and impossible—that Eliza is false to Yorick, or Yorick is false to Eliza." But through evil dreams and periods of hemorrhages he doggedly continued his journal.

By the middle of April he was seriously sick and weak. He recorded his trials with necessary brevity:

Monday: April 15th.

Worn out with fevers of all kinds... stayed the whole evening at home—no pleasure or interest in either society or diversions—What a change, my dear girl, hast thou made in me!—In a high fever all the night.

April: 16. and got up so ill, I could not go to Mrs. James as I had promised her.—Took James's Powder however—and leaned the whole day with my head upon my hand; sitting most dejectedly at the table with my Eliza's picture before me—sympathizing and soothing me—O my Bramine! my Friend! my— [here he cancelled *future wife*] Helpmate!

James's Powder was a famous nostrum of the day. Like Oliver Goldsmith and many other contemporaries who should have known better, Sterne placed his faith in it. The result of his assiduous dosing, Yorick would have us believe, was a painful and ridiculous occurrence. Unfortunately, after taking the medicine one day he incautiously exposed himself:

> The injury I did myself in catching cold upon James's Powder, fell, you must know, upon the worst part it could,–the most painful, and most dangerous of any in the human body.–It was on this crisis, I called in an able surgeon and with him an able physician to inspect my disaster.–'Tis a venereal case, cried my two scientific friends.–'Tis impossible. At least to be that, replied I, for I have had no commerce whatever with the sex–not even with my wife, added I, these fifteen years.–You are [poxed] however my good friend, said the surgeon....

The incredulous scientific friends, refusing to listen to his argument, recommended the usual treatment, a course of mercury. Thus the Yorkshire parson faced the painful and undignified prospect of undergoing "the chastisement of the grossest sensualist." Even before he was actually put on the mercury his treatment was severe enough. He was bled and placed on a rigid diet of water gruel. This regimen, together with the unfortunate breaking of a bandage and the consequent loss of more blood than the original bleeding demanded, came near being fatal. On April 24 Yorick was so weak that he could barely scribble a farewell to Eliza as his entry in the journal for the day. "I'm going–" he wrote; but on the next day he continued, "Am a little better–So shall not depart as I apprehended." In fact, he had by this time gathered enough strength to tell the whole story of his amazing diagnosis.

Although he persisted in regarding the occurrence as a "whimsical" story which, aside from the account in the journal, he told twice again,–once in a letter to Lord Shelburne and then in a letter to Lydia,–the whole affair may have been much more serious than he intimated. The whimsicality he might easily have attempted to use as a smoke screen, subtly providing an explanation for whatever gossip might have arisen and forestalling the presentation of the scandal to Lydia and his wife in a far different light. Of course, the diagnosis might have been wrong. On the other hand, if one traces the case history as I have already suggested, one is forced to the conclusion that the doctors might also have been right. Saintsbury was positive that Sterne had syphilis, arguing that he acquiesced to the diagnosis in treating himself with *extrait de Saturne*, a French nostrum, apart from the treatment of the physicians. But the case is not quite so clear as Saintsbury assumed. Since the doctors informed Sterne that the disease might have lain dormant for twenty years, the patient might reasonably have been frightened. Patently, Sterne by his actions admitted the possibility of the disease. But an admission of a possibility and the acceptance of a fact are two different things. The real truth is almost impossible to determine on either side.

Yorick was not neglected in his illness. Perhaps he even had too much company; for his room seemed always crowded with friendly visitors and his door-knocker rapped incessantly. After seven days of a water-gruel diet he was allowed chicken, and the next day a glass of wine. His periods of delirium continued, and he imagined Eliza beside him talking of the progress of their friendship. On April 27, not yet able to walk across the room from his armchair, he recorded that he spent much time poring over the ever-present picture of Eliza and longing for reunion with her. ("Jesus! grant me but this, I will deserve it–") The next day Mrs. James made one of her numerous calls. In spite of her glowing kindness, she could be stupidly indiscreet in the sick-room:

> Tears ran down her cheeks when she saw how pale and wan I was–and never gentle creature sympathized more tenderly.–I beseech you, cried the good soul, not to regard either difficulties or expenses, but fly to Eliza directly–I see you will die without her.

As sick as he was, Yorick was still actor enough to assume his best melodramatic manner. "Tell her, my dear friend," he whispered weakly to the accompaniment of Anne James's elegant sniffles, "that I will meet her in a better world—and that I have left this, because I could not live without her. Tell Eliza, my dear friend . . . that I died broken hearted—and that you were a witness to it."

The next day, thanks to his well-meaning friend, he had a relapse, and he was barely able to write, "Come!—Come to me soon my Eliza and save me."

Yet only a few days later he was able to take a drive in Hyde Park. Among the smartly dressed riders he encountered an old friend whom he designated as "Sheba" and who sounds much like the wicked and spirited Anne Stuart, Lady Warkworth. After passing Yorick twice unintentionally, the lady stopped and inquired after his health, remarking on his ill appearance:

> I *fear* your wife is dead, quoth Sheba.
> —No, you don't *fear* it, Sheba, said I
> —Upon my word, Solomon! I would quarrel with you, was you not so ill.—
> —If you knew the cause of my illness, Sheba, replied I, you would quarrel but the more with me.—
> —You lie, Solomon! answered Sheba, for I know the cause already—and am so little out of charity with you upon it—that I give you leave to come and drink tea with me before you leave town.
> —You're a good honest creature, Sheba.
> —No! you rascal, I am not—but I'm in love, as much as you can be for your life.
> —I'm glad of it, Sheba, said I.
> —You lie, said Sheba, and so cantered away.

Thus Sterne continued acting his part as Lothario. That evening he appeared once again at Ranelagh for two hours, undoubtedly looking more like a ghost than anything that had been seen in Cock Lane.

For his exertion he paid with another relapse; and the next day he had to write the entry in his diary flat on his back.

On the same day, May 3, Eliza—having arrived at Sao Thiago, Cape Verde Islands—was writing an account of her voyage to her adored Tom Sclater. She had already dispatched part of her journal to Yorick. A few days after leaving the Cape Verde Islands the *Earl of Chatham* met a Dutch vessel homeward bound from India and transferred mail to England, including a second part of Eliza's journal. Two weeks or more later—after the boat had crossed the Line—Eliza seems to have dispatched a third installment. The first two packets Yorick was to receive simultaneously on July 27 and the third on August 10. If we may judge from Yorick's reactions, in her journal Eliza went through all the requisite sentimental posturings, giving lengthy accounts of her pains and her dangers. The third letter was most heart-rending, including—

> a melancholy history of herself and sufferings since they left Iago—continual and most violent rheumatism all the time—a fever brought on with fits—and attended with delirium: and every terrifying symptom—the recovery of this has left her low—and emaciated to a skeleton.

To Mrs. James, too, she had written of illness at the beginning of the journey. But her letter to Tom Sclater—more reliable because less affected—gives a different picture. One gets the impression that during the course of the voyage her ill health and her melancholy state of mind had vanished. She had found Miss Light an engaging and stimulating companion, and she had probably taken delighted interest in Hester's approaching marriage to the promising George Stratton. She assured Sclater that she was "all life and air and spirits"—although she admitted, naturally enough, that her heart heaved with sighs and her eyes betrayed agitating emotions when she thought of England and her dear "connections" there. She even undertook to rally her cousin for taking his friendships too seriously.

Running ahead of our story, we do not get a further glimpse of the lady until November 29 in another letter to her cousin. The boat had called at Madras where Miss Light had disembarked and where Eliza had had a visit of some two months. Then Eliza had set out again on her way home. As the "belle Indian" she felt that she had been a considerable social success. "I have endeavoured to make myself popular everywhere," she wrote with a vanity not unlike her forgotten Bramin's; "success has attended me. . ." She intimated that there was a serious breach between her husband and herself; but she no longer regarded her plight sentimentally. With cool realism she resolved to make the best of a bad situation for the sake of her children, for the sake of her honor, and for the material advantages that such a course would bring. After all, Daniel Draper promised to be a real nabob. His excellent position and his fine country house, "High Meadows," near Bombay were not unpleasant to contemplate. Who knew that Eliza might not one day be able to return to England as the mistress of a proud fortune?—This was the paragon of sensibility, the delicate and ingenuous spirit to whom Yorick cried out in his loneliness.

Sterne's health improved slowly. By May 6 he was able to dine out again; but after his exertion he complained again of disordered health. In spite of his weakness he was looking forward to the return to Coxwold and to the beginning of work on *A Sentimental Journey*. When it was noised about that he was planning once more to leave for Yorkshire, invitations came in handsomely. He dined with Lord and Lady Belasyse, breakfasted with Lady Spencer, and appeared again at Ranelagh for an hour. On May 17 he felt strong enough to attend Court at St. James's Palace. He had planned to set out for Coxwold about the twentieth, but Lord and Lady Spencer delayed him by giving a farewell dinner in his honor. He was hardly capable of enjoying the event fully, for on the following day–the day of his departure–he wrote to John Talbot Dillon: "I am ill, very ill–I languish most affectingly–I am sick both soul and body."

Sterne had made many a journey between London and York; but never had he made a braver one than that on which he set out on May 22. So weak was he that he had to lie on a huge pillow arranged in the bottom of the chaise –"like a bale of cadaverous goods assigned to Pluto and company." On the way he fared badly; as a consequence he was forced to spend two days at the Brodsworth home of Archbishop Drummond, five miles north of Doncaster.

When he arrived in Coxwold on May 28, he was so ill that he went directly to bed.

> Alas! poor Yorick!–'*remember thee! Pale Ghost* [he exclaimed in self-pity, inaccurately quoting his *Hamlet*] *remember thee–whilst memory holds a seat in this distracted world....*'

On the continued insistence of his doctors, he began the course of corrosive mercury (for what the French called an *ecclesiastic rheum*, he remarked wryly). The harsh medicine tortured him with terrible colics in stomach and bowels. He had submitted to the treatment, he assures us, "as my Uncle Toby did, in drinking water, upon the wound he received in his groin–*merely for quietness' sake*."

While he was recovering, news came that Lydia and her mother were coming home. Although a few months earlier Sterne had been urging their return, he could not now feel that their coming was entirely altruistic, especially since they had consented on the condition that they be allowed to return to France for a permanent residence. Because they seemed particularly concerned about settling financial matters, the sick Yorick feared that they were on a mission of pillage. In the *Journal* he assured Eliza that he would be plucked bare of money, linen, and plate:

> Eliza, what say you, Eliza! [he continued] Shall we join our *little capitals together?*—Will Mr. Draper give us leave?—He may safely—if your virtue and honour are only concerned.—'Twould be safe in Yorick's hands, as in a brother's.

Seized by such madness, Sterne began a letter to Draper himself. It is a document to make one sick at heart, so full it is of false starts, cancellations, and general indirection. "I <am> fell <really dear Sir>in love with yr Wife—but tis a Love, You would honour me for. . ." Such was the burden of the abortive attempt, the futility of which Sterne certainly must have recognized in a saner moment. There is no reason to believe that the letter was ever revised for the post.

During this period Sterne seemed often suspended between the world of actuality and that of day dreams, failing to distinguish between them. He communed with the spirit maiden Cordelia. Eliza visited him as he sat writing in his library. He built (in imagination and to some extent in actuality) a "sweet little apartment" for her in Shandy Hall:

> 'Tis a neat little simple elegant room, overlooked only by the sun—just big enough to hold a sofa,—for us—a table, four chairs, a bureau—and a book case.—They are to be all yours, room and all—and there Eliza! shall I enter ten times a day to give thee testimonies of my devotion—

Yet there are indications that by the end of the first week in June he was showing signs of marked improvement. To a friend back in London he wrote on June 7 in such a way as to indicate that his recovery had been miraculously rapid or that much of the heaviest sentimentality in the *Journal* had been studied, or both.

> I am as happy as a prince, at Coxwold—and I wish you could see in how princely a manner I live—'tis a land of plenty. I sit down alone to venison, fish and wild fowl, or a couple of fowls or ducks, with curds, and strawberries, and cream.... I am in high spirits.—Care never enters this cottage. I take the air every day in my postchaise, with my two long-tailed horses—they turn out good ones; and as to myself, I think I am better upon the whole for the medicines, and regimen I submitted to in town.

Nearly a month later he included the same description in the *Journal*—when it was more appropriate than it would have been to the sentimental day-dreaming concerning Eliza written on the same day!

In the *Journal* the day-dreaming continues. By making financial readjustments and buying annuities for his wife and his daughter, Yorick at this point concludes that he will "purchase peace" and will leave the way clear for Eliza to come to Yorkshire. He expects her, he says, in the fall of the next year. He dreams of her swinging to his arm in his walks to his "convent"—the "delicious mansion of our long lost sisters" and the haunt of "Cordelia," his imaginary confidante; and, as if Eliza were expected to return immediately, he speaks of having plucked up a score of briars from the path so that they may not "scratch or incommode" her. The object of his "evening walks" and of his fantastic meditations was the ruins of Byland Abbey, which had been built about two miles northeast of Coxwold by twelfth-century Cistercian monks. Since a walk of four miles an evening would be a formidable undertaking for a weakened man, it is reasonable to believe that these sentimental jaunts were also more a matter of fancy than of fact. Nevertheless, Yorick affected a daily communion with the ghostly sisters and the equally ghostly Cordelia, baring to them the open secrets of his sleeve-worn heart.

In spite of his illness, he had not neglected the work for which he had planned. Before he left London he had busied himself with getting subscriptions for *A Sentimental Journey*, and on February 20 he had boasted in his usual manner that "all the nobility here almost have honoured me with their names." Some, it is true, honoured him with their names but failed to include their half-guineas. Six days before he left the city he commissioned his black friend Sancho, who had already been energetic in his behalf, to dun the Duke and Duchess of Montagu and their son, Lord Monthermer, for the cash.

When shortly after his return to Coxwold he first attempted to set pen to paper, he affected to find his preoccupation with Eliza a serious deterrent:

> Cannot write my travels [he entered in his journal on June 3], or give one half hour's close attention to them, upon thy account of my dearest friend—Yet write I must, and what to do with you, whilst I write—I declare I know not—

By June 13, however, he had enough manuscript to make some fifty pages of print. For Eliza's first appearance in the book, he composed on June 17 a remarkable annotation to be used by future editors and scholars:

> [She]—was handsome—genteel—engaging—and of such gentle dispositions and so enlightened an understanding,—that Yorick, (whether he made much opposition is not known) from an acquaintance—soon became her admirer—they caught fire, at each other at the same time—and they would often say, without reserve to the world, and without any idea of saying wrong in it, that their affections for each other were

unbounded—Mr. Draper dying in the year xxxxx—this lady returned to England, and Yorick the year after becoming a widow—they were married—and retiring to one of his livings in Yorkshire, where was a most romantic situation—they lived and died happily.—and are spoke of with honour in the parish to this day—

Just at this point Yorick did a baffling thing. Fresh from writing such an expression of devotion to his Bramine, he seems to have picked up another sheet to write a letter to an unidentified Countess, declaring his love to her in the same terms in which he had been expressing his affection for Eliza—even to the point of using Cordelia and the nuns of Byland Abbey as part of the sentimental "machinery." At some later date Sterne, with an eye on future publication, went through the letter and substituted for the Countess his pet name for Eliza. Accepting Lydia's erroneous date of 1767 for the letter that Sterne had written from Mount's Coffee House to Lady Warkworth two years earlier, Thackeray was quick to charge flagrant duplicity. Eliza's ship was hardly out of the Downs, he declared, before Laurence was hurrying away to make an assignation with another woman. If Thackeray had seen the letter to the unknown Countess he would assuredly have used it as evidence for his general contention. And, indeed, it is difficult to explain away. There is, however, a possible explanation that seems not to do too much violence to inherent probability. One may observe that the letter was written just when Sterne was composing the portion of *A Sentimental Journey* in which Yorick was tempering his affection for Madame de L*** by remembering his vow to Eliza and in which the sentimental traveler was attempting to compose the letter to which La Fleur's gallantry had committed him:

> I begun and begun again; and though I had nothing to say, and that nothing might have been expressed in half a dozen lines, I made half a dozen beginnings, and could no way please myself.

With such ill success, he finally gave up and copied the amusing letter from La Fleur's collection. Whether originally Sterne had planned to give the incident its extremely clever turn—burlesquing the sentimental billet-doux—it is impossible to say. He may easily have planned at the outset to include in the chapter a letter or a part of a letter written by Yorick to Madame de L***. In that event he may have sat down to the task directly after a little evening walk in the direction of the ruined abbey. But, carried away by the spirit of the evening, he was led into a meditation on the grave of Cordelia with attendant luxuriation in sentimentality. If we examine the letter we shall see that, throughout, the addressee serves as little more than a stimulus to the writer's narcissistic delight in his own sensibility. Early, Eliza and the putative addressee probably became thoroughly confused and, in fact, lost in the rhapsody. And the letter turned into a sentimental exercise addressed to a figment of the writer's enthusiastic imagination—an abstraction who in one paragraph is capable of conquest and who in the next is coldly indifferent. ("Why have I never received—one gracious nod, from you?") The final paragraph tapers off weakly:

> I want to hear you say, you have something more than cold esteem for me—in short, I know not what I want—

When the letter was finished Sterne quickly realized that it was unsuitable for either Madame de L*** or for Eliza and thus could find no place either in *A Sentimental Journey* or in his journal. Yet since he would often plagiarize from himself and since he might therefore want to preserve a sentimental *jeu d'esprit* for future use, he copied the letter in his letter book, addressing it to the Countess of ****** to give it the air of having arisen from a fashionable intrigue. His later attempt to adapt the letter to Eliza came when he saw the value of preserving some consistency in the great love story that he wanted to leave to posterity.

This explanation may not be satisfying at all points. Nevertheless, the chief argument for the letter's being little more than a sentimental exercise should rest on the confused tone permeating it. It is all but impossible to associate it directly with any one person whom Sterne knew. And it is always possible that a letter which might be written to anybody might also be written to nobody.—But if we must believe that it *was* written to a flirtatious lady of rank—like the Countess of Edgcumbe, for example, a daughter of Archbishop Gilbert whom the Yorkshire parson had known for years and to whom he admittedly wrote many letters—one does not have to believe that his defection was extremely serious. "Great wits jump" might have been the explanation of one who was always under the necessity of having some Dulcinea in his mind. Devotion to Eliza he undoubtedly had. But only one whose sentimentality is far more egregious than Sterne's would believe unreservedly that Yorick was dying of love rather than of physical disease. He had been and he remained the connoisseur of sensibility, and he should normally be expected to take his sensibility where he found it.

To return to the story of Sterne's health, on June 19 the indomitable man was in unusually good spirits, and several days afterward he reported that he had quit all medicine. Earlier in his journal he had told of purchasing a milk ass in order to live "by suction." The diet of ass's milk seemed a wonderful restorative. The only thing that concerned him now was the return of his wife—on which count he reported receiving commiseration from all his friends.

In the last week of June he was so much revived that he hitched up his chaise and two fine horses for a proposed ten-day visit to "Crazy Castle"—packing with his luggage the manuscript of *A Sentimental Journey*, the journal, and his *vade mecum*, the picture of Eliza. As usual, Hall-Stevenson's table was surrounded with much company. Part of his visit Sterne enjoyed, especially when he engaged with his friend in his old sport of racing chaises over a five-mile beach "as even as a mirror." But no longer did he find the company and the dissipation to his liking. Especially disagreeable to him was Peter ("Bombay") Lascelles, a director of the East India Company, a friend of Commodore James, and a nabob of hard rind and no sensibility. Undoubtedly, Lascelles, who knew Eliza's family connections, refused to be sympathetic with the lady's eccentric admirer. Another disconcerting circumstance to Yorick was a night of fever in which he dreamed that Eliza had married the captain of the *Earl of Chatham*. So he cut short his visit by several days and went home.

Back in Shandy Hall he lapsed once more into dreams of redecorating and renovating the house for Eliza's reception:

> Your little temple I have described—and what it will hold—but if ever it holds you and I, my Eliza—the room will not be too little for us—but we shall be *too big* for the room.—

Thus runs the poetry of sentimental love! The youthful John Donne had written of a more virile passion:

> For love, all love of other sights controls,
> And makes one little room, an everywhere.

CHAPTER XVII

FAREWELL TO SHANDY HALL

THE REMARKABLE CONTRAST between the two almost simultaneous productions of Yorick's last months has frequently been pointed out. Most often the *Journal* has been regarded as a unique exhibition of sentimentality in the raw, uninhibited and unrevised; and *A Sentimental Journey*, as an exquisitely conceived masterpiece of sensibility in charming prose. However, adequate warning has already been sounded against regarding the *Journal* as a purely spontaneous overflow of powerful feelings. Sterne himself plainly intimated almost at the outset that he was intent upon creating another love legend, at least in the tradition of Swift and Stella if not in that of Abelard and Heloïse. If one needs additional proof that he conceived of the whole affair dramatically, one has only to turn to an entry made in the *Journal* early in July:

> –be assured my Bramine that ere everything is ripe for our drama–I shall work hard to fit out and decorate a little theatre for us to act on–

In writing the *Journal*, it is true, Sterne was not thinking of immediate publication. Nevertheless, both the *Journal* and the *Journey* must be regarded as conscious literary productions, the main difference being in the degree and kind of artistry applied. Thus they were rivals for the time of the author; and when it became more important to write for the guineas of the present than for the sympathetic tears of posterity, the *Journal* was broken off. It is also important to remember that the *Journal* might have been broken off for another reason: namely, that the author had become wearied by the strain of recording distorted sentiments.

In regard to the *Journey*, Sterne's decision to interpolate it among installments of *Tristram Shandy* calls for some consideration. We have already observed that two years previously the *Monthly Review* had settled upon Sterne's mastery of the "pathetic" as the most significant element of his genius and had singled out the episode of Le Fevre as being of more honor to Yorick than all his sermons. "Give us none but amiable or worthy, or exemplary characters," the reviewer had continued; "or, if you will, to enliven the drama, throw in the *innocently humourous*... Let morality, let the cultivation of virtue be your aim—let wit, humour, elegance, and pathos be the means." Although the advice was given in a far more amiable manner than that in which Warburton's earlier advice was given, it has been apparent that Sterne was not quick to follow it. But in two years the tide of disapproval had swelled, finally engulfing even such a staunch friend as Mrs. Montagu. And the agitation caused by Book IX of *Tristram*, especially among the clergy, was enough to give the author some alarm. The typical clerical reaction found expression in the verses of the Reverend Dr. William Dodd (who a decade later might have been seen swinging at Tyburn for forgery):

> Yes, they will laugh;—but who, vain Sterne, inquire!
> The wretched sons of vice and foul desire;
> To these your page immoral may be dear,
> But virtue o'er it sheds the conscious tear:
> The wise, the modest, view it with concern,
> Detest the matter, and the master mourn.

Thus when Sterne wrote to Lydia on February 23, 1767, that he had laid a plan for "something new, quite out of the beaten track," his resolution may have covered more than a continuation of his banter of travel books in substituting the sentimental adventures of the traveler for the usual accounts of nations, peoples, and sights of historical and aesthetic interest. Such treatment had been so thoroughly anticipated in Book VII of *Tristram* (aptly called "The First Sentimental Journey" by Professor Cross) that it could hardly be called new. What Yorick had apparently decided to do was to give the public the pathos it demanded—at least on the surface; at the same time actually to relinquish none of the devices that made *Tristram* successful. He took pains to create the right attitude toward the book even among his friends. To Richard Griffith he advertised the new work as a work of "redemption"; and he wrote to another friend, "If it is not thought a chaste book, mercy on them that read it, for they must have warm imaginations indeed!" The moral purpose he stated in a letter to Mrs. James: "I told you my design in it was to teach us to love the world and our fellow creatures better than we do. . ." The measure of his success in this new venture in "innocence" is seen in a remark that Mrs. Montagu made, unfortunately too late for Yorick to know about it: "Poor Tristram's last performance was the best, his sentimental journey would not have misbecome a young Ensign."

Was Sterne, then, merely shedding crocodile tears over the dead ass and "Poor Maria," and was the whole book the result of trickery and sham? Thackeray thought so, and others have concurred. On the other hand, Professor Cross has been willing to assert: "Sterne's emotions are . . . always sincere." Perhaps it is wiser to take neither position; for in taking either, one would seem to neglect Sterne's dramatic approach to his material. It is always well to remember that Sterne was constantly an artist seeking for effects and that his purpose was often not so much to render emotions as to educe them. Thus it appears that the relationship between his own emotions and the question of his artistic sincerity is of less importance than many have chosen to make it. The fact that he produced a work of astonishing stylistic finish in a period of physical suffering and mental confusion is magnificent testimony to his will to achieve his artistic purpose. Here, at least, there is no insincerity.

Back to the *Journal*, the entry for June 30 is, on first glance, well established in the devotional mood. It had been almost three months since Eliza's sailing. Imagining her approach to India, Yorick now expressed concern lest Mr. Draper should receive his wife with such caressing gentleness that she would give up the idea of quitting him! But even in the midst of a very sentimental passage comes a hint—a bare hint, it is true—that Sterne was developing a a sense of futility about the journal. He had mentioned a letter that he had written to his friend Dillon, the recent happy winner of a "fair Indian" like Yorick's Bramine:

> I have wrote him a whole sheet of paper about us [he confessed]—it ought to have been copied in this Journal—but the uncertainty of your ever reading it, makes me omit that, with a thousand other things, which when we meet, shall beguile us of many a long winter's night.

On the same day he wrote in a letter to an unidentified friend a statement suggesting that his immediate concerns must be other than those of luxuriating in his affection for Eliza:

> I ought now to be busy from sun rise, to sun set, for I have a book to write—a wife to receive—an estate to sell—a parish to superintend, and what is worst of all, a disquieted heart to reason with—

It may also be worth observing that on the same June 30—a day on which he seems hardly to have left his writing table—he wrote an unusually calm and unsentimental statement of his philosophy to the Negro, Ignatius Sancho:

> I am a resigned being, Sancho, and take health and sickness as I do light and darkness, or the vicissitudes of seasons—that is, just as it pleases God to send them—and accommodate myself to their periodical returns, as well as I can—only taking care, whatever befalls me in this silly world—not to lose my temper at it. This I believe, friend Sancho, to be the truest philosophy—for this we must be indebted to ourselves, but not to our fortunes.

During the next few days much of the heaviest sentimentality vanished completely from the *Journal.* Yorick's health seemed better. He delighted in the life of Coxwold. Only the cloud of Mrs. Sterne's visit hung over him, but even that hard prospect was ameliorated by the sympathy of his friends for him. Hall-Stevenson had even written verses about his plight. Sterne's own testimony leaves little doubt that his work on *A Sentimental Journey* was now his most important concern, from which he *stole* "something each day . . . to obey a more sentimental impulse" and to write to Eliza. The writing did not go so rapidly as he would have liked, for his head was too full of other matters; but he was determined to finish before returning to London in order not to "break faith with the world." No satirist should be able to write of him as Churchill had written of Johnson when the learned doctor delayed in bringing out his edition of Shakespeare:

> He for subscribers baits his hook,
> And takes their cash—but where's the book?

The relative pleasantness of life was upset by two letters from the South of France. The ladies in Avignon had not received Yorick's last letters, and their tone of marked coolness was disturbing. In propitiation Sterne rushed off a letter of "consolation and good will," begging the two to take post immediately and to arrive in York in time for the August races. His harassment brought a resurgence of tender feeling toward Eliza for whom he affected to maintain daily devotional exercises, kissing her picture, her shawl, and other oddments that she had left him—the fervor of the rites having been increased by the knowledge that he must soon hide the sacred relics from the curious eyes of his wife. As the days went on his vexation toward Bess grew:

> She has now entered upon a new plan of waging war with me [he complained], a thousand miles off—thrice a week this last month, has the quietest man under heaven been outraged by her letters—I have offered to give her every shilling I was worth, except my preferment, to be let alone and left in peace by her—Bad Woman!

When he did not turn to Eliza for consolation, he accepted the good offices of his tom-cat, purring *pianissimo* beside him. And, again, he pictured himself walking in his garden like a disturbed spirit, calling on heaven and his fair Indian to come to his succor. However, a more practical idea came to him—that of taking sanctuary at Skelton, where Garrick and Coleman were already reported to be guests.

The visit was good for his spirits. There was no "Bombay" Lascelles to chill his enthusiasm. His friends at Skelton allowed him to play his game of reciting Eliza's virtues and showing her picture. On the day after his arrival he dined with Charles Turner of Kirkleatham, an eccentric country squire whose house was overrun with dogs and whose passion for hunting was so great that he was rarely found out of his odd sports costume of Kersey coat, leather breeches, and straw boots. Yorick hardly risked the precious picture on the uncouth squire. However, Mrs. Turner was given the privilege of gazing on the oval face. Her response was a polite compliment. "O my dear lady," exclaimed Yorick, needing only a mild stimulus, "did you but know the original!" "But what is she to you, Tristram?" asked the lady. "Nothing," he replied; "but that I am in love with her."

Before the visit was over the master of Skelton had proposed a jaunt to Harrogate in order to acquire strength for the coming racing season in York. When Yorick agreed, Hall-Stevenson accompanied his old friend back to Shandy Hall.

A day with Archbishop Drummond served as a pleasant interlude. It was a gratifying occasion for Yorick. His Grace's chaplains took him aside to tell him that Drummond was continually talking about him; and the Archbishop himself showed keen interest in the progress of *A Sentimental Journey*.

On July 15 Yorick had arrived at Harrogate and was taking the waters. Although for purposes of the *Journal* he insisted, shortly after his arrival, that none of the women at the spa attracted him and that he loved Eliza "more than the heart of man ever loved woman's," he neglected entries in his daybook for a week. Whether some Dulcinea of the springs may have been the cause there is no way of knowing.

When Sterne arrived in York on July 27 the two packets from Sao Thiago were awaiting him. His own dramatization of the event omits none of the requisite stage business:

I instantly shut the door of my bedchamber, and ordered myself to be denied—and spent the whole evening, and till dinner the next day, in reading over and over again the most interesting account—and the most endearing one, that ever tried the tenderness of man—I read and wept—and wept and read till I was blind—then grew sick and went to bed—and in an hour called again for the candle—to read it once more....

And he yearned to flee the festivities of York and to return to his simple retreat, to Cordelia, and to his unimpeded day-dreams of his Bramine.

So ran the last great sentimental splurge in the *Journal.* Sterne himself could not have failed to recognize that he had exhausted every emotional device, that he had pulled every quavering stop in the organ of sensibility. Therefore, as one should have expected, in a few more days he left off writing in his journal. He picked it up once again, but he did so for a brief time only; and the old urge was gone.

Back in Coxwold, he wrote on August 4:

> Hurried backwards and forwards about the arrival of Madame, this whole week—and then farewell I fear to this journal—till I get up to London—and can pursue it as I wish. At present all I can write would be but the history of my miserable feelings—She will be ever present—and if I take up my pen for thee—something will jar within me as I do it—that I must lay it down again—I will give you one general account of all my sufferings together—but not in Journals—I shall set my wounds a-bleeding every day afresh by it—and the story cannot be too short.—So worthiest best, kindest and [most] affectionate of Souls farewell—Every moment will I have thee present—and soothe my sufferings with the looks my fancy shall cloth thee in.—Thou shalt lie down and rise up with me—about my bed and about my paths, and shalt see out all my ways.—Adieu—Adieu—and remember one eternal truth, My dear Bramine, which is not the worse, because I have told it thee a thousand times before—That I am thine—and thine only, and forever.

Such a quick and passionate close would convince the reader that Mrs. Sterne's arrival was momentarily expected. But only a few weeks earlier Sterne had written asking Panchaud to forward letters to his wife at Avignon, and only two days before he had written to Mrs. James that his wife and daughter were still in France. Since Mrs.

Sterne's health was none too good, Yorick could not have expected the arrival of his family in less than three or four weeks. As early as July 11 he had mentioned the end of September as the most likely date, and on August 11 he repeated the prediction to Hall-Stevenson. Actually it was two months before the ladies finally arrived. The assumption that Sterne was deliberately guilty of untruth is strengthened by the fact that when he resumed the journal on November 1 he intimated that his family had been with him since the first of September.

The subterfuge cannot be completely justified. But one can understand the exigencies under which the *Journal* was actually broken off. Yorick had a book to write. Within several months his labors would be interrupted by a wife who gave promise of being on the warpath. Every ounce of creative energy was needed for the immediate task. To himself Yorick probably found little difficulty in justifying the slight manipulation of dates. Eliza was thousands of miles away and would never know the difference. To nobody's harm and with the gain of valuable time for himself the beautiful legend could be preserved.

Even the third packet from Eliza on August 10—with the story of rheumatism and delirium—did not cause Sterne to reopen the journal, which had presumably been packed with the picture and the trinkets "for the duration." His health still seemed to be holding up remarkably, and his spirits were high. Wraith-like though he was, he once again mustered enough energy to appear at the York races between August 17 and 22. But he did not escape without finally spitting blood and having a temporary relapse.

Earlier in August Sterne had encountered in York the Reverend Dr. Jemmett Brown, Bishop of Cork and Ross. To this whimsical and "anti-sublime" dignitary, Yorick had spun out his story of Eliza, and the Bishop had sympathized to the extent of offering Sterne preferment in Ireland and of expressing a desire to bless the union of the sentimental pair when the time was ripe. Of more immediate importance, however, was an invitation that he extended to Yorick to be "one of his family" in Scarborough for ten days in September.

Sterne naturally found such an invitation difficult to refuse, especially since the Bishop's guests included his charming compatriots, Lady Anne Dawson and Yorick's old friend, Mrs. Vesey. A third guest was Richard Griffith, minor author and future imitator of Sterne. The ten days went by most pleasantly. Every morning Yorick went sea-bathing (jumping "into Venus's lap," as he put it to Sir William Stanhope). His fragile frame was in ludicrous contrast to that of his ungainly host who floundered and sprawled in the surf much to the amusement of the ladies. During the day there were numerous opportunities to continue an old conquest with Mrs. Vesey, to hold her perfumed hand and to make delicious phrases. He might easily have recognized that she was daintier and more intelligent than his Eliza. Griffith provided literary stimulation. Sterne took interest in his work, not neglecting to shed a sympathetic tear over his autobiography. And in his turn Yorick produced some of the manuscript of *A Sentimental Journey*, taking the opportunity at the same time of soliciting a subscription.

The impetus of his sentimental diversion, strengthened by a letter in which his friend Sir William Stanhope banteringly assumed that his eroticism at Scarborough had been of body as well as of mind, impelled the parson upon his return to Coxwold to compose a whimsical note to a lady thus far identified only as "Hannah":

People think [wrote Yorick in his *jeu d'esprit*] that I have had many [affairs], some in body, some in mind, but as I told

> you before, you have had me more than any woman—therefore you must have had me H[annah], both in mind, and in body. —Now I cannot recollect where it was, nor exactly when—it could not be the lady in Bond-street, or Grosvenor-street, or ——— Square, or Pall-mall.—We shall make it out, H[annah,] when we meet—I impatiently long for it.

In his reply to Sir William, Sterne described the note, maintaining at the same time that in spite of his *badinage* his heart was innocent:

> The past is over—and I can justify myself unto myself [he continued half seriously, half jestingly]—can you do as much? —No faith!—'You can feel!' Aye so can my cat, when he hears a female caterwauling on the house top—but caterwauling disgusts me. I had rather raise a gentle flame than have a different one raised in me.

"I had rather raise a gentle flame. . ." This, indeed, was the essence of his sentimental scheme.

Early in October the event that he affected to dread took place: Mrs. Sterne and Lyd arrived in Yorkshire. The actuality Sterne found to be much more agreeable than the prospect. Lydia delighted her father by showing piquancy and vivacity tinctured not a little by elegance and poise. Some touches of French manners she undoubtedly brought. But no French rouge added to her natural blush, for her father had specifically warned her to throw her rouge pots into the Sorgue before she left for England. Any touch of flagrant coquetry he refused to tolerate in his beloved daughter. Mrs. Sterne, too, was on her best behavior. The return of Mrs. Draper to India had manifestly removed much of the cause for Bess' anxiety; therefore, the lady was willing to make some show of cordiality and amiability, especially so long as provisions for her future were being worked out to her satisfaction. If Sterne was not actually pleased, he was at least relieved by his wife's attitude. "My wife," he wrote archly to the Jameses, "–but I hate to praise my wife–'tis as much as decency will allow to praise my daughter."

The household spent a busy month arranging affairs so that Mrs. Sterne could eventually retire to France on a comfortable income. By the first of November most of the arrangements had been made, and Bess and Lydia had been settled for the winter in a house in York. "She leaves me, more than half in love with me," wrote Yorick, delighted that everything had moved so smoothly. And he was willing to confer tender blessings on his wife's old age–to be spent at a safe distance from him! Lydia's departure from Coxwold had its lachrymose aspects. When her doting father offered her ten guineas for spending money in York, she made one of her prettiest speeches: "No my dear papa, our expenses of coming from France may have straitened you–I would rather put an hundred guineas in your pocket than take ten out of it." Coming from Lydia, the speech was indeed overwhelming. No wonder Yorick burst into tears.

Almost before the two ladies had disappeared in the direction of York, the journal came out of its hiding place. But there was only one entry–an entry in which Yorick tells of the unexpectedly favorable winding up of affairs. He ends with an exclamation more suggestive of emotional exhaustion than of renewed passion:

> –And now Eliza! Let me talk to thee–But what can I say, of what can I write–but the yearnings of heart wasted with looking and wishing for thy Return–Return–Return! my dear Eliza! May heaven smooth the way for thee to send thee safely to us, and soj[ourn] forever.

Sterne now planned to return to London just before Christmas. As he had anticipated, the work on *A Sentimental Journey* had been seriously delayed. Since his strength was definitely ebbing, he could no longer expect to write at such a furious pace as he had formerly done. When he began again, he found the effort miserably exhausting. At the end of November, 1767, he wrote that he had worn out both body and spirit and that he had torn his "whole frame into pieces" by his feelings. Toward the first of December a hemorrhage and accompanying fever put him in bed for three weeks, thus delaying his southward journey. The seriousness of his illness must have been apparent to him. But his old courage remained.

From Coxwold he moved on to York to be nearer his physicians and his wife and daughter. Three days after Christmas he wrote Mrs. James that in a few days he would start out for London with Hall-Stevenson. "You'll see me enter like a ghost," he wrote, "–so I tell you beforehand, not to be frightened." Once again he did not flinch from the ordeal of the journey. Notwithstanding his usually sanguine outlook, he may have sensed that the journey would be his last. The only tangible evidence that he did, however, is the fact that he scribbled off a memorandum concerning the whereabouts of his letters, in anticipation of an edition after his death for the benefit of his wife and child.

Shandy Hall, the deal table and the quills, the purple jerkin, the purring tom-cat, and the ghostly nuns of the ruined abbey had already been bidden goodbye. Very likely Sterne had been too ill when he left Coxwold to become sentimental about his departure. And a sudden return of deceptive strength, accompanied by a resurgence of faith in the ability to elude his old pursuer, undoubtedly made his departure from York toward the end of December far less melodramatic than many a scene that he himself had delineated. His portmanteau having been packed with his London clothes and with two precious manuscripts, Yorick (we may assume) kissed Bess respectfully on the cheek, clasped Lydia warmly to his breast, and, then with Hall-Stevenson at his elbow, walked as jauntily as he dared down the steps to the waiting carriage. As the two old friends drove away from the shadow of the great Minster, across Ouse Bridge, toward Micklegate and the London highroad, a gay jest from Eugenius, extemporized for the occasion, dissolved them in laughter.

CHAPTER XVIII

THE SKULL OF YORICK

DURING THE FIRST few days of January, 1768, Sterne was for the last time installed in the house of the wig-bag maker in Old Bond Street. The wear and tear of the long journey from Yorkshire he had stood with a minimum of fatigue. Invitations were waiting for him, and again he anticipated the pleasures of the social season in London. Nevertheless, the fact that he had not this year subscribed to the assemblies at Carlisle House suggests that he expected curtailment of his activities. There was, of course, much to be done in regard to seeing two new volumes through the press. Old friends again demanded his time. The Jameses continued to lavish their hospitality on him, regularly expecting him on Sunday evenings if he happened not to be engaged elsewhere. By the middle of February he was writing in his old manner: "I am now tied down neck and heels (twice over) by engagements every day this week." He was breakfasting with Topham Beauclerk (Dr. Johnson's friend), spending an hour with Lord Ossory, visiting the studio of the American painter, Benjamin West, to see a new portrait of Anne James, and was himself sitting for another portrait (destined never to be finished) by Sir Joshua Reynolds.

But much of Sterne's old effervescence of spirit was gone, and he suffered weariness and disillusionment. In reply to Dr. John Eustace, a North Carolina physician who had sent him a curious walking stick, he wrote:

There is so little true feeling in the *herd* of the *world* that I wish I could have got an act of parliament, when the books [of *Tristram Shandy*] first appear'd, 'that none but wise men should look into them.' It is too much to write books and find heads to understand them.

His superficial licentiousness everybody had been quick to see and many had been as quick to attack. But most had failed to see that *Tristram Shandy* had a moral purpose, and that deeper than the humor and the licentiousness lay a faith in moral good and an expression of a philanthropic philosophy like the kindly philosophy of Shaftesbury and Hutcheson. Thus of gross misunderstanding the author complained to his admirer in America. To his friends in England he complained on other scores. He spoke of being physically exhausted and he referred doubtfully to his recovery and his return to Coxwold.

A Sentimental Journey appeared on February 27. Nothing that he had hitherto published had been so completely successful. The reviewers were all but unanimous in their praise, the *Monthly Review* being the most enthusiastic. The only important dissenting voice was the *Critical Review;* and it could be discounted, for it was Smollett's journal and it could, therefore, not be expected to condone a work containing such a devastating caricature as that of Smelfungus. Lydia wrote from York that everybody there liked the book. Yorick had indeed triumphed. But the triumph was hollow, for by this time he was too sick to appreciate it.

"I am ill—very ill," he exclaimed early in March to Mrs. Montagu, with whom he was again on his old footing. At the same time, however, he asserted his will to live and told of the composition of a comic romance that was proceeding as the result of his confinement. "I brave evils," he remarked with a flash of his old courage; and he intimated that when his time came to die he would go with a jest on his lips like the Emperor Vespasian or like Scarron.

Although he complained to Lydia of a "vile influenza," he was careful not to alarm her; and he spoke bravely of a return in May to his family in Yorkshire.

In the meantime, Mrs. Sterne's good humor toward her husband had suffered a reversal. When he was again out of her sight, her broodings revived her old feeling of distrust. Much of the loose chatter that Sterne had engaged in about Eliza was obliged to have reached her ears through the kindly offices of Yorkshire acquaintances and friends. Hence, in the same letter in which she mentioned the success of *A Sentimental Journey* in York, Lydia had mentioned a disturbing rumor then current to the effect that her father planned to bequeath her "as a legacy" to Mrs. Draper in case her mother should die first. There can be little doubt of Mrs. Sterne's having encouraged her daughter to pass the rumor on. Sterne quickly took pains to deny the story by saying that, on the contrary, he planned to commit Lydia to the charge of his much admired Mrs. James, from whom his daughter might learn "to be an affectionate wife, a tender mother, and a sincere friend." "But," he added significantly, "I think, my Lydia, that thy mother will survive me."

As a further peace offering he purchased a necklace and a pair of buckles for his daughter and the same for his wife:

> My girl cannot form a wish [he wrote] that is in the power of her father, that he will not gratify her in—and I cannot in justice be less kind to thy mother.

In his illness the tender nursing of a beloved daughter would have been the greatest boon that the dying man could have asked; but he accepted stoically the fact that Lydia could not leave her chronically ailing mother, and he assured her—lest his condition should occasion worry—that he was being given every attention. The assurance was not merely a brave boast. There is plenty of evidence that his friends rallied to Bond Street. Mrs. Montagu sent strengthening wines and jellies. Mrs. James, whom Sterne had come to love with real tenderness and who had in some measure supplanted Eliza in his affections, was a ministering angel. The Commodore himself was generous in his attentions. A Yorkshire parson told of making a visit to Bond Street just two days before Sterne's death. When he entered the room, he stated, a lady withdrew to the window. "Do not go out, Fanny; this is an old friend," said the sick man. "I am glad you are so carefully attended," remarked the visitor. "Had you come sooner," replied Yorick, "instead of three, the lady and the two you met on the stairs, you might have seen thirteen."

On the day before, he had written with a weak hand his last letter—a note to Mrs. James. The "vile influenza" had developed into pleurisy, and he had for several days been subjected to the stringent treatment recommended by the best medical practice of the time. Bleeding and blistering had so exhausted his strength that he could no longer muster a great deal of hope; and, most ominous of all, his old will to live was gone. There was no time for play-acting now. With touching sincerity he made his benediction and his confession to one who he felt could best understand:

> —do not weep my dear Lady—your tears are too precious to shed for me—bottle them up, and may the cork never be drawn.—Dearest, kindest, gentlest, and best of women! may health, peace, and happiness, prove your handmaids.—If I die, cherish the remembrance of me, and forget the follies which you so often condemn'd—which my heart, not my head betray'd me into.

On the afternoon of March 18 John Crauford of Errol had invited distinguished guests to have dinner with him at his house in Clifford Street. Surely, only illness kept Sterne from being included in a guest list of such an array of old friends as Garrick, Lord Ossory, David Hume, the Earl of March, Lord Roxburgh, the Duke of Grafton, and Mr. James. Upon James's arrival inquiry was made concerning Yorick's progress. Thereupon the Commodore gave the correct impression of his friend's perilous condition as he had judged it both from the note to his wife and from his own visit the day before. So much concern was expressed by all that the host summoned his footman and sent him for the latest news of Yorick's health.

The servant thus dispatched was as extraordinary a character as his gay libertine of a master. John Macdonald, a cadet of a Highland family and a world traveler, was by his own account so handsome and such a ladies' man that he caused rifts between the premier Earls of Scotland and their countesses. On another score he achieved renown, sharing credit with Beau Nash in diminishing the social evil of dueling in England by substituting the umbrella for the sword as an article of dress. "Undoubtedly," Mr. John Beresford has remarked, "John Macdonald was a social benefactor: how many duels and acts of violence received the coup de grâce from the peaceful prod of the umbrella!"—To this colorful person we are indebted for the only reliable account of Yorick's last moments.

When Macdonald arrived at Mrs. Fourmantel's house, the mistress herself opened the door. Upon his inquiry about Sterne's condition she directed him to the nurse upstairs. "I went into the room," Macdonald reported, "and he was just a-dying. I waited ten minutes; but in five he said: 'Now it is come.' He put up his hand as if to stop a blow, and died in a minute." It was four o'clock.

So Yorick fought his last fight and lost, in the same manner in which he had won many times before—courageously. In *Tristram Shandy* he had written that were he in a condition to stipulate with Death he would make only one wish:

. . . that it happen not to me in my own house—but rather in some decent inn—at home, I know it,—the concern of my friends, and the last services of wiping my brows, and smoothing my pillow, which the quivering hand of pale affection shall pay me, will so crucify my soul, that I shall die of a distemper which my physician is not aware of: but in an inn, the few cold offices I wanted, would be purchased with a few guineas, and paid me with an undisturbed, but punctual attention—

This foreshadowing of the circumstances of his death proved uncannily accurate.

Macdonald returned to give the sad news to his master and the guests, all of whom seemed deeply affected. That evening Lord Ossory, having an engagement to play loo at Caroline Howe's, reported the death to his hostess and her guests, Horace Walpole, Lord Eglinton, and Lady Mary Coke. Lady Mary included the news in her journal, quoting Lord Eglinton's somewhat lame remark that Yorick had taken his "Sentimental Journey." The situation almost inescapably suggests a paraphrase of Dean Swift's searchingly cynical lines on his own demise:

His female friends, whose tender hearts
Had better learn'd to act their parts
Received the news in doleful dumps:
"Yorick is dead: (and what is trumps?)
Then, Lord have mercy on his soul!
(Ladies, I'll venture for the vole.)
Six lords, they say, will bear the pall:
(I wish I knew what king to call.)
Madam, your husband will attend
The funeral of so good a friend."
"No, madam, 'tis a shocking sight;
And he's engaged tomorrow night:
My Lady Club wou'd take it ill,
If he should fail her at quadrille.

> Yorick he loved—(I lead a heart,)
> But dearest friends, they say, must part.
> His time was come: he ran his race;
> We hope he's in a better place."

But the lines are perhaps appropriate because of their universatility, not because they may be applied with some aptness to Yorick. In any event, they should not add weight to those apocryphal stories about Sterne's death that attempt to visit poetic justic on an "immoral" author.

The legend of the great writer who dies neglected in a garret has been so seductive that it has grown up around many literary figures. For one reason or another, Sterne did not escape. In 1783 the Shakespearean editor, Malone, wrote:

> The celebrated writer Sterne after being long the idol of this town, died in a mean lodging house without a single friend who felt interest in his fate except Becket his bookseller, who was the only person that attended his interment.

Another part of the legend gave Sterne a Falstaffian end in that he was said to have complained of coldness in his feet and subsequent coldness creeping up his body. According to Dr. Ferrier's account, while one hired hand was chafing Yorick's poor feet to kindle some warmth in them, another was stealing his gold sleeve buttons. His body was also said to have been sold to the dissectors by his landlady who was fearful of failing to collect the rent. Still another story—slightly out of the foregoing tradition—had it that Sterne was dealt his death blow at Sir Joshua Reynolds's table by the sarcastic wit of a lady who had been offended by the grossness of his conversation!

The privacy of Sterne's interment was probably the basis of a part of the legend. Since Hall-Stevenson had returned to Yorkshire and since Lord Fauconberg was not in town, the two people most likely to attend to Yorick's affairs were Becket and James. On March 22 these gentlemen seem to have been the sole witnesses of the interment in the new burial grounds of fashionable St. George's, Hanover Square—a burial ground then on the outskirts of the city, beyond Tyburn on Bayswater Road. A funeral service, however, had previously been conducted at his lodgings by the chaplain to the late Prince of Wales (if John Croft's testimony is correct). This service, one may reasonably believe, was attended by many of Sterne's closest friends. It is curious that no other record of it than Croft's bare mention remains.

The obituary notices naturally played on Hamlet's famous meditation on the skull of the King's jester, especially since Sterne himself had engaged in similar sentimentality in *Tristram Shandy*. In an indefensible continuation of *A Sentimental Journey* Hall-Stevenson pursued the device *ad nauseam*. This obvious association, together with the fact that at the time of Sterne's death resurrectionists had been plying their ghastly trade in several London burial grounds, made almost inevitable the most macabre of legends about the dead parson.

One day, the story runs, Dr. Charles Collignon, professor of anatomy at Cambridge, had invited some friends in to see the dissection of a corpse newly arrived from London. When the process was nearly finished, one of the visitors lifted the cloth that had concealed the head of the corpse. As he did so, he recoiled with horror. He had recognized the head of his friend, Laurence Sterne. The skull was said to have been kept (as indeed it would have deserved to be) as a great rarity; but among the collection at Cambridge it has never been identified. The complete disappearance of everything but the tradition should naturally cause the story to be treated with the greatest skepticism. Yet the tradition has been so persistent that it still finds credence in some quarters.

Although the alleged neglect of Sterne in his last days is plainly mythical and although the story of his exhumation is only slightly less credible, the neglect of his grave is a well established fact. Garrick wrote an epitaph admired by Lydia; but neither Sterne's wife and daughter nor his friends erected a memorial. Around 1780 a simple slab was erected by "two BROTHER MASONS," whose identities remain a mystery and whose impulse seems to have been fully as whimsical as many impulses of Sterne himself.

Yorick deserved better. A kinder fate might have given him six feet of earth in Coxwold in the churchyard near his "sweet retreat." To this little corner of the North Riding might have flocked memories of Sutton and Skelton, of Stillington Hall and Newburgh Priory, of York and Scarborough; and the simple parishioners might have shown the world to the grave of their famous rector. But London had become more nearly the home of Yorick's heart as the scene of his most brilliant triumphs; and to lie in London, even in relative obscurity, was no bitter fate. His books were his monument; and though Garrick's epitaph was not carved in stone, it was graven in the more durable material of memory:

Shall Pride a heap of sculptur'd marble raise,
Some worthless, unmourn'd titled fool to praise;
And shall we not by one poor grave-stone learn
Where Genius, Wit, and Humour, sleep with *Sterne?*

THREE WOMEN: AN EPILOGUE

TO THE THREE women whose lives were most closely tied up with Yorick's own, his death brought more consternation and chagrin than grief. Such was the ironic fate of the sentimentalist who wanted to move the female heart with only the tenderest passions. The rest of the story contains much that is unpleasant and sordid—for other reasons than that the memory of Sterne was neglected, exploited, and even reviled. If one is charitable, one will not forget that the chief actors in the afterpiece were sinned against as well as sinning. On the other hand, their crimes of self-interest necessarily weigh heavily against them; and one may see in the unhappy destiny of all three a measure of poetic justice.

The shock of Sterne's death was a great one to his wife and daughter. Feeling that their mission had been completed and that their long journey from France had been reasonably well justified, the ladies had settled for a comfortable winter in York before returning to the Continent to take up permanent residence. They had certainly been conscious of Sterne's pallor and weakness before he left for London, but he had been pale and weak so often before that such symptoms could not have been regarded with great alarm. Now came news of his death, upsetting their plans and making their future exceedingly precarious. Obviously, Sterne had not been frugal in his living. He had had neither the inclination nor the chance to be. He had borrowed right and left, both to maintain himself in the proper style and to provide for his family in France.

Thus the ladies found that in comparison with his assets his debts were tragically large. The parsonage house at Sutton was still in ruins, and claims for repairs confronted the executors of the estate. Mrs. Sterne and Lydia might well have faced their situation with some feeling of panic.

At all odds, they lost no time in advertising their distress. Yorick was hardly cold in his grave when Lydia posted a letter to Mrs. Montagu and another to the Archbishop of York, then at Dartmouth, in an effort to get whatever help she could. The Archbishop immediately promised a small pension; but he insisted upon the claims of the Reverend Andrew Cheap, who as the new incumbent of Sutton had to have a parsonage to live in. Mrs. Montagu was willing to use whatever influence she had on Dr. Drummond for additional aid; at the same time, she took a realistic view of the situation:

> The only thing for these people [she wrote to her sister, Mrs. Scott] would be to board in a cheap place, but my good cousin is si tracassiere, she puts every Town into a combustion in a month.

Needless to say, Mrs. Sterne and Lydia had little notion of accepting supinely the status of the shabby genteel. They were determined to go through with their original idea of living respectably in France if they could possibly do so by using Sterne's reputation and their own distress to the proper advantage. With some haste, Lydia moved to raise ready money. One of her first acts after her appeal to the Archbishop was to instruct her uncle, the Reverend John Botham, to dispose of her father's effects in London and to send all his papers to her. The way in which Mr. Botham executed this commission was exasperating not only to Lydia but also to every person who has ever attempted to read the character of Sterne aright. Lydia's complaint to Mrs. Montagu tells the sad story:

—not one of these directions has Mr. Botham followed . . . he has read every paper of my poor Father's and has burnt what he did not think proper to communicate to us.—it was not mama's intention that any one should read my Father's papers. Well knowing that there was some amongst them which ought not to have been seen no not even by his Daughter nor should I have wished to see one of them! mama is very much chagrined at this for not withstanding she can perhaps rely on Mr. Botham's secrecy yet it grieves that even he should be so well acquainted with certain anecdotes. But to burn any paper was very wrong. . . .

Indeed, it was—wrong and highhanded; for Mr. Botham took much of the truth about Sterne to the worms when his own pious head lay in the grave. He cannot easily be forgiven. What happened to many of the letters in the bureau in Coxwold and in garrets in York remains a mystery. Many of them may also have been thrown into the fire.

After Yorick's personal effects had been disposed of, the household goods and furniture at Shandy Hall were sold at auction. On the block went the parson's colored china, his fine chaise with the long-tailed white horses, his cow, and some remainders of his hay—not to mention his library, which was sold by the successors of Hildyard and Hinxman in York. The total proceeds Lydia reported to be £400, a sum which had to be balanced against £1100 in debts.

Obviously, money had to be raised from other sources. A suggestion that pleased the ladies was that a collection might be made at the York races in the coming August, during the race week to which Yorick had often lent his colorful presence. The idea had a special appeal, since it seemed possible to keep the scheme on an elegant plane and to avoid the stigma of small charity:

Begun with the Marquis of Rockingham and continued by the principal gentlemen of the County and nothing less than five Guineas to be received [Lydia wrote smugly to Mrs. Montagu] is putting it upon such a footing that it is an *honour* to Mr. Sterne's memory and no small one to us and cannot lessen us in the eyes of the world.

This manner of honouring Sterne's memory both ladies could best appreciate. It would be only honest to say that they wasted few thoughts on commemorating him with a tombstone.

Although Mrs. Sterne seemingly set out with the noble purpose of settling all her husband's debts, she was willing to accept the advice of her attorneys and haggle about Mr. Cheap's claim. The Archbishop felt that a compromise of a hundred guineas would be fair; but still Mrs. Sterne held out. In the course of the argument, the prelate became no less exasperated by the haggling than he was by the fact that the lady was allowing her course to be shaped by "that crooked-headed Attorney," Arthur Ricard; and he accused Bess and Lydia of depreciating their estate in order to make the race-week subscription seem more plausible. The angry Vicar of Sutton was forced to sue and finally to accept sixty pounds as a settlement.

When race week came, Mrs. Sterne and Lydia moved to the garret of their house in York ostensibly to give the landlord the advantage of demanding higher rents of the transients. The move may have also been a subtle one to suggest to Yorick's friends the real indigence of his widow and daughter. Whether or not this added touch aided the appeal, at least eight hundred guineas were collected. Even Dr. Drummond—who had previously expressed his convictions concerning the pride, vanity, and untruthfulness of the ladies—subscribed ten guineas. Perhaps he acted with a desire of appearing to do his bit rather than with any real sympathy for the widow.

The Archbishop was by no means alone in holding an

uncomplimentary opinion of Mrs. Sterne. Mrs. Montagu insisted that she was so little loved and esteemed that nobody would have contributed a guinea to the fund had not the subscribers been promised that the money would be converted into an annuity for Lydia. Some misgivings were even entertained concerning the daughter. Miss Ann Eliza Morritt, a Yorkshire lady who had known the Sterne connections all her life and who had busied herself in raising money for the fund, wrote Mrs. Montagu that Miss Sterne should be advised "not to affect wit, a desire of being distinguished" in a way that had "ruined the whole family." When Mrs. Montagu took her commission seriously and mentioned the matter to her god-daughter, Lydia denied having the least grain of Yorick's wit, which, she said, she and her mother regarded as "an unhappy turn" in her father! Even as a denial under fire, the statement does not reflect to the credit of the young lady—especially since she intended doing everything possible to exploit any shred of her father's cleverness that she could lay her hands on.

Aside from the race-week subscription, a source of income on which the Sternes naturally counted was the publication of eighteen slightly nondescript sermons that Yorick had not hitherto chosen to send to the press. The ladies sought the advice of Hall-Stevenson, who had been one of the prime movers in raising money at the York races. That gentleman advised publication and suggested that Becket be retained as publisher. Unfortunately, Sterne himself had given Becket the impression that the unpublished sermons were "but the sweepings of his study." Although Hall-Stevenson was willing to champion the remaining sermons as comparable with the published ones, Becket refused to be convinced. Thus when the publisher was approached by Lydia, he was at first unresponsive. Later he offered £400 for the copyright, provided that Lydia did not offer the manuscript elsewhere. Angered and convinced that Becket was a "dirty fellow," Lydia disregarded her obligations to her father's faithful publisher and secretly offered the sermons to William Strahan, publishing partner of Thomas Cadell. Some kind of arrangement was finally effected through which the volumes of sermons came out in June, 1769, under the joint imprint of Strahan, Cadell, and Becket. And a disagreeable episode over Yorick's remains was closed.

To get subscriptions for the sermons Lydia had employed some devices peculiarly her own and some suggestive of her father's. In the spring of 1769 she and her mother had moved down to London where they had taken rooms in the house of a paper merchant in Gerrard Street, near enough to Mrs. James to reap the full benefit of her friendship. This lady, who was flattered to assume obligations to the memory of her famous deceased friend, acted with her usual generosity. Taking the Sternes under her wing, she introduced them to as many of Laurence's friends as she could. To all, Lydia and her mother told their distressing story; and from all, they solicited subscriptions. To those unsolicited by word of mouth Lydia wrote notes suggesting the family's tragic financial plight as a part of her appeal. An example of these notes is preserved in a letter to John Wilkes, who at the time was having trouble of his own in King's Bench Prison. Lydia manages very adroitly to make the future comfort of the unhappy widow and daughter hinge directly on subscriptions to the sermons and thus to put the recipient of the appeal in a position from which he can hardly extricate himself without subscribing.

When the ladies took it upon themselves to wait upon Wilkes in his place of confinement, that notorious gentleman agreed to write the authorized biography of Sterne, provided that he could secure the collaboration of John Hall-Stevenson. Wilkes may have been honest in his promise, or he may simply have wanted to get rid of two persistent females. At any rate, Lydia took the offer in good faith and proceeded to secure the aid of Hall-Stevenson, who had just published his scurrilous continuation of *A Sentimental Journey*, with an attached memoir. The master of Skelton, doubtless flattered by the prospect of having his name coupled with that of so famous a man as Wilkes, sent back his acceptance immediately. Lydia's job was to draw frontispieces for the volumes and to arrange her father's correspondence as a supplement to the biography.

Thus with high hopes of another source of income, daughter and mother set out for France. On July 22, 1769, Lydia was writing Wilkes a coquettish letter from Angoulême, describing the idyllic way in which she spent her time–reading Shakespeare to her mother, playing her guitar, and singing. Unfortunately, the easy tenor of her life was upset in the fall by the failure of Panchaud's banking house in Paris and by the consequent threat of losing a sizeable sum of money. Also upsetting was the fact that as the months went by neither Wilkes nor Hall-Stevenson made any move to produce the promised biography. After failing to get replies from either for over six months, Lydia wrote in desperation to Hall-Stevenson on February 13, 1770:

> –but dear Sir consider that the fulfilling of . . . [your promise] may put £400 into our pockets and that the declining it would be unkind after having made us hope and depend upon that kindness.

Still there was no reply. Wilkes had too many other things to concern him; and Hall-Stevenson's indolence was notorious.

In March, 1770, Lydia was complaining to Mrs. Montagu that Angoulême lacked cultural life and that the inability of the Sternes to entertain restricted their social activities.

The narrative must now move rapidly. In the summer or fall of the same year the two left Angoulême for Albi, near Toulouse, in Langue d'Oc. Two years later we find them here. In the meantime they had fallen on evil days. Mrs. Sterne had had "epileptick" fits; and her daughter was now in serious trouble. On March 22, 1772, Lydia wrote a dutiful letter to Mrs. Montagu, who had been contributing to their support and to whom Lydia still looked for succor. The tale that she told concealed far more than met the eye. An offer of marriage had been made, said she, "which tho' not advantageous, yet was far from disagreeable. . ." Her fiancé, she continued, though a Catholic, was not a bigot; however, his father had insisted that Mrs. Sterne give up her estate immediately as a marriage settlement. Her own health Lydia reported to be "indifferent." Mrs. Montagu certainly must have been puzzled by the strange letter, and she must have sensed that something sinister was in the offing. Her reply was firm: she did not like the idea of Lydia's marrying a man of different religion or of her reducing her mother to beggary.

But it was too late to protest. Lydia was already pregnant. On April 28 she abjured the Protestant faith and married Jean-Baptiste-Alexandre-Anne de Medalle. Three months later came a son, Jean-François-Laurent (the last name a reminder of the deceased Laurence). The Communal Archives of Albi have been found to reveal, somewhat gratuitously, that the marriage was "forcé, urgent." Lydia was twenty-five at the time and her husband was five years younger. Whether she was the seducer or the seduced one must judge for himself; however, the youth of the husband and the fact that old Medalle took an aggressive interest in immediately getting Mrs. Sterne's estate for his son may allow the uncharitable to put the worst construction on Lydia's behavior.

For more reasons than one poor Bess was too ill to witness the sad ceremony. The circumstances were enough to unhinge her precariously balanced mind. There is no record of what she did and where she lived for the rest of the year. We do know that in January, 1773, her unhappy life was ended in Albi at No. 9 Rue St. Antoine, the house of a local physician named Lionières. Thus the vivacious parson's daughter who had married a spindle-legged young clergyman after a sentimental courtship breathed her last far from the gay Assembly Rooms in York, after having spent her final days in greater loneliness and depression of spirit than her famous husband could have imagined.

The facts known about Lydia now grow exceedingly sparse. On December 23, in the year of her mother's death, she gave birth to another son. Her husband died a year or more later. In the spring of 1775 she had returned to England. Since Wilkes and Hall-Stevenson had failed her in the project of the biography, she took upon herself the publication of her father's letters. Need for money and the success of Mrs. Stanhope with the letters of Lord Chesterfield in the preceding year provided sufficient stimulus.

In London Mrs. Medalle established herself in respectable quarters, had her portrait painted by Benjamin West, and set about promoting interest in the forthcoming volumes by advance advertising. The letters and miscellanies (including Sterne's invaluable little autobiography) came from the press in three volumes in October, 1775. They contained the richest treasure of Sternian material that existed apart from the previously published works. But the shape in which the volumes were presented was a credit neither to Lydia's intelligence nor to her integrity. On account of the slight attempt at consistent chronological sequence, the collection was a hodge-podge. There were numerous mistakes and misprints. Names of living people were replaced by dashes; and deliberate tampering with the text took place when there was an indiscreet reference either to Mrs. Draper or to Mrs. Sterne. In some of the most sentimental passages on Eliza, Lydia either inserted her own name or rendered the passages innocuous by rephrasing. Other changes seem to have been purely matters of whim. Since many of the originals no longer exist, the whole of Lydia's edition has presented many complicated and apparently insoluble problems for editors.

When the letters had been safely seen through the press, Lydia returned to France. Here the thread of her story is lost. In 1783 one of her sons died. The other survived the mother. But nothing else is known regarding the fate of Yorick's daughter and his French grandson. Obscurity has swallowed them up with ironical completeness.

For the fate of Eliza we must retrace our steps.

When Mrs. Draper arrived in Bombay in the early months of 1768, she found that she had not misjudged her husband's success. Since Daniel was rising rapidly in the company, his wife found it possible to return to "High Meadow" with a glow of satisfaction in the family's increasing importance. She was also delighted to have once again the company of her sister Louisa, who having been widowed after an unfortunate marriage was on the point of making an excellent match with a Colonel Pemble. While Sterne lay dying in Bond Street his Bramine was luxuriating in sea bathing with her sister or galloping along bridle paths on a properly elegant Indian mount—all in all, delighting in her rôle as a lady of quality.

In the autumn Draper had another promotion, being sent to Tellicherry as chief of the factory there. This spot—the "Montpelier of India"—his wife found delightful and exciting. Their house within the fort was a magnificent one; and there was a thrill in living on the dangerous edge of territory controlled by the gallant and treacherous

Hyder Ali. Here also Eliza bathed in the sea and continued her riding, accompanied by an impressive "guard of six sepoys with drawn sabres and loaded pistols." When she rode out she was always faced with the enchanting possibility of being captured by Ali, who had the reputation of treating English ladies gently if they submitted cheerfully "to the laws of his seraglio." Her time indoors was spent reading and writing. The flattery of Yorick and other friends in England had gone to her head; therefore, she had visions of being a Bluestocking, with the fabulous Mrs. Montagu as her model. Reams of prose issued from her pen.

In the midst of one of the most idyllic periods of her life came the news of Yorick's death. For several months her contacts and her indiscretions in England had seemed a closed chapter. But now the memory of her last days in London was revived in an aspect that was not entirely pleasant. There is slight evidence that she felt any real pangs of grief. But her first act suggests that she was carrying out in somewhat quixotic faith a promise made to her famous admirer. On her own testimony, she sent by the first boat a letter to Lydia offering a home in India. Tactlessly, she made no reference to Mrs. Sterne. Nothing could have been more inept, for the letter merely served to confirm both for Lydia and Bess the rumors which Sterne himself had taken pains to deny. One can see why both were infuriated.

Here, indeed, was an occasion for one of Bess's tantrums, if ever there was one. Lydia expressed her contempt in a scornful rejection of the offer. This rejection, together with rumors from England that Mrs. Sterne planned to publish the correspondence, filled Eliza with frantic fear. Having established herself in a comfortable way of life, she quaked lest the breath of scandal should deprive her of the wealth and position that she seemed destined to attain. The horrible thought that the widow of whom Sterne had painted such an unattractive picture had her letters "in her power" and thus was in a position to subject her to "disgrace and inconvience" moved Mrs. Draper to dispatch a letter to Becket, offering him "a reward equal to his expectations" if he turned the letters over to Mrs. James—"in case they were offered him for sale." In her desperation she conceived of Mrs. Sterne in the most uncomplimentary way. "—the widow, I was assured," she wrote to Mrs. James, "was occasionally a drinker, a swearer, exceeding unchaste." But this wretched character, she continued, was "in point of understanding, and finished address supposed to be inferior to no woman in Europe"—a fact which offered slight consolation to one who feared blackmail! Against Yorick, too, Eliza turned in a manner of petulance, because the subtle flattery of a sentimental old man had led her into silly indiscretions now threatening her happiness:

> I believed Sterne implicitly, I believed him! [she wrote in the same interminable letter to Mrs. James] *I had no motive to do otherwise than believe him just, generous and unhappy—till his death gave me to know, that he was tainted with the vices of injustice, meanness, and folly.*

Nor did her assurance grow stronger when she learned that Mrs. James was extending her hospitality to the arch-enemies of her peace. To her friend, Eliza wrote in April, 1772, the long and incoherent letter just cited. In this "rigamarole" (to borrow an apt description from Saintsbury) she defended her own position and vented her spleen upon the Sternes, living and dead.

Few letters have contained a greater number of glittering contradictions, not the least of which was the fact that while Eliza was pouring her scorn on Bess and Lyd to Mrs. James ("It is true my friend! I love not these ladies!")

she admitted that a few days earlier she had recommended the acquaintance of the ladies to her young friend Colonel Donald Campbell. Aside from her invitation to Lydia and her offer to Becket, Eliza had further attempted to avert scandal by initiating a subscription for the Sternes in India. In this effort Colonel Campbell had been one of the most zealous coadjutors. In a letter to the Colonel, Eliza had puffed the Sternes magnificently in an apparent attempt to make a match between him and Lydia when he arrived in England. This kind of duplicity is either too callous, too subtle, or too desperate to be easily comprehended.

By the time Eliza wrote her verbose letter to Mrs. James her marital difficulties were moving toward a melodramatic climax. From Tellicherry the Drapers had been transferred to Surat, where Daniel was chief agent for the government and where Eliza continued to play queen–riding in a palanquin attended by running footmen or taking part in the royal Guzerat sport of chasing antelopes with leopards. Then Draper's fortunes suffered reverses. He lost his post at Surat and returned to Bombay. Here the family lived at "Marine House," overlooking the harbor of the city. Marked coolness had developed between Daniel and his wife, who now fretted to return to England and to her daughter. (Her little son had died.) Soon Eliza had ceased conjugal relations with her husband. The morose Daniel Draper, of whom one would have expected little "gallantry," apparently had not only had a series of affairs but he had especially outraged his wife by daring infidelity with one of the female servants named Leeds. No doubt, Eliza was righteously indignant; but she herself may not have been entirely guiltless. To friends in England she had admitted blandly that the convention of the "gallant" was a popular one in India; and her success in attracting young men to her as "close" friends had not gone unobserved by scandal-mongers. Her attachment for young George

Horsley, to whom she entrusted jewels to be sold in England, is suggestive of her friendships. This gentleman she enthusiastically describes to Tom Sclater:

> ... a very intimate friend of ours, and very much approved by your favourite cousin.—You are not to suppose from this, that he is either handsome, genteel, or remarkably well bred, so far from it, that he more resembles my idea of the Knight of la Mancha than that of an Adonis—or Man of Fashion;—and yet, take him, for all in all, I shall not see his like again.... You'll find him sensible, conversible, and truly worthy....

At "Marine House" Eliza spent a most unhappy year. Constantly she begged to be allowed to return to England; but her husband just as constantly turned a deaf ear. Finally on January 14, 1773, she eloped from her husband's house by a rope ladder swung from a second-storey window and took refuge with Commodore Sir John Clarke, whose flagship—ironically named H.M.S. *Prudent*—was anchored in the harbor. It was a desperate act which Eliza undertook with calm deliberation. On the night of her departure she wrote three extraordinary letters—two in interest of rewarding a faithful servant and the third to Draper:

> O! Draper! [she wrote in part to her husband] a word, a look, sympathetic of regret on Tuesday or Wednesday would have saved me the perilous adventure, and such a portion of remorse as would be sufficient to fill up the longer life. I reiterate my request that vindictive measures will not be pursued. Leave me to my fate I conjure you, Draper, and in doing this you will leave me to misery inexpressible, for you are not to think, that I am either satisfied with myself or my prospects, though the latter are entirely my own seeking.

Just what Sir John's actual relations with Eliza were is not clear. Draper instituted proceedings against the Commodore but dropped them when he saw that he would not profit by being forced to wash his own dirty linen in public. Eliza went to Masulipatam to live with her wealthy uncle, John Whitehill.

In 1774 the Bramine returned to her beloved England and to her daughter. From all appearances, she lived in quasi-retirement at 3 Queen Anne Street, West Cavendish Square—an address that was ultra-respectable and that was sufficiently distant from Gerrard Street and Soho to enable her to avoid, if she chose, the Jameses and other Anglo-Indian friends of her husband. There is no reason to believe that her path crossed Lydia's when Mrs. Medalle came to London to edit the letters.

The fact that Eliza lived quietly should not be taken to mean that she was without attention. John Wilkes admired her and made some advances; and she exchanged visits with his daughter, "Polly." William Combe, the scurrilous author of the *Tours of Dr. Syntax*, boasted of favors that few believe he received. He ungallantly told the poet Samuel Rogers that he used to meet Eliza often beside a windmill near Brighton—

> ... that he was once surprised in her bed-chamber, and fled through the window, leaving one of his shoes behind him; that some days after he encountered her as she was walking with a party on what is now the Steyne (at Brighton), and that, as she passed him, she displayed from her muff the toe of his shoe!

Eliza's most important friend was the Abbé Raynal, ex-Jesuit and apologist of British imperialism, who had met her in Bombay and who now fell completely under the spell of her combined "voluptuousness" and "modesty":

> When I saw Eliza [he exclaimed], I experienced a sensation unknown to me. It was too warm to be no more than friendship; it was too pure to be love. Had it been a passion, Eliza

would have pitied me; she would have endeavoured to bring me back to my reason, and I should have completely lost it.

Only Yorick himself could have improved on the strain. Eliza had an amazing power of eliciting sentimentality from old men. What kind of affection she bestowed on the Abbé is not a matter of record; but Raynal maintained that his relationship with Mrs. Draper was so close that at the time of her death she was planning to go to France and live with him.

The last years of Yorick's Bramine are almost as obscure as the closing days of Lydia. We know merely that her death occurred on August 3, 1778, in Clifton, a suburb of Bristol, and that she was buried in the Cathedral. Why she was in Bristol no one has satisfactorily explained,—unless she was visiting a kinsman of her husband there, General Sir William Draper.

The Abbé Raynal may have erected the memorial tablet in the British Cathedral. At all odds, he included in the great edition of his *Histoire des Deux Indes*, published in Geneva in 1780, a wildly rhapsodic eulogy on his sentimental love. The occasion was a discussion of her birthplace, Anjengo:

> Eliza ended her days in the land of her forefathers [ran part of the eulogy], at the age of three and thirty. A celestial soul was separated from a heavenly body. Ye who visit the spot on which her sacred ashes rest, write upon the marble that covers them: In such a year, in such a month, at such an hour, God withdrew his spirit and Eliza died.

With such a benediction we leave the oval-faced lady to her rest.

SELECTED BIBLIOGRAPHY

INDEX

SELECTED BIBLIOGRAPHY

For further reading one can supplement the following brief list of Sterne material by referring to the *Cambridge Bibliography of English Literature* (Cambridge: The University Press, 1941), II, 521–23, and its *Supplement* (Cambridge: The University Press, 1957), V, 452–53; and especially for the latest material by referring to Lodwick Hartley's *Laurence Sterne in the Twentieth Century* (Chapel Hill: The University of North Carolina Press, 1966).

EDITIONS

Letters of Laurence Sterne, edited by Lewis Perry Curtis. Oxford: The Clarendon Press, 1935.

The Life and Opinions of Tristram Shandy, Gentleman, edited by James A. Work, New York: The Odyssey Press, 1940; other editions edited by Samuel Holt Monk, New York: Rinehart and Company, 1950; by Alan D. McKillop, New York: Harper and Brothers, 1962; by Ian Watt, Boston: Houghton Mifflin Company, 1965.

The Life and Works of Laurence Sterne, edited by Wilbur L. Cross. 12 vols. New York: J. F. Taylor Company, 1904. [Includes *Life* by Percy Fitzgerald.]

A Sentimental Journey through France and Italy, edited by Gardner P. Stout, Jr. Berkeley: University of California Press, 1967.

The Works of Laurence Sterne. 7 vols. Oxford: Basil Blackwell; Boston and New York: Houghton Mifflin Company, 1926–27.

BIOGRAPHY AND BIOGRAPHICAL MATERIAL

Connely, Willard. *Laurence Sterne as Yorick*. London: The Bodley Head, 1958.

Cross, Wilbur L. *The Life and Times of Laurence Sterne*. New Haven: Yale University Press, 1929; and New York: Russell and Russell, 1967 [Reprint].

Curtis, Lewis P. *The Politicks of Laurence Sterne*. Oxford: Oxford University Press, 1929.

———. "Sterne in Bond Street," *Times Literary Supplement*, March 24, 1932, p. 217.

Elwin, Whitwell. "Sterne," in *Some Eighteenth-Century Men of Letters*, II. London: J. Murray, 1902.

Fluchère, Henri. *Laurence Sterne*. Paris: Gallimard, 1961.

Hewins, W. A. S., ed. *The Whitefoord Papers*. Oxford, 1898.

Kuist, James M. "New Light on Sterne: An Old Man's Recollections," *Publications of the Modern Language Association*, LXXX (1965), 549-53.

Montagu, Elizabeth Robinson. *Elizabeth Montagu, the Queen of the Blue Stockings: Her Correspondence from 1720 to 1761*, edited by Emily J. Climenson. London: John Murray, 1906.

Ollard, S. L. "Sterne as a Young Parish Priest," *Times Literary Supplement*, March 18, 1926, p. 217; also May 25, 1933, p. 364 and June 1, 1933, p. 380.

Pottle, Frederick A. "Bozzy and Yorick," *Blackwood Magazine*, CCXVII (1925), 297-313.

Quennell, Peter. "Laurence Sterne," in *The Profane Virtues*. New York: The Viking Press, 1945.

Shaw, M. R. B. *Laurence Sterne: The Making of a Humorist, 1713-1762*. London: Richards Press, 1957.

Sichel, Walter. *Sterne*. London: Williams and Norgate, 1910.

Stapfer, Paul. *Laurence Sterne*. Paris: Fischbacher, 1882.

Traill, H. D. *Sterne*. New York: Harper, 1887.

Watkins, W. B. C. "Yorick Revisited," in *Perilous Balance*. Princeton: Princeton University Press, 1939. Pp. 99–156.

Wright, Arnold, and W. L. Sclater. *Sterne's Eliza*. London: Heinemann, 1922.

CRITICAL

Bagehot, Walter. "Sterne and Thackeray," in *Literary Studies*, II, 94–130. London: J. M. Dent, 1910.

Baird, Theodore. "The Time-Scheme of *Tristram Shandy* and a Source," *Publications of the Modern Language Association*, LI (1936), 803–20.

Booth, Wayne C. *The Rhetoric of Fiction*. Chicago: University of Chicago Press, 1961. Pp. 221–40.

Cash, Artrur H. "The Lockean Psychology of *Tristram Shandy*," *English Literary History*, XXII (1955), 125–35.

———. *Sterne's Comedy of Moral Sentiments*. Pittsburgh: Duquesne University Press, 1965.

Drew, Elizabeth. *The Novel: A Modern Guide to Fifteen English Masterpieces*. New York: Dell Publishing Company, 1963. Pp. 75–94.

Fluchère, Henri. *Laurence Sterne: From Tristram to Yorick, An Interpretation of "Tristram Shandy."* Translated and abridged by Barbara Bray. Oxford: Oxford University Press, 1965.

Hammond, L. V. H. *Sterne's Sermons of Mr. Yorick*. New Haven: Yale University Press, 1948.

Howes, Alan B. *Yorick and the Critics: Sterne's Reputation in England, 1760–1868*. New Haven: Yale University Press, 1958.

Jefferson, D. W. *Laurence Sterne*. London: Longmans, Green, 1954.

Landa, Louis A. "The Shandean Homunculus," in *Restoration and Eighteenth-Century Literature*, edited by Carroll Camden. Chicago: University of Chicago Press, 1963. Pp. 49–68.

Lehman, B. H. "Of Time, Personality and the Author," *Studies in the Comic, University of California Publications in English*, VIII, No. 21 (1941), 233–50.

McKillop, Alan D. "Laurence Sterne," in *Early Masters of the English Novel.* Lawrence: University of Kansas Press, 1956. Pp. 182–219.

MacLean, Kenneth. *John Locke and English Literature of the Eighteenth Century*. New York: Yale University Press, 1936.

Parrish, Charles. "A Table of Contents for Tristram Shandy," *College English*, XXII (1960), 143–50.

Piper, William B. *Laurence Sterne*, New York: Twayne, 1965.

Putney, Rufus. "Laurence Sterne, Apostle of Laughter," in *The Age of Johnson.* New Haven: Yale University Press, 1949. Pp. 159–70.

———. "The Evolution of *A Sentimental Journey*," *Philological Quarterly*, XIX (1940), 349–69.

Reid, Ben. "The Sad Hilarity of Sterne," *Virginia Quarterly Review*, XXXII (1956), 107–30.

Stedmond, John M. *The Comic Art of Laurence Sterne*. Toronto: University of Toronto Press, 1967.

Stout, Gardner B., Jr. "Yorick's *Sentimental* Journey," *English Literary History*, XXX (1963), 395–412.

Traugott, John. *Tristram Shandy's World.* Berkeley: University of California Press, 1954.

Van Ghent, Dorothy. *The English Novel, Form and Function.* New York: Rinehart and Company, 1953. Pp. 83–98.

Watt, Ian. *The Rise of the Novel.* Berkeley: University of California Press, 1957. Pp. 290–95.

INDEX